Medieval America

Medieval America

FEUDALISM
AND LIBERALISM IN
NINETEENTH-CENTURY
U.S. CULTURE

Robert Yusef Rabiee

The University of Georgia Press
Athens

Paperback edition, 2023
© 2020 by the University of Georgia Press
Athens, Georgia 30602
www.ugapress.org
All rights reserved
Designed by Melissa Bugbee Buchanan
Set in Garamond Premier Pro

Most University of Georgia Press titles are
available from popular e-book vendors.

Printed digitally

Library of Congress Cataloging-in-Publication Data
Names: Rabiee, Robert Yusef, 1981– author.
Title: Medieval America : feudalism and liberalism in
nineteenth-century U.S. culture / Robert Yusef Rabiee.
Other titles: Feudalism and liberalism in nineteenth-century U.S. culture
Description: Athens, Georgia : The University of Georgia Press, [2020] |
Includes bibliographical references and index.
Identifiers: LCCN 2020032135 | ISBN 9780820358369 (hardback) |
ISBN 9780820358376 (ebook)
Subjects: lcsh: United States—Civilization—19th century. | Literature and history—United States—History—19th century. | Medievalism—United States—History—19th century. | Feudal law—Miscellanea. | Liberalism—United States—History—19th century. | United States—Historiography.
Classification: LCC E169.1 .R235 2020 | DDC 973.5—dc23
LC record available at https://lccn.loc.gov/2020032135

Paperback ISBN 978-0-8203-6489-6

I started in Old World
Have come now to New.
But all my actions, behaviors,
They've come with me, too.
> —Bonnie "Prince" Billy,
> "So Far and Here We Are"
> (2014)

CONTENTS

Acknowledgments ix

INTRODUCTION
Feudalism and Liberalism in the U.S. Imaginary 1

CHAPTER ONE
Plantation Romance and Southern Medievalism
in Poe's Magazine Fiction 25

CHAPTER TWO
Melodrama of Primitive Accumulation:
Cooper's Feudal Claims 60

CHAPTER THREE
Marriage, Chivalry, and Feudal Law:
Harriet Jacobs and E. D. E. N. Southworth 95

CHAPTER FOUR
Resistance to the Feudal-Liberal Alliance:
Ridge's *The Life and Adventures of Joaquín Murieta*
and Melville's *Benito Cereno* 128

CHAPTER FIVE
Feudalism, Individualism, and Authority
in Emerson's Later Works 158

CONCLUSION
The Kentucky Castle 181

Notes 189

Index 213

ACKNOWLEDGMENTS

Thank you to my dissertation committee at the University of Southern California: John Carlos Rowe, Bill Handley, David Rollo, and William Deverell. Michelle Yvonne Gordon, who helped walk this project through its infancy before she departed USC, remained in the back of my mind throughout the writing process.

Thanks also to David Dowling at the Emerson Society; Alan Nadel of the University of Kentucky and Futures of American Studies; Chris Castiglia and Dana D. Nelson at *J19*; and Johanna Heloise Abtahi, Laura Dassow Walls, and Denise G. Stripes at *ESQ*. And, of course, and endlessly, thanks to Walter Biggins at University of Georgia Press.

Thank you to Will Oldham and Brett Sova at Drag City Records for use of lyrics from "So Far (And Here We Are)" by Bonnie "Prince" Billy as the epigraph to this book.

My colleagues Stephen G. Pasqualina and Alex T. Young have, between them, read and commented on almost every word in this manuscript. Thank you also to Jessica Mummert, who read and offered comments during the final stages of revision. Svetlana Zill provided helpful feedback on the introduction and conclusion to this text.

My parents, Lydia Jane McNamara-Rabiee and Massoud Rabiee, made all of this possible, financially and personally. They fostered a love of learning, helped guide me through choppy waters, and insisted that the study of language, history, and ideas was worth pursuing.

Finally, to Melissa Leigh Scott-Rabiee: on long hikes and road trips, from Lexington to Los Angeles to Philadelphia, in long discussions on labor and society, and in quiet moments spent listening to music or just hanging around, you have kept me alive and awake to the world. Without your support—and without our dreaming about the kind of world we want for our child—I couldn't and wouldn't have done this.

Medieval America

❧ INTRODUCTION ☙

Feudalism and Liberalism in the U.S. Imaginary

> The immigrants settling in America at the start of the seventeenth century somehow unlocked the democratic from all those other principles it had to contend with in the old communities of Europe and they transplanted that alone to the New World, where it has been able to grow freely and develop its legislation peacefully by moving in harmony with the country's customs.
> —Alexis de Tocqueville, *Democracy in America* (1835–1840)

> Whilst in ordinary life every shopkeeper is very well able to distinguish between what somebody professes to be and what he really is, our historians have not yet won even this trivial insight. They take every epoch at its word and believe that everything it says and imagines about itself is true.
> —Karl Marx and Friedrich Engels, *The German Ideology* (1846)

Of the many myths that have supported U.S. exceptionalism, the most persistent may be that the United States lacks a feudal tradition. Alexis de Tocqueville states the claim plainly in the passage quoted above. While recognizing the persistence of ideas and ways of living transplanted from the Old World to the New, he argues that Anglo-American economic, juridical, and governmental structures freed themselves of the feudal baggage that other European powers dragged behind them like atrophied tails. An earlier French observer, Hector St. John de Crèvecouer, came to similar conclusions in his *Letters from an American Farmer* (1782): "Strangers to the honours of monarchy," Americans "do not aspire to purchase founding titles, and frivolous names."[1] Out with the old fineries, in with rugged republican virtue: this, for Tocqueville, Crèvecouer, and many today, was the moral of the founding of the United States.

Tocqueville and Crèvecouer are not incorrect in their observations. The antifeudal project exercised a profound impact on U.S. political and cultural development. Thomas Jefferson aimed to dismantle feudal remnants when, in 1776, he proposed to eradicate primogeniture and entail in Virginia as the first step in establishing "a system by which every fibre would be eradicated of ancient or future aristocracy and a foundation laid for a government truly republican."[2] But Jefferson's desire to eradicate feudal privilege in the colonies somewhat troubles Tocqueville's enthusiastic belief that Anglo-Americans brought only "the democratic form" with them from Europe. If the feudal element hadn't been transported to the Americas, then Jefferson would have had no need to dismantle it. However, both authors would certainly agree that the revolution and subsequent legislation had the power to remove feudalism as a determining factor in U.S. life.

Tocqueville's, Crèvecouer's, and Jefferson's statements share an assumption about the new nation's relationship to history. Like the iconoclasts in Nathaniel Hawthorne's "Earth's Holocaust" (1844), the United States would burn "all the rubbish of the Herald's Office; the blazonry of coat-armor; the crests and devices of illustrious families; pedigrees that extended back, like lines of light, into the mist of the dark ages," not to mention "the patents of nobility of German counts and barons, Spanish grandees, and English peers, from the worm-eaten instruments signed by William the Conqueror, down to the bran-new parchment of the latest lord."[3] The new nation, born through armed struggle with an English monarchy whose symbolic power seemed to diminish exponentially by the decade, could not accommodate the elaborate and decaying feudal system any more than a Puritan divine could wear the regalia of a Catholic cardinal.[4]

Medieval America questions this narrative, arguing that feudal law and medieval literature were structural components of the U.S. cultural imaginary in the nineteenth century. The racial, gender, and class formations that emerged in the first era of U.S. nation building were indebted to medieval thought— an observation that challenges the liberal consensus model and allows us to better grasp how social roles developed. Far from casting off feudal tradition, the early United States folded feudalism into its emerging liberal order, creating a knotted system of values and practices that continue to structure the U.S. experience. Sometimes, the feudal residuum contradicted the United States' liberal values. Other times, the feudal residuum bolstered those values, revealing deep sympathies between so-called modern and premodern political thought.

The optimistic belief in the ability of the United States to cast off feudal tradition in favor of a natural law doctrine has deep roots in seventeenth- and eighteenth-century English and French historiography, both of which held that an emergent modernity was set to correct ancient power structures.[5] The idea made its way into the Constitution's provision in Article 1, Section 9, Clause 8, that "[n]o Title of Nobility shall be granted by the United States," a clear bulwark against European-style aristocracy.[6] The provision received its first major test when Major General Henry Knox, the second U.S. secretary of war, attempted to make the Society of the Cincinnati, a "chivalric order" made up of Revolutionary War officers, the basis for a titled nobility.[7] With George Washington as its founding president general, the Society of the Cincinnati seemed, for a time, to pose a genuine threat to the antifeudal principles from which the U.S. system was putatively derived. As was the fashion of the time, a lengthy pamphlet debate ensued, and the Cincinnati, while still in existence today, was never able to establish for itself the power or prestige Knox had dreamed of. However, the very existence of such an organization indicates the fragility of the U.S. claim to be a truly postfeudal nation.

By the mid-nineteenth century, the constitutionally enshrined belief that the United States had skipped feudalism served to differentiate Anglo-American power from that of other European colonizers on the continent. In his *History of the United States* (1854), George Bancroft identifies the Mayflower compact of 1620 as "the birth of popular constitutional liberty" and then compares the compact to similar medieval documents: "The middle age had been familiar with charters and constitutions; but they had been merely . . . patents of nobility, concessions of municipal privileges, or limitations of the sovereign power in favor of feudal institutions."[8] In *The Old Regime in Canada* (1874), Francis Parkman describes the feudal land system of French Canada in the seventeenth century to set the stage for a Gothic conflict between innocent New England villagers and debauched Canadian lords: "[The feudal lord] was at home among his tenants, at home among the Indians, and never more at home than when a gun in his hand a crucifix on his breast, he took the war-path with a crew of painted savages and Frenchmen almost as wild, and pounced like a lynx from the forest on some lonely farm or outlying hamlet of New England."[9] In Parkman's telling, the purity of the Yankee's spiritual, communitarian task is threatened by two ancient forces: the "painted savages" and their feudal Catholic partners in terror. The Puritans' nascent democracy must defend itself against incursions from these residual forces.

Two decades later, Frederick Jackson Turner would elevate Parkman's conflict between free U.S. soil and artificial European social constructions to mythic heights in "The Significance of the Frontier in American History" (1893): "The wilderness masters the colonist. It finds him a European in dress, industries, tools, modes of travel, and thought.... The advance of the frontier has meant a steady movement away from the influence of Europe, a steady growth of independence on American lines. And to study this advance,... and the political, economic, and social results of it, is to study the really American part of our history."[10] While Turner recognizes that the Anglo-American transported the "political, economic, and social" structures of Europe to the New World, he still stresses that the only "really American part of our history" concerns the growth and development of liberal notions of independence and personal industry. The necessary precondition for the emergence of a "really American" populace is that moment in the wilderness when the man of refinement and Euro-American sensibility is denuded of European tradition. For Turner, U.S. history is liberal history: the story of a nation that emerged as a land of yeoman farmers and then transitioned to industrial capitalism. With the absence of feudalism and its institutions a foregone conclusion, the sole political problem faced by the nation was to cultivate democratic institutions against neofeudal perversions. As Richard Hofstadter puts it in *The Age of Reform* (1956), U.S. politics were able to focus on "popular causes and ... reform" because it "had always been relatively free of the need or obligation to combat feudal traditions and entrenched aristocracies."[11]

While historians and political leaders told a national origin story in which the United States was a postfeudal republic, some literary authors saw the young nation in a different way. Jefferson, the great enemy of Virginian feudal institutions, might have been surprised to read Harriet Beecher Stowe's account of the Gordon family in *Dred: A Tale of the Great Dismal Swamp* (1856):

> Among the first emigrants to Virginia in its colonial days, was one Thomas Gordon, Knight, a distant offshoot of the noble Gordon family, renowned in Scottish history.... Inspired by remembrances of old ancestral renown, the Gordon family transmitted in their descent all the traditions, feelings, and habits, which were the growth of the aristocratic caste from which they had sprung. The name of Canema, given to the estate, came from an Indian guide and interpreter, who accompanied the first Col. Gordon as confiden-

tial servant. The estate, being entailed, passed down through the colonial times unbroken in the family, whose wealth, for some years, seemed to increase with every generation.¹²

What is of interest in Stowe's depiction of the Gordon family tree is not her insistence that they are members of a neofeudal aristocracy in the South; this claim was made both about and by southerners in the nineteenth century and proved to be a major trope in the decades leading up to the Civil War. What should raise eyebrows is Stowe mentioning *entail*, the feudal law that dictated that estates pass unbroken from father to eldest son, as the source of the Gordon family's fortune. It is tempting to breeze past Stowe's evocation of feudal law here, but in the context of nineteenth-century political and social thought, the word "entail" would have sounded an alarm for U.S. liberals who believed, like Jefferson, *"that the earth belongs in usufruct to the living"* (emphasis in original).¹³ Writing to James Madison while serving as minister to France in 1789, Jefferson argues that Americans must "change the descent of lands holden in tale," a process to be accomplished by "taking reason for our guide instead of English precedents."¹⁴ The conflict between "reason" and "English precedents" is a theme we'll return to again and again in this book, primarily through the vexed relationship between common law and statutory law. Stowe's casual evocation of entail in describing the central family in her radical antislavery novel troubles Jefferson's hope that the United States would opt for post-Enlightenment statutes rather than common law precedent; by the mid-nineteenth century, it seems, elements of U.S. law had indeed favored the traditions of the past over the imperatives of the present.

THE LIBERAL CONSENSUS IN U.S. HISTORIOGRAPHY

As the selection of documents above indicates, nineteenth-century thinkers insisted that the United States lacked a feudal class system. It's not surprising, then, that twentieth-century literary and cultural criticism inherited and perpetuated the myth of an always already liberal America. Louis Hartz, a leading figure of the "liberal consensus" school of political theory that gained traction during the Cold War, asserts in *The Liberal Tradition in America* (1955) that "America was settled by men who fled from feudal and clerical oppressions of the Old World." Hartz's "liberal society analysis" thus "stresses the absence of the feudal factor in America."¹⁵ C. Wright Mills, while opposing Hartz's laudatory assessment of U.S. liberalism, nonetheless stresses in *White Collar: The American Middle Classes* (1951) that North America was "occupied by men whose absolute individualism involved an absence of traditional fetters, and who, unhampered by the heirlooms of feudal Europe, were ready and eager to realize the drive toward capitalism."[16]

The myth and symbol school of U.S. literary criticism folded Hartz's liberal consensus into their readings of U.S. literature and history. As Donald Pease suggests, the myth and symbol school emphasized an imagined "cohesion of the national community" through "foundational signifiers" such as "Virgin Land, American Adam, Errand into the Wilderness" that were promulgated through collaborations with "the press, university system, publishing industry, and other aspects of the cultural apparatus that managed . . . such value-laden terms as the nation and the people."[17] This "cohesion of national community" also required a unified vision of U.S. cultural development and, more important, a linear, progressive view of the national community's relationship to the past. Liberalism—imperfectly defined as a political ideology emphasizing belief in free market capitalism, the "one man, one vote" vision of universal suffrage, and the defense of individual liberties (however those liberties may be defined)—became the cohesive glue that held the mythic United States together despite the fissures and contradictions evident from the republic's earliest days. To that end, myth and symbol Americanists recapitulated Hartz's notion of liberal consensus even as they offered stinging critiques of the nation that supported their scholarly efforts.

A cursory review of key texts in twentieth-century American studies reveals how hegemonic the liberal consensus thesis has been. Henry Nash Smith asserts in *The Virgin Land: The American West as Symbol and Myth* (1950) that the "Virgin Land," "where nature loomed larger than civilization," called to settlers because it was a place "where feudalism had never been established."[18] Following Smith, Leo Marx makes the struggle between "the feudal past, perpetuated by corrupt, repressive institutions" and "the pristine landscape of Virginia," which is "conducive to the nurture of democratic values," a central premise in his reading of Jefferson in *The Machine in the Garden* (1964).[19] Despite a rigorous effort to connect U.S. literature to its European sources, Leslie Fiedler's *Love and Death in the American Novel* (1967) argues that the central conflict of the bourgeois novel—the representational struggle between an emergent middle class and a decadent feudal class—is lost in U.S. literature due to the nation's lack of "debased aristocratic codes."[20] Writing thirty years after Smith, Marx, and Fiedler, Sacvan Bercovitch reaffirms the old liberal consensus view: "In Europe, capitalism evolved dialectically, through conflict with earlier and persisting ways of thought and belief. It was an emerging force in a complex cultural design. Basically, New England bypassed the conflict."[21] Though Bercovitch goes on to point out moments when U.S. liberalism cannibalized elements of the feudal order, his vision of an Anglo-American liberal consensus erases the active struggle between capitalist modernity and its premodern antecedents that was essential to the formation of national identity in the United States.

Beginning in the late twentieth century, American studies began to question the hidden assumptions undergirding older approaches to U.S. culture. A "comparative" model, which insisted that literary critics expand their archives to include global authors and theorists and types of knowledge (e.g., economic, scientific) drawn from other disciplines, offered new perspectives on texts central to myth and symbol studies, and introduced texts that fell outside of the older methodology's purview.[22] Yet the liberal consensus model endured in postmodern critiques of liberalism. Critics accept that U.S. liberalism represented a wholly new political form and then perform critiques that demonstrate contradictions within this new form, all the while neglecting to assess transhistorical structures of economic and social order that shed new light on how our cultural institutions have developed.[23] When critics do seek to assess the impact of medieval traditions on the United States, they often do so in formalist terms. Most would agree with literary critic Kim Moreland, who argues that "the medievalist impulse clearly runs counter to the major U.S. cultural tradition at every point. Medievalism is feudal and aristocratic rather than capitalistic and democratic, Roman Catholic rather than Puritan, European rather than nationalist American, and regressive rather than progressive."[24] As Moreland usefully notes, for the United States in the nineteenth century, "medievalism" defined a constellation of interrelated cultural forms—political, literary, architectural, religious, and economic—that all signaled a bad past that must be overcome. If this study seems to slide between "feudalism" and "medievalism" somewhat haphazardly, that is due in part to the ease with which nineteenth-century thinkers themselves failed to distinguish between feudalism and the culture of Catholic Europe from roughly the fall of the Roman Empire to the fifteenth century.

Nineteenth-century thinkers conflated feudalism and medievalism partly as a conscious act of distancing (from Europe, monarchies, and rigid aristocracies) and partly due to their still-evolving knowledge of the Middle Ages.

Those who claimed that the United States had overcome the medieval were not lying; as we will see, many truly believed that the nation had done just that. Similarly, liberal consensus political scientists, their myth and symbol colleagues in American studies, and contemporary scholars working in these traditions do not make their claims from a place of ignorance: they argue from deep readings of American literature, much of which openly professes a distaste for feudal institutions. In a sense, my thesis in this book is perverse: it asks us to read against the grain of the upper-class Anglo-American's assertions of historical sovereignty and political novelty. Lingering beneath this method is an earnest desire to avoid the mistake Karl Marx and Friedrich Engels warn against in *The German Ideology*: I never want to take the upper-class Anglo-American at his word, believing what he believed of himself to be true. A key assumption of this book is that a given culture often either has little idea what is happening to itself during periods of radical transition, or (more darkly) that cultural luminaries will perform endless backbends to make themselves appear more radical than they really are.

FEUDALISM IN THE NINETEENTH-CENTURY IMAGINARY

In reality, and against claims from eighteenth- and nineteenth-century Americans to the contrary, the United States inherited a robust feudal tradition from Europe and allowed that tradition to shape the nation's literary, juridical, and social discourses. Intellectually, Anglo-America inherited a set of philosophical and social precepts that had been worked out by men of the old feudal elite; politically, Anglo-America derived its laws and institutions from models with genealogies reaching back to the Middle Ages; and, culturally, Anglo-America deployed aesthetic modes that emerged from medieval literary and visual traditions.

These ideas carried through the Revolution and brought with them class antagonisms and hierarchies meant to keep those antagonisms at bay. As Tocqueville admits in his assessment of U.S. populism, "Beneath the conventional enthusiasm and amid this ingratiating ritual toward the dominant power, you can easily perceive a deep distaste for the democratic institutions of their country. The people are a power they both fear and despise."[25] Tocqueville here troubles his earlier claim that aristocracy yielded power to the populace out of fear of uprising and a well-honed survival instinct, thus ensuring that "the thrust of democracy proved all the more irresistible in those states where aristocracy had been most deeply rooted."[26]

Another French historian, François Guizot, would go even further than Tocqueville, insisting that the federative approach to U.S. political life was a nineteenth-century iteration of arrangements developed under feudal states. In his fourth lecture on European civilization, Guizot lays out the fundamentals of the feudal system, proceeding from small landed baronies set up to protect individual interests to the "federative system" that finally bound them all together and made them the precursor of a modern nation. Toward the end of the lecture, Guizot takes an unexpected turn to the western hemisphere:

> The federative system, then, is that which evidently requires the greatest development of reason, morality, and civilization, in the society to which it is applied. Well, this, nevertheless, was the system which feudalism endeavoured to establish; the idea of general feudalism, in fact, was that of a federation. It reposed upon the same principles on which are founded, in our day, the federation of the United States of America, for example. It aimed at leaving in the hands of each lord all that portion of government and sovereignty which could remain there, and to carry to the suzerain, or to the general assembly of barons, only the least possible portion of power, and that only in cases of absolute necessity.[27]

For Guizot, the federative system, a cornerstone of liberal polity, is not the radical negation of feudalism, but instead an outgrowth of unresolved contradictions within the feudal conception of the state. That the balance tipped in favor of liberalism as the struggle played out does not indicate that the old feudal institutions could be entirely overcome, especially not by the Revolutionary Generation, who were (by and large) the New World's equivalent of the landed class that had always constituted the basis for feudal power.

This view was not lost on the framers of the U.S. Constitution. Alexander Hamilton noted during the ratification debate in New York that the federal government's structure would reflect that of the feudal state: "In the antient feudal governments of Europe, there were in the first place a monarch; subordinate to him, a body of nobles; and subject to these, the vassals or the whole body of the people. The authority of the kings was limited, and that of the barons considerably independent." Hamilton warns that the old feudal states collapsed because of overreach on the part of the monarch and nobility, but that the U.S. republic may sidestep these upheavals by protecting "the vassals or the whole body of the people" from the more outrageous abuses of the ancient regimes. "These very instances" of abuse, Hamilton writes, prove "that in whatever direction the popular weight leans, the current of power will flow: wherever the popular attachments lie, there will rest the political superiority."[28] Hamilton does not shy away from comparing the U.S. government to the feudal state. Instead, he insists that America must not overextend its sovereignty and thus risk alienating its citizenry in the same ways that European monarchies outraged their vassals and peasants. As historian Gordon S. Wood observes, Hamilton's semifeudal view of the federal government, in which the secretary of the treasury would serve "as a kind of prime minister to Washington's monarchical presidency," reflected Hamilton's view of history, which predicted that as U.S. institutions developed, they would follow the model of European royal courts.[29] At the very birth of constitutional democracy, then, we find a transhistorical impulse that makes the United States resemble a great clearinghouse of historical tendencies: more like Whitman's nation that "cheerfully" accepts the feudal past than the revolutionary holocaust Hawthorne envisioned. What the liberal consensus school overlooks is precisely what Guizot and Hamilton emphasize: the ways in which the foundational principles of liberalism developed *within* and not *against* feudalism.

Viewed from the long range, we see that U.S. liberalism did not effect a radical break from the feudal past: instead, the liberalism of the seventeenth, eighteenth, and nineteenth centuries sought a source in "antient" feudal precedent even as it critiqued that decadent feudalism's excesses. To take an English example, Locke's response to Robert Filmer in the *Two Treatises of Government* (1689) does not seek to alter the domestic relation of master and servant, nor does it break up the landed gentry that constituted the power base of seventeenth-century England; instead, Locke realigns that aristocracy's relationship to the monarch, empowering the feudal class against abuses on the part of the sovereign. As David Wooton puts it, Locke did not "believe in any inalienable right other than the right to freedom of religion." Indeed, Locke "[sees] the task of the philosopher as being to preserve the existing order against the subversive threat of change," not to radically overhaul existing social relations.[30] Locke therefore diffuses sovereignty among the landed powers, but does not seek to establish an egalitarian relation between citizens.

This had a direct bearing on the development of U.S. political culture. One of Locke's most important contributions to U.S. politics, the *Fundamental*

Constitutions of Carolina (1669), while establishing the liberal precedent of religious toleration in the New World also "erect[s] the first hereditary nobility on North American soil."³¹ The *Fundamental Constitutions* also establishes a strong link between black slavery and feudal privilege, guaranteeing the landed aristocrat "absolute power and authority over his negro slaves," and introduces a new class of white laborers, "leet-men," whose progeny would serve in perpetual bondage to their lords.³² For Locke, as for Hamilton, harmonizing contradictory social forces, *not* resolving those contradictions, is the state's primary function.

Edmund Fawcett, whose recent *Liberalism: The Life of an Idea* (2014) synthesizes several strands of liberalism from the 1820s to our own moment of crisis in the global liberal order, places this struggle between contending social forces at the heart of all subsequent liberal ideologies. Fawcett observes that for liberals of the nineteenth century, society was "a field of inescapable conflict" between contending classes and factions within those classes.³³ Liberalism was thus a "practical response by state and law to the predicament of capitalist modernity"—namely, the struggle between contending classes that so many Americans believed the nation had skipped over or dismantled by revolutionary reform.³⁴ It wouldn't have been difficult, then, for a liberal of the nineteenth century to understand that landed wealth posed a threat to labor and capitalist development any more than it would have been difficult for a tenant farmer or property-less urban laborer to understand that his class interests were in direct opposition to the class interests of his landlord or employer. The point wasn't to end social antagonism, but to prevent further abuse leading to further revolution. Liberalism's relatively recent alliances with progressive economics, welfare states, and social justice have little to do with liberalism in its nineteenth-century context.

If all of this was evident to so many nineteenth-century lights, why do we have such difficulty understanding it in our accounts of U.S. history? The major difficulty is terminological. What do we mean by "feudalism"? What do we mean by "liberalism"? Readers living in the world that liberalism made can more intuitively grasp the latter. The former, however, is a mare's nest of innuendoes, half-thoughts, and clichés. As Elizabeth A. R. Browning has made clear, our understanding of feudalism bears little resemblance to actual social relations in the Middle Ages; it is instead a reductio ad absurdum that serves as scholarly and political shorthand for all that modernity has supposedly overcome. Browning observes that scholars use terms such as "feudalism" and "the feudal system" in order to "grasp . . . a subject known or suspected to be complex." This tendency has "[encouraged] concentration on oversimplified models that are applied as standards."[35] An oversimplified view of feudalism has saturated the West's popular imagination. Susan Reynolds puts it succinctly: "Feudalism, to any members of the general public, stands for almost any hierarchical and oppressive system. Bosses or landlords who bully their employees or tenants are being feudal. If they bully them fiercely they are worse: they are positively medieval."[36]

In order to properly situate the key terms through which I will assess antebellum U.S. culture, I therefore must pause to define "feudalism" in its nineteenth-century context. The term has intellectual origins in seventeenth-century French and English historiography, which attempted to codify the overlapping and sometimes contradictory jurisdictions of the Middle Ages into a unitary system of values and laws.[37] Notable English scholars such as Henry Spelman (1595–1623) and Edward Coke (1552–1634) offered full-throated defenses of Anglo-Saxon liberty, rooted in an imagined Anglo-Saxon constitutionalism, against the importation of Norman *féodalité* after 1066.[38] In the English context, then, "feudalism" also implied a racial historiography that pitted Anglo-Saxon tribalism against Norman feudalism, the latter understood as a foreign usurpation of the primitive liberty of the former.

The English conception of feudalism received its first thorough elaboration in Adam Smith's *An Inquiry into the Nature and Causes of the Wealth of Nations* (1776). Smith explains feudal law in terms that would have appealed to Jefferson and his contemporaries in the Revolutionary Generation. For Smith, feudal law is "founded upon the most absurd of all suppositions, the supposition that every successive generation of men have not an equal right to the earth, and to all that it possesses; but that the property of the present generation should be restrained and regulated according to the fancy of those who died perhaps five hundred years ago."[39] Put another way: "life belong in usufruct to the living." The absurdity Smith finds in imposing feudal law on contemporary circumstances is based in his stadial theory of history. Book 3 of *The Wealth of Nations* relies on this theory, which charts the progression of Europeans from the "disorderly times [when] every great landlord was a sort of petty prince" to the collapse of that system due to the "silent and insensible operation of commerce and manufactures."[40] Smith finds in the supposed collapse of the feudal order a moral lesson: the feudal lords lost their estates because the allure of foreign manufactures was too great, causing them to squander their fortunes in "the wantonness of plenty, for trinkets and baubles, fitter to be the play-things of children than the serious pursuits of men."[41]

Understood in terms of a stadial historiography, the Revolutionary Generation's claim to have overcome feudalism is perfectly valid. Simply by being in the eighteenth century and not, say, the thirteenth, America had moved beyond feudalism. But this is a little like someone taking a chess board, assigning new names and moves to the pieces, and then confidently declaring herself the world champion of the resulting game. By positing one's own time as the apex of a progressive historical narrative, one can confidently disregard inheritances from the past, or (even better) demonstrate that these inheritances predicted the present moment's ideal synthesis. Simply by living, now, we have overcome all the residual social forces from way back then.

Perhaps, being so close to the major upheavals that have traditionally been taken as signs of feudalism's decline, the Revolutionary Generation could not see how their own concepts of social order related to premodern aristocratic ideas. The Revolutionary Generation engaged in a pitched battle against monarchy, which was, beyond the Catholic Church, the most durable symbol of medieval power. But, for the historian and political theorist Ellen Meiksins Wood, the monarchical sovereignty that the Revolutionary Generation associated with feudalism was, in the European context, a development *against* feudal power and the "parcelization of sovereignty" that characterized feudal social relations.[42] In Wood's account, seigniorial authority in the Middle Ages was based on "a complex network of competing jurisdictions," whereas the protomodern state sought to establish a "single unitary jurisdiction, the civic corporation" that would guarantee inalienable rights for all citizens, however citizen may be defined.[43]

This is distinct from the forms of democracy-among-nobles that characterized feudal social relations. As Marx writes in the *Critique of Hegel's Doctrine of the State* (1844–1843), "In the Middle Ages there were serfs, feudal property, trade guilds, scholastic corporations, etc. That is to say, in the Middle Ages property, trade, society and man were *political*. . . . Man was the real principle of the state, but man was *not free*. Hence there was a *democracy of unfreedom*, a perfected system of estrangement."[44] Trade, as Smith, Marx, and Wood all agree, erodes this "democracy of unfreedom" by shifting the locus of wealth production from the feudal estate to the marketplace. In volume 3 of *Capital*, Marx skews from his earlier ideological critique to offer a material analysis of the process of defeudalization: "With money rent, the traditional relationship fixed by customary law between the landowner and his dependent... is necessarily transformed into a contractual relationship, a purely monetary relationship determined by the firm rules of positive law."[45] (Marx's insistence that money rent represented a new economic relationship isn't exactly correct; *scutagium*, or scutage, and *obliae*, both forms of money rent, were common in England and France from at least the second half of the twelfth century.)[46] Positive law in Marx's formula is related to the Enlightenment conception of natural law and is to be separated from custom and custom's Burkean, ritualistic overtones. In the end, finance forces feudal lords to share their political leverage with the absolutist state and the nascent bourgeoisie, both of which control the markets and therefore the economic vitality of the country. Sometimes, the more recently minted nobles became bourgeoisie themselves, as was the case in eighteenth-century France, where wholesale trade (but not shopkeeping), real estate speculation, stock trading, and industrial mine operation carried no threat of *dérogeance*, or loss of noble title.[47] Over time, the movement away from the manor to the urban market erodes feudal power, leaving the bourgeoisie to seize control of a country's political, economic, and cultural institutions. The bourgeoisie stand between the feudal crown and the remaining feudal lords, carving out an ever-increasing space that eventually threatens the structural integrity of the older rival powers. We may call this the classic Marxist narrative of European defeudalization.

However, the Marxist narrative does not necessarily mean that the aristocracies erected under feudalism merely recede into the fog of history. Wood is careful to note that the "civic corporation" model was not inimical to the ongoing consolidation of power in the hands of a landed aristocracy. So, even as feudalism as a system of production and mutual obligations was replaced by capitalism and its emphasis on positive law, the feudal power structure was allowed to transition into the new market economy. Instead of creating a system wherein small producers brought their goods to the market—the storybook version of capitalist relations that persists as a central tenet of primary education in the United States—capitalism produced a system whereby the wealthiest landowners could transition from military powers to economic powers.[48]

As Wood notes in her analysis of political institutions during the English

Civil War, "Both monarchy and aristocracy were strengthened by the bargain in which the demilitarization of the aristocracy . . . was compensated by the state's defense of landed property, underwriting and protecting the aristocracy's purely economic powers of exploitation."[49] By sacrificing some degree of sovereignty for the social stability provided by a central governmental authority, the aristocracy created favorable conditions for their continued relevance under the emerging commercial society of early capitalism. But maintaining a system whereby political power rests in the hands of landowners ensured that this central authority would not "act in the traditional ways of a feudal monarchy."[50] The English system's division of governing power between Parliament's wealthy landowners and the Crown does not, therefore, represent a full dismantling of feudal power, but instead a compromise that allowed feudal wealth to make a smooth transition into commercial society.

It should go without saying that the young United States inherited all of these European developments and developed them further into the federative system that for Guizot was a mirror of medieval governance. As Leon Trotsky succinctly puts it in his *History of the Russian Revolution* (1930), "The European colonists in America did not begin history all over again from the beginning. The fact that . . . the United States [has] now economically outstripped England was made possible by the very backwardness of [its] capitalist development."[51] The U.S. landed class scavenged elements of feudal law and governance and combined them with the dynamism of a powerful young capitalism. Just as the feudal nobility of Europe used elements of the market to support itself in the transition to capitalist modernity, the capitalist United States used elements of feudal law and tradition to secure its position and guarantee its world-historical dominance.

THE FEUDAL IDEA OF ORDER

I will argue in the coming chapters that the elements of feudalism that persisted in the United States were both practical and abstract. Practical neofeudalism manifests in legal decisions pertaining to land ownership, women's roles, and master/servant relations that were inherited from the Middle Ages and filtered through the common law. These specific regulations and precedents were used in U.S. courtrooms when statutory regulations were not in place, troubling the belief that U.S. legal and political thought evolved free from feudal baggage. The legal manifestations of America's feudal-liberal synthesis are covered most carefully in chapters 2 and 3, in relation to land law and marriage law, and in chapter 5, in relation to employee/employer relations. But the legal traces of feudalism only tell half the story.

Of more lasting importance is the structural influence feudal precedent played on the U.S. social imaginary. I call this the *feudal idea of order*, and it is this inheritance that will occupy the majority of my argument in *Medieval America*. This phrase captures six core inheritances from European social ideology, inheritances that without exception trouble the United States' belief that it is the telos of liberal political and economic development. The feudal idea of order includes:

1. A *structure of nature* (including racial, class, and gender hierarchies) that insists intellect and the ability to own and manage property are inheritable traits, predominantly associated with one type of human;
2. A *property structure* that emphasizes private ownership, and argues that sovereignty derives from the ability to hold, manage, and extract profit from private property;
3. A *family structure* that places sovereign power in the hands of a patriarch or matriarch, coupled with a household structure that affords the patriarch or matriarch economic and quasi-judicial rule within the home;
4. A *managerial style* that instills employee deference to great men or women;
5. A *political structure* that emphasizes the sovereignty of discrete political units in the form of a weak federalism organized by, for, and with the consent of a strong landed class;
6. An *aesthetics* that models the poet-genius on the feudal lord, and the work of art to a well-ordered and internally consistent estate.[52]

These six elements of feudal order do not contradict the Revolutionary Generation's belief that they were enacting Enlightenment principles in the New World; in fact, they come from the heart of Enlightenment philosophies of society, history, and individuality. As the progressive historian Carl Becker points out in *The Heavenly City of the Eighteenth-Century Philosophers* (1932), the very philosophers that inspired men like Jefferson were themselves inheritors of a medieval worldview that their works updated but did not fundamentally contradict. Conceptions of ideal social order borrowed from St. Augustine's *The City of God* (426) and a doctrine of natural law repurposed from St. Thomas Aquinas's *Summa Theologica* (1265–1274) were as instrumental in shaping the Enlightenment worldview as were scientific advances and the emergence of the market economy.[53] The dichotomous terms we so often use to describe the development of capitalism and its concomitant political institutions do not adequately represent the historical and ideological upheavals that have been underway from the fifteenth century to today.

None of this was lost on keen nineteenth-century observers. As early as 1834, an unsigned editorial in the pro-Jackson *United States Telegraph* questions the view of the United States as the exemplary postfeudal republic:

> To Europe, and especially to the friends of freedom in Europe, our country is the *Eldarado* of modern times. They read our excellent republican and paper Constitutions, our bills of right, the results of our popular elections, and the glowing eulogises [sic] upon all these and some other things, delivered by our holiday trumpeters, our fourth of July orators, and they sigh to be among us, to partake of such unparalleled blessings. But alas! they know nothing of our degeneracy since the days of '76 and of '89. They know not, that while feudal principles and feudal tyranny, with hierarchy, and monarchy, are rapidly declining among them, that here feudalism and monarchy are advancing in rather a different shape, but the same, if not worse, in the end.[54]

The author frames his quarrel with "advancing" feudalism in a spirit of nostalgic reaction; he seeks a return to the days of declaration writing in 1776 and constitution writing in 1789 without understanding that actions undertaken by the Revolutionary Generation laid the groundwork for the consolidation of capital that motors the nation's "degeneracy." Another anonymous editorial writer, writing in a January 1834 issue of the *Providence Patriot*, offers a similar warning to working people:

> [History] presents examples of some attempts on the part of [the working class] to rescue it from thralldom, and those efforts might have changed the whole order of society in Europe four or five centuries ago, if it had not been put down by combinations among those who possessed the military force that belong to the feudal system. This country is exempt from such interference.... There is, however, the same general tendency to the concentration of wealth in a few hands here as elsewhere, and that concentration will produce here the same effects on society and political institutions. So that the people have got something to do for themselves, and something

which cannot be done but by a great effort, and by the effective exercise of the powers of government in behalf. The government only can UNDO what IT has done amiss and place the commercial interests of the whole people on a just and safe basis.[55]

The author of "To the Working Men" is more astute than the Jacksonian. Seeing a "general tendency" at work underneath the accumulation of capitalist wealth in the hands of a few who also maintain a monopoly on the use of force, the author of this editorial reaches toward a full-throated demand for universal equality and suffrage on some "just and safe basis" other than private property.

Both editorials make an observation that speaks forcefully to our own political moment: in the West, wealth and privilege are astonishingly good at rearticulating their authority under ever-evolving conditions. But how do they go about this, especially in a country that so prides itself on free and open institutions? Aristocracies—whether military, agrarian, industrial, or "postindustrial"—marshal a culture's representative apparatuses to make their political and economic dominance seem like the result of a natural process of power consolidation by the "best and brightest" of any given historical epoch. Through narratives that emphasize temporal rupture and radical change in ever-more-particular historical moments over broader, centuries-long arcs of historical development, aristocracies are able to conceal the persistence of their power and privilege. But when we look at the West from a long historical vantage point, the social upheavals of the past five hundred years take on the character of a struggle between an astonishingly small group of key global players who have "protested too much" that their power has been reduced by every victory of the people over their oppressors. Whereas we tend to view the power shifts brought on by capitalism as flattening out social influence, making it more democratic and diffuse, in reality the system looks more like a triangle, with the pinnacle being lifted ever higher and higher as the middle and base grow. The very existence of that triangular distribution of political and economic power is the essence of the feudal idea of order.

MEDIEVAL INHERITANCES IN U.S. LITERARY FORMS

Most of us don't bother to think about our cars until we hear the first rumble that portends a pricey visit to the mechanic. Likewise, one may choose to ignore ideological forms as long as they are functioning as intended. We can best undertake the analysis of an ideology when its motor breaks down, whether as the result of an irresolvable internal contradiction rising up or an open rebellion breaking out against its core mechanisms. My analysis in the coming chapters will focus on those moments when the détente between feudalism and liberalism breaks down, and the artificiality and unsustainability of the feudal-liberal synthesis becomes plain.

Hungarian philosopher Georg Lukács observes in *History and Class Consciousness* (1923) that, more often than not, "the real motor forces of history are independent of man's (psychological) consciousness of them."[56] Following Lukács, I assume throughout this book that the vast majority of historical actors are unaware of the real conditions in which they labor. To extend the metaphor above, they might believe their car has no engine at all and instead runs on magic. They may mistake their car for a horse. Or they may, more troublingly, not see that there's anything moving them forward at all: living in an eternal now, they believe that they have always been and will always be fixed in one place even as they are being propelled to the next.

If Lukács is correct and most historical actors are unaware of what's happening around them, then cultural critics have a weird (and tough) job. On the one hand, we need to work through cultural archives with the knowledge that the people we are reading do not fully understand what they are writing. At the same time, we must be conscious of the ways in which we are also unaware of "the real motor forces of history" influencing our analyses. This mode of criticism can be, in the words of literary critic Fredric Jameson, "a practice of allegorical enlargement rather than one of reduction."[57] It can also be a mess. The line between the useful critique (a productive "unmasking of cultural artifacts as socially symbolic acts") and the mess (a queasy mix of historical false consciousness with contemporary false consciousness) is thin.[58] It's all very confusing.

This perplexity has everything to do with how we view our relationship to the past. Marx writes in *The Eighteenth Brumaire of Louis Bonaparte* (1852) that a revolutionary generation "cannot begin with itself before it has stripped off all superstition about the past," and therefore "in order to arrive at its own content, the revolution . . . must let the dead bury their dead."[59] This process requires prior acts of recognition—we admit that the past existed, that it persists into our moment, and that we must demystify its aura in order to move forward from it. But Marx doesn't demand that the present generation bury (or smash, or leap from, or overcome) the past. Nor does he encourage us to treat the past as an object of disinterested, formal inquiry. Instead, Marx conjures an image of a great procession of past eras, finally receiving their proper funeral rites after generations of use and abuse: not a cultural revolution but a revolutionary Tenebrae, during which the light of past eras is granted recognition and then snuffed out. The past is tired and ill; it deserves rest. The critical futurist is Antigone demanding the right to bury her brother; the uncritical futurist is Creon sowing the seeds of his own collapse by insisting that the past rot out in open.

Anglo-Americans in the nineteenth century were, I will suggest in the following pages, more like Creon than Antigone—they chose to leave the feudal past's corpse rotting on the balustrade even as they claimed that it had vanished, utterly, from their nation. The literary authors I cover attempted to solve anachronistic persistence of feudalism in the United States by employing direct allusions to medieval literature, romantic and gothic tropes, and detailed (if sometimes disingenuous) rejections of feudal governance. Sometimes they did so consciously. Other times, their reliance on archaic literary forms indicates an uncritical assumption of past modes of expression. Literature, which then as now allows its practitioners to play fast and loose with historical time and contexts, offers a space in which writers can reconsider the nation's relationship to the past, and how that relationship determines America's national consciousness.

In a time of rapid social and economic change, medievalism served a crucial role in this process of mediation. For Lukács, the medievalism emerged in Europe in the eighteenth and nineteenth centuries as a form of protest: "The inhumanity of capitalism, the chaos of competition, the destruction of the small by the big, the debasement of culture by the transformation of all things into commodities—all this is contrasted, in a manner generally reactionary in tendency, with the social idyll of the Middle Ages, seen as a period of peaceful co-operation among all classes, an age of the organic growth of culture."[60]

We can find many instances of this "generally reactionary" mode in American letters, from the feudal apologias of southerners such as George Fitzhugh through to the antitechnological impulses of Henry Adams. Scholarship pertaining to American medievalism has traditionally favored such figures because they allow scholars to quickly delineate between those authors who saw themselves as contributing to the United States' liberal program and those who formulated nostalgic reactions against that program. Kim Moreland argues that "the Middle Ages served largely to provide a direct contrast to contemporary U.S. life. This contrast was evaluative, many writers assuming that medieval values were superior to contemporary American values."[61] Other critics, from T. J. Jackson Lears to Tison Pugh, have approached the problem with the similar assumption that American medievalism reacted against, and not with, the emergence of bourgeois modernity.[62] The assumption underwriting all such studies is, to return to Lukács, that bourgeois modernity had already done away with the vestiges of feudal order and class structure and could therefore turn its attention toward "smoothing out the sharp division" between the worker and the employer and thus move human history "on to a bourgeois path."[63] Those authors who chose to turn their attention to the past did so as conscious retreat from social forces developing around them.

My argument moves away from a reading of U.S. cultural history that locates in the medievalist impulse an antimodern tendency like that described by Lukács. The authors discussed here all agree that U.S. democracy shared a complex and shifting relationship to feudal tradition. Southerners such as George Fitzhugh, Edgar Allan Poe, and John Pendleton Kennedy held that slaveholders represented an organic aristocracy, one uniquely capable of maintaining an economic and racial order that was under siege by the specter of slave rebellion and meddling abolitionism. Like his southern contemporaries, James Fenimore Cooper also championed the need for a class of great landowners to tamp down radical energies unlocked by the cult of popular sovereignty. His novels and political writings both celebrate U.S. democracy and warn against its excesses, but by the 1840s Cooper would move further and further toward the latter valence of his thought. Cooper's last major literary production, the three-novel Littlepage novels sequence, argues that only a feudal elite can prevent poor white settlers from undermining the nation's republican project. Ralph Waldo Emerson, whose early Transcendentalist works were so instrumental in the formation of white middle- and upper-class U.S. identity, would by the end of his career make a similar feudal turn. In the 1860s and 1870s, Emerson would replace his "American Scholar" with the corporate noble, a figure he repeatedly links to medieval precedents. Emerson's feudal turn came at the cusp of the Gilded Age, an era when "robber barons" amassed great fortunes, became prolific patrons of the arts, and imported crates of medieval art and manuscripts to the New World. From one perspective, the actions of these corporate nobles seem like anachronisms in democratic America. But, when understood from the perspective of America's synthesis of feudal tradition with liberal ideology, we see that they are really the fruits of a century-long process.

Not every author I analyze celebrates the United States' synthesis of feudalism and liberalism. Harriet Jacobs's *Incidents in the Life of a Slave Girl* argues that the construction of white southern nobility—including its valorization of the white southern woman as moral and social paragon—was predicated on the creation of a peasant class whose labor was stolen and bodies were open to any and all abuse. E.D.E.N. Southworth's *The Hidden Hand* reaffirms slavocracy and aristocratic order, yet its author nonetheless objects to the treatment of women under America's semifeudal system, which forced them to relinquish rights to their husbands under the ancient law of "baron and femme." Herman Melville troubles the aristocratic pretensions of U.S. capitalists by portraying the violence necessary to maintain the feudal order of slave and merchant ships. By portraying violence at the heart of capitalism's means of trade, Melville asks readers to reconsider the premises on which their seemingly more polite society is constructed. The Cherokee novelist, poet, and newspaperman John Rollin Ridge also discovers violence at the heart of capitalist accumulation, even as he frames indigenous sovereignty through feudal-romantic language. His works slide between pro-feudal and pro-settler stances, an ideological disunion bred by Ridge's subject-position, which was likewise pitched between the center and fringes of U.S. social life. These major authors—along with lesser-known voices from the popular press and mass literature—offer stinging critiques of U.S. feudalism that illustrate how ancient precedent was central to U.S. political and social development.

Near the end of chapter 5, I briefly discuss Harvard president Charles W. Eliot's decision to deploy the Harvard riflemen in 1877. No one event covered in the following pages so succinctly illustrates the tangible results of U.S. feudalism. Picture a trained militia deployed in front of Harvard College in 1877, the university's armed response to strikes in nearby Lowell. The soldiers stand at ready to quash any mob of immigrant laborers who might cross their path. One newspaperman opined that the rioting workers "constituted a separate racial group, like blacks or Indians, who were incapable of altering their inherently uncivilized and uncivilizable behavior."[64] In other words, they were monsters. The monstrous racial other that bedeviled the slavocrats;

the riotous false "Injuns" who made claims to landlords' estates; the indigenous revenant who stalks white settlers pursuing their own petite kingdoms; the specter of women run riot, insisting that they too can aspire to your heights—these forces, newly constituted as a mob of immigrants demanding economic equality, must have loomed in Harvard president Charles W. Eliot's mind when he deployed the Harvard riflemen. Similarly frightful figures continue to loom in the collective imagination of so many white Americans who subconsciously suspect that their privilege is not a product of natural law but an ancestor's good luck.

Finally, the figure of the mob emboldens these men of privilege. As political theorist Corey Robin puts it, "What the conservative ultimately learns from his opponents... is the power of political agency and the potency of the mass. From the trauma of revolution," conservatives "learn that men and women can order social relationships and political time."[65] The privileged therefore mimic the riotous crowd and embrace their Anglo-Saxon ancestor's "immigrant" status in the Americas, all the while working diligently to further consolidate social and productive power. The Harvard riflemen, knights framed by Memorial Hall, stood guard over a profound symbol of the Western intellectual and economic tradition and kept the monsters at bay.

If it is a grim image, it contains in it a kernel of hope. Übermenschen are fragile things, after all: prone to fits of melancholy and violent reaction, it is as if they somehow sense that their power is ephemeral. Poe's grotesques, avatars of slave revolt, are his greatest inventions. The endless procession of pale aristocrats and their frail lovers cannot compare to the genius of Hop-Frog, the Red Death victim, or Vondervotteimittiss's anarchic harper. Poe's texts therefore work against themselves to produce characters and scenarios that exceed their author's intentions. Cooper's "Injuns," offensive as their assumption of indigenous identity is, nonetheless stand as an example of tenants who would not let landlords determine their fates. Capitola Cap snatches her equal share of power and fame, even if it is a power based in the economic exploitation of others. Linda Brent is certainly a better model: she not only discovers a network of supportive women to help her raise her daughter in freedom, but she also uses her master's rhetorical and intellectual tools to dismantle his manor. Joaquín's bloody vengeance may shock, but it is profoundly cathartic for generations of immigrants whose families have been targeted and harassed. Babo's messianic death points toward a transhistorical alliance of laborers, sailors, slaves, and tribesmen who may one day conspire to seize the master's ship and sail it into new ports. Poe's artist-geniuses, Cooper's enlightened landlords, Melville's lordly captains, and Emerson's poetic businessmen cannot stand up to such forces for very long, no matter how many riflemen are deployed to defend the manor.

CHAPTER ONE

Plantation Romance and Southern Medievalism in Poe's Magazine Fiction

> Great literary movements are never consciously directed; they are always the expression through art of some fresh energy of conviction, some new and large hope of a race or an epoch. The general development of literature is, therefore, in its main directions inevitable and beneficent; if it were not so, progress would be a blunder and life a stagnant pool rather than a running stream.
>
> —Hamilton Wright Mabie, *Essays in Literary Interpretation* (1893)

Speaking in 1898 at the unveiling of George Julian Zolnay's bust of Poe at the University of Virginia, literary critic Hamilton Wright Mabie argued that Poe's works would help educate a "superior" caste of men who could help the nation "eradicate the provincialism of taste" that in Mabie's opinion was "the bane . . . of the whole country." Mabie's description of Poe's legacy emphasizes genetic aristocracy and ownership by birthright: "One of the greatest privileges of the average man," he says, "is to recognize and honor the superior man, because the superior man makes it worth while to belong to the race by giving life a dignity and splendor which constitute a common capital for all who live."[1] For Mabie, Poe is the sort of "superior man" that the literate masses must recognize and honor. Mabie's Hegelian conception of historical progress as an ascent from ignorance toward universal self-identity—in his *Essays in Literary Criticism* (1892), he lauds his century for having "come to maturity, and the self-consciousness which is the power of maturity"—is related to a cultural project that enshrines aesthetic production as the highest expression of human imaginative capability, and thus the genius-artist as the highest human type.[2] Mabie's comments assert that white racial pride and a refined aesthetics are the real fruits of Poe's artistic maturity.

If, as Mabie asserts, great art such as Poe's is the expression of "some new and large hope of a race," then we are left with a question: What "race-hope" do Poe's works strive toward, and how does that hope shape the form and content of his tales? Poe's aesthetic project, bound up as it is with his aristocratic fantasies and antidemocratic impulses shared by several of his Northern contemporaries, derives from the proslavery literary circles of his day.[3] Mabie's flattering portrait of Poe can thus be resurrected as a damning critique of an author who has for too long been regarded as disengaged from the pressing historical and political issues he and his contemporaries took up in the long "culture war" that preceded Confederate secession.[4] Poe's proslavery aesthetics are so subtle and persuasive that they have also been important in the contemporary southern elite's seemingly endless attempts to rehabilitate the Confederacy; it's no small coincidence that Zolnay, the Hungarian American sculptor whose bust of Poe occasioned Mabie's speech, was known as "the sculptor of the Confederacy" and was responsible for several monuments to Confederate luminaries, including Jefferson Davis.[5] Both in the nineteenth century and today, the "fresh energy of conviction" that Poe's works channel is of a piece with the prettified sadism, political disingenuousness, and historical arrogance of the proslavery cause.

For lovers of Poe's stories, myself included, it is tempting to make a "separate the artist from the man" argument here. So what if Poe was dedicated to the work of developing a distinct southern regionalism as a forerunner to a full-throated southern nationalism, as the archival evidence of his time at the *Southern Literary Messenger* makes clear? Can't we say that Poe's politics—and the way he made his money for a time, as the editor of a proslavery magazine—were one thing, and his enduring tales another? Don't all of us in one way or another do one thing for money and another for passion? And, anyway, do aesthetics necessarily follow from politics, or can the two be separated? I want to argue that, at least in Poe's case, it's not possible to separate the aesthetic from the political, for the very simple reason that Poe's literary aesthetics rely on pseudomedieval tropes drawn from the plantation romances and political treatises produced by proslavery thinkers who profoundly shaped the trajectory of his career.

Poe's fiction dramatizes, with a regularity that borders on monomania, the decline of a magnificent semifeudal realm after the displacement of a patriarchal genius who maintains the realm's sense of order. The allegory of feudal decay that Poe wrote again and again in the magazine fiction of the 1830s and 1840s concretely aligns his works with the literary precedents and rhetorical devices deployed by other southern regionalists of his generation. Not quite "medievalist"—that word implying at least some earnest study of actual conditions of life during the European Middle Ages—this approach to the premodern European history is more aptly described as *medievalesque*, a hash of elements drawn largely from a fairy-tale vision of castles in the mist and knights on the battlefield. By displacing the reality of medieval social life and culture for an illusion summoned up from postmedieval literary representation, southerners fashioned a fantastical vision of their social life in a naked attempt to disguise the cruelty of the region's social organization. The practical effect of this simulacrum was to integrate the commodity-producing southern plantation into a "chivalric" vision of history that was as garbled as it was grandiose.

Medievalesque tropes were essential to southern efforts to present the plantation as a transcendent space that exceeded its specific material context as a working farm that relied on slave labor. Literary authors like Poe and his benefactor John Pendleton Kennedy, as well as polemicists like George Fitzhugh and Thomas Roderick Dew, appealed to the sympathies of Northern readers by characterizing chattel slavery as feudal in organization and paternalistic in intent. The technique helped abstract the racial and political dynamics of the planter aristocracy by tapping into medievalist nostalgia and a yearning for feudalism's supposedly more ordered social relations. The idealized plantation is a romantic fairy-tale kingdom in miniature; Poe's kingdoms are plantations idealized out of all historical specificity, into mist and fantasy. It is a trope that survives to this day. If you happen to visit a Disney theme park after reading this chapter, consider the image of Splash Mountain, a ride based on Joel Chandler Harris's Jim Crow–era Uncle Remus stories, looming to the left of Sleeping Beauty's castle.

The conflation of the plantation home with the feudal estate is based on sheer historical fabrication. The black bondsman, whose body was a commodity to be bought and sold on the marketplace, does not share an organic legal relation to the feudal villein, who willfully entered into a contract with his lord and was thus free (in theory, at least) to break that contract.[6] And, despite repeated claims for the homeliness of domestic slavery, the South was not autarkic in even the most liberal definition of the word. Between its large-scale commodity exports and its internationalist imperial ambitions, the region was a fully fledged global actor whose aggregate wealth outstripped even that of residual feudal landlords in the Old World. As economist Thomas Piketty puts it, "Southern slave owners in the New World controlled more wealth than the landlords of Old Europe. Their farmland was not worth very much, but since they had the bright idea of owning not just the land but also the labor force needed to work that land, their total capital was even greater." By factoring in the market value of chattel ("human capital"), Piketty determines that, with a male slave commanding an average of two thousand dollars on the market, the wealth of southern slaveholders "exceeded four years of [average] national income" until abolition in 1865.[7] By connecting the plantation system with feudalism, proslavery authors softened the truly exceptional atrocities committed by the U.S. slaveocracy—and disguised the reality of slavery as a structural component of nineteenth-century capitalist economics.

Popular literary history has excluded the romances produced by authors such as John Pendleton Kennedy, Caroline Lee Hentz, and William Gilmore Simms, who are read largely by academic specialists writing about the antebellum South and a distressingly persistent klatch of racists who continue to perpetuate the "Lost Cause" myth by publishing the plantation romances in new (albeit cheap and poorly edited) editions. The reason is clear: the thesis they share is monstrous. Poe's talents, and his influence on modernist literary aesthetics, place him well above the authors whose success he envied and forms he plundered. And that's why it's so difficult to evaluate his works for their political content. Other southerners sought to obscure their intentions, but did a poor job of it: any perceptive reader can tell that the benign master Frank Meriwether of Kennedy's proslavery novel *Swallow Barn* (1832) is, despite his performance as a bumbling noble, a trafficker in human chattel, and that his lordly pretensions do not mix well with the Republican rhetoric deployed elsewhere in Kennedy's descriptions of Virginia social life. But, by evacuating his works of their immediate political content, Poe is able to perform an impressive sleight of hand: he produces plantation romances that do not explicitly take up slavery and yet more effectively argue the planter class's pro-aristocratic thesis than its blunter champions could. Southern authors sought to aestheticize their political ends, but their grasp of the aesthetic was poor, and therefore the obfuscation is a hash; Poe, on the other hand, brought his superior talent to bear on the project and therefore proved to be the most durable proslavery author the South produced.

This chapter moves fluidly through Poe's career, from his early success at the *Southern Literary Messenger* to the years of his greatest artistic production in the North, and finally to the "landscape fictions" produced in his final years. By freely moving between the various stages of Poe's career, I hope to illustrate the persistence of proslavery, pro-aristocratic thought in his writing, and therefore to erase any distinction that may be made between Poe's southern period and his later work in the North. First, I read the cultural production of the proslavery antebellum South through its medievalist self-representations and connect Poe's own aesthetic philosophies to the plantation romance through his landscape tale "The Domain of Arnheim" (1847), whose title is an allusion to Arnheim Castle in Walter Scott's *Anne of Geierstein* (1829), a medievalist romance that held considerable influence in the South. Next, I read Poe's editorial work at the *Southern Literary Messenger* against southern medievalism, revealing Poe's own part in trumpeting a cult of chivalry and romance that has proven so important in the formation of southern identity. This section concludes with brief readings of "Berenice," "King Pest" (both 1835), and "The Devil in the Belfry" (1839), a Northern production that bears striking thematic similarities to his southern works.

I next follow Poe to the North, where, away from the immediate influence of his proslavery peers, the author continued to rewrite the tale of feudal decline he had begun to perfect in his Richmond years. This section is devoted to readings of "The Masque of the Red Death" (1842) and "Hop-Frog" (1849), tales that at first glance seem to bear little relation to the plantation romance and its reactionary politics. My readings foreground the persistence of proslavery thought in these two popular works. The very fact that these tales seem to bear no relation to the southern literary scene out of which their aesthetics and plot mechanics emerge is the point of my argument here. The pernicious genius of Poe's works is the ways in which they seem to evade material concerns and social realities even as they put forward an unfailingly aristocratic and racialist thesis. If, as Walter Benjamin writes in "Theses on the Philosophy of History" (1940), "there is no document of civilization which is not at the same time a document of barbarism," then the planter aristocracy's "documents of civilization" represent a particularly radical attempt to occult the material conditions that undergird their fantasies.[8] Poe's fiction—complex, ironical, poetic, and nightmarish by turns—is, in several key ways, the apex of the southern elite's continuing historical legerdemain regarding slavery and race.

PLANTATION ROMANCE, MEDIEVALISM, AND THE PROSLAVERY CULTURAL FRONT

While none of Poe's works take place on a plantation, by choosing pseudomedieval locales for his tales, Poe signals his allegiance with the plantation/estate metaphor developed by slavery's apologists. In this section, we'll look at examples of the plantation/estate metaphor drawn from the writings of George Fitzhugh, John Pendleton Kennedy, Caroline Lee Hentz, and William Gilmore Simms and then conclude with readings of two of Poe's late-career "landscape fictions." Throughout, we'll disperse the fog of historical inaccuracy with which southern elites shrouded the region's economic base by placing the facts of slavery against the view of the institution that southern partisans hoped to promulgate.

Early in *Swallow Barn*, John Pendleton Kennedy pauses for a brief sociological sketch of Virginia's political institutions and the manners of its citizenry. This moment of parabasis, when all of the main actors in the story are set aside in order for Kennedy to directly address his reader, is called "Traces of the Feudal System." Kennedy here attempts to demonstrate how the Old Dominion's "genial atmosphere ... gradually matured the sober and thinking Englishman into that spirited, imaginative being" who would make the state "a predominant star in the Union" (*SB*, 70).[9] He does so by establishing the source of Virginia's wealth, and the political institutions that grew from this economic base: "Her wealth is territorial; her institutions all savor of the soil; her population consists of landholders, of many descents, unmixed with foreign alloy.... In policy and government she is ... a republic: in temper and opinion ... she is aristocratic" (71).

The apparent contradiction between a republican system and a landed aristocracy is not lost on Kennedy. Instead of working out a solution, however tenuous, to the paradox, Kennedy makes the contradiction an integral part of the Virginia's gentleman's worldview. Accordingly, Kennedy holds that the masters of the Old Dominion harbor "a constitutional fondness for paradoxes" (*SB*, 72). Later, the family's tutor, Mr. Chub, will express this same "fondness for paradoxes" when he tellingly names two political theorists in a "short but vehement panegyric": "'Mr. Burke—Cicero'" (73). By leveling the ancient theorist of natural law and the eighteenth-century defender of the ancien régime, Chub provides an intellectual itinerary for proslavery thought. Southern partisans must navigate treacherous waters, avoiding a total embrace of natural law (which could provide a basis for universal emancipation of slaves) by laying this potentially radical thought at the foundation of an aristocratic cultural superstructure.

As Kennedy's discussion of Virginia above indicates, elite southerners liked to imagine themselves both as being on the forefront of the century's republican political projects and as protecting the last vestige of a benign aristocratic order. Few proslavery authors would go as far as George Fitzhugh, who in *Sociology for the South* (1854) asserts that "the barons of Runimede have their exact prototype in the Southern farmer."[10] Most would instead take Kennedy's path and attempt to suspend the contradiction between democratic institutions and aristocratic culture. Feudal history is cast as both a benevolent, residual force and the motor for U.S. history. For Kennedy, this means he must pause his discussion of Virginia's feudal "traces" to remind readers that "when the Revolution broke out, [Virginia] was among the first of its champions," and that subsequently, "Four Presidents have been given to the Union from her nursery" (*SB*, 70). Virginia's manners and institutions may be anachronistic, Kennedy admits—and yet it is this very backwardness that motored Virginia's early defense of the United States' democratic experiment. Only aristocratic gentlemen could be entrusted with protecting the young democracy.

Despite the region's evidently backward-looking tendencies, Coleman Hutchison characterizes southern literature as employing what he calls "a rhetoric of futurity" that stems from its status as "a literature of aspiration."[11] What both pre- and postsecession southern literature aspired toward is clear enough: the preservation of slavery and the strengthening of the relatively small planter aristocracy that benefited from the institution. But Hutchison's characterization of southern culture as aspirational and future oriented, insightful as it is, belies the reactionary character of the region's futurity. As Tison Pugh puts it in *Queer Chivalry: Medievalism and the Myth of White Masculinity in Southern Literature*, "The U.S. South's conflicting turn to chivalric medievalism as regressive and progressive, depending upon the circumstances of its enactment, reflects the amorphousness of the past when used to construct the present."[12] Like Pugh, Susan J. Tracy characterizes southern intellectual culture as existing in a complex relationship to the past and present: "Primarily, they saw themselves as the inheritors of English intellectual traditions; yet they also saw themselves connected with and to the Romantic movement."[13] Tracy defines this "English intellectual tradition" as one stemming from Burkean conservative thought that emphasizes an aristocracy based on the rule of "natural superiors" over "natural inferiors."[14] Belief in natural aristocracy, paired with a romantic interest in past modes of social life and cultural expression, provides the ideological basis for southern literary aesthetics, which consist of an uneasy commingling of a "progressive" emphasis on liberty (for propertied white citizens), a backward-looking fondness for Old World art and architecture, and a future-oriented interest in the extension of southern political and cultural influence in the western hemisphere Southern conservatism fixated on the estate, the patriarchal family, and a pastoral image of agricultural labor as the core of its attempted cultural counterrevolution against bourgeois industrialism and liberalism in the North.[15]

Southern medievalism emphasized the antimodern, preindustrial nature of southern culture: the commodity-producing plantation finds its original in the feudal estate, and the slave, or human commodity, in the master's vassal or child.[16] But this southern view is out of step with the realities of the feudal mode of production: feudal production was, in Perry Anderson's formula, "dominated by the land and a natural economy, in which neither labour nor the products of labour were commodities."[17] Economic historians Robert William Fogel and Stanley L. Engerman explain that, contrary to the southern propagandist's claims, chattel bondage was directly tied to not only global capitalism, but also served as an alternative to wage labor in both urban and rural settings. Frederick Douglass emphasizes the national reach and modern nature of slave labor in his famous address "The Meaning of July Fourth for the Negro" (1852):

> Is it not astonishing that, while we are ploughing, planting and reaping, using all kinds of mechanical tools, erecting houses, constructing bridges, building ships, working in metals of brass, iron, copper, silver and gold; that, while we are reading, writing and cyphering, acting as clerks, merchants and secretaries, having among us lawyers, doctors, ministers, poets, authors, editors, orators and teachers; that, while we are engaged in all manner of enterprises common to other men, digging gold in California, capturing the whale in the Pacific, feeding sheep and cattle on the hill-side, living, moving, acting thinking, planning, living in families as husbands, wives and children; and, above all, confessing and worshipping the Christian's God,

and looking hopefully for life and immortality beyond the grave, we are called upon to prove that we are men![18]

Douglass's continental portrait of black labor and his emphasis on the variety of slave employment reveals the big lie at the heart of the southern elite's feudal pretenses. Bondsmen and women allowed the South to grow along capitalist lines without the use of wage labor; the southern propagandist's characterization of the plantation as a feudal desmene cannot be taken seriously. But this lie did serve a strategic rhetorical purpose: slaveholding characterized as paternalistic and "homely" allowed slavery's defenders to project the unique institution of nineteenth-century black chattel slavery across temporal boundaries. As Fitzhugh asserts in *Sociology for the South*: "It is *domestic slavery* alone that can establish a safe, efficient, and humane community of property. It did so in ancient times, it did so in feudal times, and it does so now."[19]

Fitzhugh's claim suggests the historical arrogance that paternalism afforded southern writers. If southerners were to recognize that slaves allowed their economies to function without the use of wage labor—in other words, if they admitted that slavery was a form of wage theft in which the black laborer was reduced to an *instrumentum vitale* and prevented from becoming a proletarian wage laborer—then their defenses of slavery as a "positive good" would necessarily have collapsed. Instead, proslavery authors borrowed liberally from Western historical precedent—Christian scripture, Greco-Roman architecture, Revolutionary-era rhetoric, romantic pastoral, medieval English legend—leading to a prewar southern culture that appears almost postmodern in its elaborate bricolage.

Of these interlinking strategies, an amorphous "medievalism," popularly associated with well-maintained feudal estates, chivalry, the colorful characters of medieval romance, and chaste maidens, proved to be the most enduring scheme for transcendentalizing the slave plantation.[20] Unlike the more studied academic medievalism that would emerge in the North, the southerner's vision of the European Middle Ages bore next to no resemblance to fact. Mark Twain captures the absurdity of southern medievalism in his assessment of antebellum southern culture in *Life on the Mississippi* (1883): "[In the South], the genuine and wholesome civilization of the nineteenth century is curiously confused and commingled with the Walter Scott Middle-

Age sham civilization; and so you have practical, common-sense, progressive ideas, and progressive works; mixed up with the duel, the inflated speech, and the jejune romanticism of an absurd past that is dead, and out of charity ought to be buried."[21] Like Scott's Cedric, the twelfth-century Saxon lord in *Ivanhoe* (1820) who bucks Norman tyranny while saddling his vassals, Wamba and Gurth, with heavy brass collars bearing his mark, the antebellum South saw no contradiction in arguing liberty for lords and subjection for slaves. Fitzhugh equates the slave with the feudal villein in a passage that, had Twain encountered it, would have confirmed his suspicions regarding the South's self-imagination: "The feudal Barons were more generous and hospitable and less tyrannical than the petty land-holders of modern times. Besides, each inhabitant of the barony was considered as having some right of residence, some claim to protection from the Lord of the Manor. A few of them escaped to the municipalities for purposes of trade, and to enjoy a larger liberty. Now penury and the want of a home drive thousands to towns. The slave always has a home, always an interest in the proceeds of the soil."[22] The thrust of Fitzhugh's work is a justification of slavery that strongly echoes Thomas Carlyle's *Occasional Discourse on the Nigger Question* (1849). Fitzhugh rehearses the argument of Carlyle's pamphlet in his "Appendix," but as a southern paternalist takes occasion with Carlyle's own phobic hatred of slaves: "We love and respect the negro. He is eminently docile, imitative and parasitical.... He knows he is the ivy, and would cling to the white oak, not to the ivy, for support."[23] Slavery here is an organic social relationship between master and servant and an ennobling force that transforms the nineteenth-century plantation from a working farm into a picturesque English manor.

Fitzhugh's paternalistic metaphor of the slave clinging to the white oak also reveals the distinctly masculinist bent to southern medievalism. Southern medievalists emphasized, even more than their Northern analogues, the role of the strong man in feudal social organization. Pugh observes that "the myths of the U.S. South converge with myths of the medieval past, and cultural fantasies unite as a glorified vision of southern masculinity merges with a glorified vision of the Middle Ages."[24] This "glorified vision of southern masculinity" gave rise, inevitably, to a gendered antipode. The southern cult of chivalry rose alongside the intertwined struggles for abolition and women's suffrage in the North. The same proslavery theorists who argued for the continued "fatherly" subjugation of black men and women also (unsurprisingly) imagined their benign influence as embracing their wives.²⁵ Thus in a key sequence in Caroline Lee Hentz's *The Planter's Northern Bride* (1854), Eulalia Moreland realizes her role in the management of her husband's slaves: "She had known him as the fond, devoted bridegroom; now he was invested with the authority and responsibility of a master. And she must share that responsibility, assist him in his duties, and make the welfare, comfort, and happiness of these dependent beings the great object of her life."²⁶ Eulalia's obligation is moral, not practical; in reality, however, planters' wives were often more responsible for the day-to-day maintenance of "standards of order and efficiency" than their husbands were.²⁷ With southern wives, then, we encounter another form of obfuscation: the person in charge of the practical management of the slave household is disguised as an imperiled maiden who must be protected by a manly cavalier.

The idyllic plantation, childlike slave, and angelic planter's wife were all bulwarks against slave rebellion, a specter that haunts the plantation romance no less than it did the imaginations of the planter aristocrats. Insurgencies such as Denmark Vessey's 1822 rebellion and Nat Turner's 1831 uprising forced the planter aristocracy to consider adopting a more "humane" standard of conduct toward their slaves.²⁸ The opposite of the naturalized slave is the insurgent: Nat Turner prowling the Great Dismal Swamp, Harriet Tubman leading night raids on the Combahee River. Southerners were right to fear slave insurrection; as Herbert Aptheker demonstrated half a century ago, slave rebellions were a constitutive political factor throughout early U.S. history.²⁹ Paternalism sought to naturalize the institution of slavery and infantilize the slave in order to quash rebellion, and the false comparison of the slave to the feudal subject served this process well. In *Swallow Barn*, Kennedy refers to slave children as "young serfs" who are "drilled into a kind of local militia" by Rip Meriwether, the master's son. (That Strother's accompanying illustration depicts the "young serfs" in a lineup that brings to mind a Revolutionary War regiment once again emphasizes the paradox of Virginia's feudal-liberal synthesis.) Under the master's influence, slaves are as harmless as pets or as dedicated as soldiers; left to their own devices, they congregate in "herds," "swarms," and "hordes" (310). In William Gilmore Simms's *The Sword and the Distaff* (1854), a slave also comes to defend the protagonist's plantation against an ill-intentioned sheriff out of a sense of chivalric fealty: "He had come to stand up beside, and for, his feudal lord—such was really the sort of relation between the parties—and to break spear for him, and peril life, against all comers."[30] While none of the plantation romances depict a slave uprising, the threat of one looms large. Without the social regulation of the plantation and its concomitant infantilization of the slave, the tamed and drilled militias of slave labor could reorganize for their own purposes. These authors contend, as Thomas Jefferson puts it in his 1820 letter to John Holmes, that slave masters "have the wolf by the ears, and... can neither hold him, nor safely let him go."[31] The fear of slave rebellion is where Poe's tales most openly intersect with his those of his peers: the intrusion of a havoc-wreaking, racially marked other is the engine of many of his most famous horrors.

As demonstrated above, the plantation romance—with its idealization of white femininity, valorization of the heroic feudal strongman, deployment of medievalesque imagery, and anxious negotiation of slave rebellion—occult the material conditions of life in the South. Where the plantation boosters see dignity and refinement, history sees depravity and want. Throughout the 1820s, the Old Dominion witnessed a mass exodus of white propertied men and their families into new slave territories. "Prompted by declining fertility of the soil," historian Daniel Walker Howe writes, "Virginia's sons and daughters migrated out of state—about a million of them in the antebellum era, by far the most from any state."[32] Despite the continued political clout of Virginia's aristocratic "Richmond Junto" in sectional debates surrounding slavery, the institution's base of power was shifting to the Old Southwest. Slaveholding in the Old Southwest was a far cry from the relatively mannered form of the institution that had developed through the gradual adoption of paternalism in the Upper South; the new territories were brutal and lawless, constituting "a violent society, even by American standards."[33] It is no coincidence that so many plantation romances are set in the Carolinas and Virginia; to go further South was to face the barest violence possible under the slave system. Geographic dislocation thus afforded these authors a buffer between slavery as it was and as they would like it to have been seen. This is not peculiar to southern culture, but is instead baked into the entire nation's political discourse.

From the Revolution onward, U.S. politicians and businessmen developed a rhetoric of obfuscation that allowed the classes who had a material interest in slavery (financiers, plantation owners, land speculators, and the like) to defend slavery without ever speaking its name or referring to its human chattel. The process began early on, when Jefferson revised out of the first draft of the Declaration of Independence a crucial clause that blamed George III for encouraging the Atlantic slave trade. As Douglass points out in his 1852 address, slavery likewise appears nowhere in the Constitution—and yet it's simply not possible, from our historical vantage point, to separate that document from the *types of property* it was drafted to protect. In both the Declaration of Independence and the Constitution, then, we have oblique references to property—including, of course, property in human chattel—without any use of the words "slaves" or "slavery" at all.

This rhetoric of obfuscation saturates the legal logic of the early republic no less than it does its founding documents. *Fletcher v. Peck* (1810), a signal moment in the development of U.S. capital markets and property law, nominally takes up the question of whether land contracts made in bad faith ought to be protected when the voters of a state oust the representatives who made those agreements. But, as economic historian Edward E. Baptist tells us, slavers were quick to recognize a hidden purpose in the ruling: even if public opinion in the South shifted toward abolition, plantation owners could plausibly argue that the contract between themselves and the slavers, which in substance concerned the right to trade in humans, was constitutionally protected. In this way, slavery was allowed to expand across the young nation—to become an institution that "find[s] no geographical limits, only political ones."[34] Slavery's reach was bound only by the imagination of the entrepreneurial slavocracy; it's no surprise, then, that it would find its way into the artistic works produced by their culture.

Poe perfects the process of geographic dislocation and the rhetoric of obfuscation by completely removing his tales from the U.S. landscape. But, while the tales seem to take place very far away from the geographic United States and its political concerns, Poe's themes and images often derived directly from his immediate social context. In substance and style, Poe wrote plantation romances, sharing their aspirations and nightmares.

The aristocratic vein in Poe's thought runs so deep that it forms the basis for his preference for the short tale over the novel. In his 1852 review of Nathaniel Hawthorne's *Twice-Told Tales* for *Graham's*, Poe explains his preference for the tale as a literary form: "The ordinary novel is objectionable, from its length, for reasons already stated in substance. As it cannot be read at one sitting, it deprives itself, of course, of the immense force derivable from totality. Worldly interests intervening during the pauses of perusal, modify, annul, or counteract, in a greater or less degree, the impressions of the book.

... During the hour of perusal the soul of the reader is at the writer's control. There are no external or extrinsic influences."[35] There is nothing dialogic in Poe's imagination of literary production; the tale is an estate, the author is its master, and the reader is in the author's thrall. Later, in a self-plagiarizing 1847 review of both *Twice-Told Tales* and *Mosses From an Old Manse* for *Godey's Lady's Book*, Poe makes this point more forcefully. He argues that "true or commendable originality" is produced only through the agency of a totalizing imagination: he praises the "ever-present force of imagination, giving its own hue, its own character to everything it touches, and, especially, *self impelled to touch everything.*" After self-plagiarizing his 1842 review of *Twice-Told Tales* (the paragraph quoted above), Poe elaborates his philosophy of the short story. "In the whole of the composition," he writes, "there should be no word written of which the tendency, direct or indirect, is not to the one pre-established design"; the creative author strives for this autonomy until "the idea of the tale, its thesis, has been presented unblemished."

Given the racial anxieties we will trace through Poe's plantation romance period, and the proslavery literati's related emphasis on the autarkic, paternal home as a social ideal, we should place special weight on Poe's choice of the word "unblemished" and his emphasis on "pre-established design."[36] Poe casts the author as master of his domain, and his stories allegorize what happens when the power of these masters is undermined by forces that he is meant to tame, drill, and divide into methodized fancy. The effect of Poe's theory of prose composition, when paired with his political and racial views, is a startling lack of variety in plot mechanics and theme. Central mechanisms change—here we have a live burial, there a *sub-rosa* plague carrier—but the story remains the same: some stain, interloper, or otherworldly force undermines what would otherwise be a Domain of Arnheim, leading to chaos and horror. Poe's fiction, which has been praised again and again for its inventiveness, reveals upon further scrutiny a sameness that borders on monomania.

Only in two relatively neglected set of works, "The Landscape-Garden" (1842) and its revision, "The Domain of Arnheim" (1847), does Poe give us a feudal domain of the imagination that remains "unblemished." Perhaps owing to a landscape gardening craze sparked by the publication of architect Andrew Jackson Downing's *A Treatise on the Theory and Practice of Landscape Gardening* (1841), "The Landscape Garden" and "The Domain of Arnheim" were extensively reprinted and even yielded a complementary fragment, "Landor's Cottage: A Pendant to 'The Domain of Arnheim'" (1849).[37] Poe held the works in high esteem. In an 1848 letter, he says the "story contains more of myself and of my inherent tastes and habits of thought than anything I have written."[38] The texts concern a wealthy aesthete, Ellison, who finds, "under certain unusual and highly fortuitous conditions," a happiness that defies "the present darkness and madness of all thought on the great question of social condition."[39] Ellison secures his contentment through a set of aristocratic tenets that ally him with the patriarchal master of plantation romance, including "the love of woman," "the contempt of ambition," and a predilection for "free exercise in the open air" that leads to his singular interest in landscape aesthetics ("DA," 856). "The Landscape-Garden" and "The Domain of Arnheim" contain lengthy treatises by Ellison in which he lays out an aesthetic theory that dovetails with Poe's own theory of composition in "The Poetic Principle" (1848).[40]

Like Poe's conception of poetry, Ellison's landscape aesthetics emphasize the role of a genius who, "by the show of order and design," cultivates his work and thereby evidences a "moral" sense of "care and human interest" in it ("DA," 862). To illustrate his theory, Ellison asks the narrator to imagine "a landscape whose combined vastness and definitiveness—whose united beauty, magnificence, and *strangeness*, shall convey the idea of care, or culture, or superintendence, on the part of beings superior, yet akin to humanity" (863). The culmination of Ellison's aesthetic project is a harmonious medievalesque kingdom, the centerpiece of which is "a mass of semi-Gothic, semi-Saracenic architecture, sustaining itself as if by a miracle in mid air . . . and seeming the phantom handiwork, conjointly, of the Sylphs, of the Fairies, of the Genii, and of the Gnomes" (870). Poe's use of the conditional "as if" here reveals a key deception: like the palace's *seeming* to sustain itself in mid air, its construction also *seems* to have been miraculous—but was not. As in the plantation romance, the actual labor that went into the fabrication of Ellison's estate is omitted and replaced with a fantastic, otherworldly provenance. In Ellison's Arnheim, labor is purely an act of the imagination, not a material undertaking.

"The Domain of Arnheim" is an outlier in Poe's body of work and thus affords us a valuable vantage point from which to assess his other works. Arnheim remains immaculate because, unlike other fantasy worlds Poe constructs, the feudal authority that structures it has not yet been compromised. Free from the "present darkness and madness" of his times, Ellison is able to construct a dreamworld that is not unlike Kennedy's pastoral Virginia: chivalric, at peace, and fundamentally romantic. Ironically, Poe's late-life dream of a peaceful, autonomous kingdom of pure aesthetic production caps a career that was based on exploiting his reader's fears of realms like Arnheim devolving into horror and chaos. Over his two years as editor of the *Southern Literary Messenger* (1835–1837), Poe developed the formula that would continue to inform the horror tales that would bring him fame in Northern publications throughout the 1840s. While there have been several studies of Poe's work at the *magazine*, none have read that work against the backdrop of southern medievalism out of which his post-*Messenger* fame emerged. In the following section, I will read the progress of the *Southern Literary Messenger* under Poe's editorship as taking the magazine from the organ of a southern literary nationalism that sought to reject European and Northern U.S. models to one that embraced a medievalesque aesthetic—and that aesthetic's concomitant nostalgia for feudal order.

POE AT THE *SOUTHERN LITERARY MESSENGER*: "BERENICE" AND "KING PEST"

A December 1835 article in the *Southern Literary Messenger* finds the law professor Lucian Minor (1802–1858) lamenting the decline of aristocratic Old Virginia in words that would doubtlessly have stirred the author of *Swallow Barn*: "The most lukewarm friend of the State must perceive—if he perceives anything—that the glory of the Ancient Dominion is in a fainting—is in a dying condition. Her once great name is becoming, in the North, a bye-word for imbecility—all over the South, a type for 'the things that have been.' And tamely to ponder upon times gone by is not to meet the exigencies of times present or to come. Memory will not help us. The recollection of our former high estate will not benefit us. Let us act."[41]

This speech, republished in an issue of the *Southern Literary Messenger* that Poe was involved in assembling, is anxious over the passing of a glory that cannot be regained.[42] The grammatical parallelism of the ante- and penultimate sentences and the concise imperative that ends the passage give this selection the feel of a political manifesto. The damp terror of "The Fall of the House of Usher" rests in that paragraph, and the horror at time's all-effacing power animates Minor's sentiment as much as it does Poe's doleful "Annabel Lee." The "fainting" or "dying" condition of Virginia—the pervasive sense of decline shared by his southern colleagues—haunts Poe's horrors as much as any other concern.

The political and historical fears of southerners like Minor find creative expression in the horror stories Poe published in the *Southern Literary Messenger*, and Poe's tenure at the magazine allowed him to develop ideas about the function and form of the short story that would shape his fiction until his death. The two years Poe spent working at Thomas Willis White's publication marked his only period of career stability and set in motion the pursuit of his own magazine that would consume the author. It also marked the high tide of the *Southern Literary Messenger*'s circulation; Poe's caustic reviews and ingenious tales greatly expanded the journal's readership, a mutually favorable relationship that ended only because of publisher Thomas Willis White's objection to Poe's alcoholism.[43] Poe assumed the editorship knowing full well what the magazine stood for: the *Southern Literary Messenger* was conceived from the beginning as an organ of Southern literary nationhood. Its first issue (August 1834) opened with a salvo of quotes from literary luminaries, including the proslavery novelists John Pendleton Kennedy and James Kirke Paulding. Paulding's notice calls for a break from the imitative strand in southern literature that Twain would later savage: "If your young writers will consult their own taste and genius, and forget there ever were such writers as Scott, Byron, and Moore, I will be bound they produce something original." James Ewell Heath's long essay on "Southern Literature" likewise calls for southern authors to break away from Northern and European models: "Are we to be doomed forever to a kind of vassalage to our northern neighbors—a dependence for our literary food upon our brethren, whose superiority in all the great points of character,—in valor—in eloquence and patriotism, we are no wise disposed to admit? . . . Let the hundreds of our gifted sons, therefore, who have talents and acquirements, come forth to this work of patriotism, with a firm resolution to persevere until victory is achieved."[44]

Heath's comparison of Northern tastemakers to feudal masters and southern authors to their aesthetic vassals, and his emphasis on the patriotic nature of the magazine's work, set the tone for the issues he would edit until Poe took his position. In a later issue, Heath would reject a story on the grounds that it bore too much of a resemblance to a fairytale: "We have no 'dilapidated castles,' nor any 'last heirs of Ardendale,' in our plain republican land."[45] Heath's editorial policy stands in stark contrast to Poe's, whose first signed work in the *Southern Literary Messenger*, "Berenice" (March 1835), has its narrator—who is, coincidentally, the last heir of his estate—being born from "what seemed, but was not, nonentity" into "the very regions of fairyland—into a palace of imagination—into the wild dominions of monastic thought and erudition."[46] Owing to southern literature's increasing emphasis on the plantation as an autonomous, semifeudal kingdom, Poe would push the magazine away from the "plainly republican" and into phantasmagoria during his time as editor.

The period of Poe's editorship brought the *Southern Literary Messenger* and its proslavery views to national prominence.[47] Like other authors of plantation romances, Poe argues for the southern cause by comparing it to Old World precedent—a sharp editorial swerve from the Heath days. Given the long history of Poe reception in European letters, and his continuing prominence in "continental" literature and theory, it might be tempting to read Poe's editorial policies as part of an antinationalist project: despite the expected gestures toward a uniquely American literature, Poe is really arguing for the superiority of European authors over "native" ones. But this reading does not stand up to the biographical or contextual evidence that this period in Poe's life provides. As J. Gerald Kennedy argues, Poe sought throughout this period to "define a U.S. literary nationalism that superseded regions," and to "promote a literary America" that he continued to theorize until his death.[48] Poe was also at this time vying for a position in the proslavery Tyler administration, further giving the lie to the old assumption that Poe was disengaged from his era's politics.[49] Economic necessity and career ambition, paired with an earnest belief in the U.S. national literary project as he imagined it, led Poe to embrace southern regionalism and its emphasis on the false equation of the slave plantation with the feudal estate. Whether or not Poe himself was actively proslavery or sold a slave on behalf of his aunt Maria Clemm is to some extent beside the point; "smoking gun" evidence isn't necessary to prove that Poe was deeply imbricated in the proslavery cultural vanguard of antebellum America. As he toiled for White and planned hopeless prospectuses for his own literary magazine, Poe fantasized about an elite class of slaveholding readers: "I know from personal experience that lying perdus among the innumerable plantations in our vast southern and Western countries were a host of well-educated men peculiarly devoid of prejudice, who would gladly lend their influence to a really vigorous journal."[50]

With the *Southern Literary Messenger*, Poe inherited a patriotic, proslavery, and antifeudal publication. He sought to change only the last of those three qualities. One of Poe's first unsigned reviews for the *Southern Literary Messenger* was of *Calavar: Or the Knight of the Conquest, A Romance of Mexico* by Robert Montgomery Bird (February 1835). In his review Poe asserts, "If

Sir Walter Scott himself were living, he would have the candor and honor to acknowledge that 'Calavar' was vastly superior to some five or six of the last litter of his own great genius," and that "'Calavar' is an American production, which will not shrink from competition with the very best European works of the same character."[51]

This short, favorable review of a romantic imitation—one Heath would not see as fitting in with his proslavery southern nationalism—initiates a series of increasingly antiquarian and fantastic tales and reviews. Poe praises Edward Lytton Bulwer's *Rienzi, The Last of the Tributes* (1835), a story of political intrigue set in thirteenth-century Rome, for "the rich and brilliant tints of its feudal paintings" and its "pervading air of chivalry, and grace, and sentiment." He then heightens his praise from an appreciation of Bulwer's literary form to a panegyric for Bulwer's romantic take on medieval history: "[*Rienzi*] is History. We hesitate not to say that it is History in its truest—in its only true, proper, and philosophical garb.... We shall often discover in Fiction the essential spirit and vitality of Historic Truth—while Truth itself, in many a dull and lumbering Archive, shall be found guilty of all the inefficiency of Fiction."[52] Finally, in an 1836 review of German historian Friedrich Ludwig Georg von Raumer's *England in 1835* (1836), Poe reveals an antibourgeois aspect of his view of the Middle Ages: "[Raumer's] remarks on the absence of all finance in the middle ages will arrest attention. In these days men had no money, and yet did more than in modern times—they effected everything, and we can effect nothing, without the circulation of the 'golden blood.'"[53] Poe appeals to the antibourgeois bias of his readership by praising medieval England for its lack of circulating capital and therefore insinuates that the South's self-conception as a collection of semiautarkic fiefdoms may yet produce a greater glory than its Northern competitor. Heath's prior defenses of "states' rights" and emphasis on the South's patriotism align him and the publication with the Old Republican, Jeffersonian proslavery rhetoric that had dominated the debates since the late eighteenth century. Poe's editorial swerve toward the medieval points to a stranger, more diffuse, and ultimately more effective strategy for defending the South's economic and social regime.

While Poe theorized his medievalesque aesthetic in the reviews, he put them into practice in the handful of stories he published in the *Southern Literary Messenger* while editor. Of these tales, "Berenice," which is indebted to both the actual Middle Ages and the false Middle Ages of southern romance, has deservedly received the most critical attention. The tale's Latin epigram may be Poe's own translation of a saying by the ninth-century Arab government functionary Abān al-Zaiyāt (d. 847).[54] Egaeus's scholarly predilections are likewise medieval: he claims that his frequent readings in grammarian Coelius Secundus Curio (1503–1569), Augustine of Hippo (354–430), and the important early Christian theologian Tertullian (160–225) occupy him "for many weeks of laborious and fruitless investigation" ("Berenice," 228). In keeping with the southern medievalist character of Poe's *Southern Literary Messenger* writings, the tale contains a reference to Scott's *Anne of Geierstein*, which also served as a source for Poe's most private fantasy, "The Domain of Arnheim": first seeing Berenice, Egaeus declares, "Oh! gorgeous yet fantastic beauty! Oh! sylph amid the shrubberies of Arnheim!" (226). Evoking Scott's late novel—which commanded a prodigious readership in the South that would only grow with time—anchors "Berenice" squarely in the cultural milieu of the planter aristocracy.[55]

The tale's atmosphere is likewise antique. Egaeus, last descendant of a "race of visionaries," takes pride in his family's mansion and its accouterments, finding evidence of his family's status in "the tapestries of the dormitories— in the chiselling [*sic*] of some buttresses in the armory—but more especially in the gallery of antique paintings—in the fashion of the library chamber— and, lastly, in the very peculiar nature of the library's contents" (225). Egaeus's description of the family manse proceeds from the practical (living rooms, armory) to the visual arts (the family portraits) and finally to the intellectual (the contents of the library), replicating the interplay between the material and the immaterial that obsesses him throughout the tale. Egaeus is consumed by a "monomania" that effectively strikes out the material object over which he obsesses and concretizes the metaphysical object of his musing: "The realities of the world affected me as visions . . . while the wild ideas of the land of dreams became, in turn,—not the material of my everyday existence—but in very deed that existence utterly and solely in itself" (226). This "relentless physicalizing," as Joan Dayan puts it, has a double effect: Egaeus at once (again in Dayan's words) "denies the transcendence of the '*speculative*' mind" even as he concretizes the transcendent world of his own imaginative process.[56] The family mansion may not be the "source" of Egaeus's mental habits, but Egaeus's description of it frames the Gothic setting as falling somewhere between reality and imagination.

Berenice is described in terms that heighten the tension between the material and immaterial: "In the silence of my library at night, she had flitted by my eyes, and I had seen her—not as the living and breathing Berenice, but as the Berenice of a dream—not as a being of the earth, but as the Berenice of a dream—not as a being of the earth, earthy, but as the abstraction of such a being—not as a thing to admire, but to analyze—not as an object of love, but as the theme of the most abstruse although desultory speculation" (229). Egaeus's description proceeds by a terse antithesis that is interrupted twice: first by the repetition of "the Berenice of a dream," and second by the strangely weak adjective "earthy." "Earthy" foreshadows Berenice's live entombment and indicates the ambiguity between the material and immaterial that Poe teases out repeatedly in the tale. Berenice is not "of the earth," but "earthy," something *like* an earthbound being, related to but not necessarily of humanity.[57] In this way, Berenice occupies much the same position as the plantation wife in southern romance: she is both an "earthy" object of physical desire and a figure of masculine desire around which a whole system of metaphysics is constructed. The symbolic violence Egaeus commits against Berenice is not, however, a revolt against this construction; it is instead an admission of defeat, of Poe's own inability to reconcile the reality of woman's material existence with the metaphysical scaffolding upon which he repeatedly hangs her idealized/brutalized effigy. Egaeus cannot reconcile the "obstinate oils and waters" of his physical obsession with/fantastical valorization of his lover, and Poe's art consequently flowers into a display of violence that stands unrivaled in his prose.

"Berenice" dramatizes the fallout from feudal masculinity's inability to master its feminine antipode. The next medievalesque story Poe published in the *Southern Literary Messenger*, "King Pest," concerns a similar theme: the results of that master class's inability to foreclose racial intrusion and rebellion. The tale is set in fourteenth-century London at the height of the Black Plague, where two sailors, Legs and Tarpaulin, skip out on a bill at their local pub. Poe's description of Hugh Tarpaulin resonates with familiar racist tropes used to describe black characters throughout American literature: Tarpaulin has a "round, full, and purple face," and his "thick upper-lip rested upon the still thicker one beneath with an air of complacent self-satisfaction."[58] Tarpaulin and his companion stumble through a desolate, near-abandoned London and into an undertaker's shop, where they are admitted into the court of King Pest and his circle. The main action of the story occurs in the shop's wine cellar. After a cross-examination, Pest sentences

Tarpaulin to consume an enormous cauldron of ale; Tarpaulin protests and accuses Pest of being no more than a stage actor, Tim Hurlygurly, who has set up court in the undertaker's basement. A member of Pest's court hurls Tarpaulin into the hogshead of ale, an action that prompts his companion Legs to assault the gathered nobles. The tale concludes, as so many of Poe's tales do, in chaos: "Out burst a deluge of liquor so fierce—so impetuous—so overwhelming—that the room was flooded from wall to wall—the loaded table was overturned—the tressels were thrown upon their backs" ("KP," 251). Unable to maintain control over his illusion, Pest/Hurlygurly drowns in his own ale. Legs and Tarpaulin raise riot back to their ship—with Arch Duchess Ana-Pest and another lady of the court as their booty.

William Whipple, the first critic to detect a satire of Andrew Jackson in Poe's tale, sees in the elaborate set piece of the undertaker's wine-cellar both echoes of the raucous festivities held on the White House lawn for Jackson's inauguration and a direct allusion to a January 8, 1835, banquet held in Jackson's honor.[59] Poe's disdain for mass movements is well documented; the rhetoric of Jacksonian populism would have, we can reason, utterly repelled him.[60] That Jackson himself was a violent slaver and proponent of extending slavery into new territories does not seem to upset Poe's satire; Jackson's proslavery is not of the aristocratic caste of Poe's, and therefore leaves the demagogic president open for attack. As a political satire, Poe seems to be warning Jackson that if his illusion of mastery is not sustained well enough, then the same crowds he invited to celebrate his inauguration could well turn against him.

Poe's readers in the *Southern Literary Messenger*, however, may have seen another side to this "allegory." Tarpaulin and Legs's rebellion is both classed and racialized, and while we assume that no plantation owner would like to see himself as master of a realm of skeletons and debauchery, the threat the sailors pose to Pest's domain nonetheless mirrors the slave rebellions that the planter aristocracy feared. That the tale ends with the abduction of Pest's wife would likewise emphasize the lurking peril to white womanhood that animated (and still animates) so much racist thought. As a horror tale evacuated of its immediate political content, "King Pest" uses a medievalesque setting and a racialized other to play on the slave owner's anxiety over the precariousness of his mastery. As we've seen throughout this chapter, southern aristocrats lived in perpetual fear of their social system—which they saw alternately as either reinstating feudal grandeur or championing democratic institutions, depending on the cultural climate—collapsing through assault or "contamination" by Northern liberal meddling.[61] Even as Poe moved away from the overtly political and regionalist climate of the *Southern Literary Messenger* and into the publishing worlds of Philadelphia and New York, he continued to exploit this southern medievalist formula to structure his most famous tales of the grotesque.

This formula is elevated to absurd heights in a work produced after Poe's time at the *Southern Literary Messenger*, the comic vignette "The Devil in the Belfry: An Extravaganza" (1839). Originally published in Philadelphia's *Saturday Chronicle and Mirror of the Times* on May 18, 1839, the byline reads, "By Edgar A. Poe, Esq., *Late Editor of the Southern Literary Messenger*." This byline, beyond its obvious function of alluring readers by announcing Poe's credentials, situates "The Devil in the Belfry" squarely in a proslavery, southern regionalist milieu. In the tale, the well-ordered village of Vondervotteimittis descends into anarchy after a foreign intruder crosses its border. The "foreign-looking" interloper is a composite of global and racial types: Poe's description splices elements of Jim Crow caricature with familiar aspects of the "Wandering Jew" (his face is "of a dark snuff colour," he has "a long hooked nose," and he shows off his "excellent set of teeth" by "grinning from ear to ear"), while his clothing and behavior suggest both a liberal revolutionary and an itinerant Irish laborer (he wears a Toussaint Louverture-esque *chapeau-de-bras* and plays "Judy O'Flannagan and Paddy O'Raferty" on his oversized fiddle).[62] In this character, Poe bundles all of the racial anxieties of the white southern master class into one anarchic figure.

The interloper plunges Vondervotteimittis first into political chaos by ousting the village's bell ringer, holder of "the most perfect of sinecures" in town, and then into temporal chaos by ringing the bell at odd intervals ("DB," 302). The entrenched burgher class goes mad, and Vondervotteimittis descends into "the most abominable din and confusion which it is possible for a reasonable person to conceive" (305). The social order of Vondervotteimittis immediately collapses. "Memory will not save" Vondervotteimittis. Poe's narrator, fleeing "in disgust," therefore calls for an aristocratic rebellion to "restore the ancient order of things in Vondervotteimittis by ejecting that little fellow from the steeple" (306).

"That little fellow" may have textual precedents in Jupiter the slave and Hafen Bok the white itinerant worker in Kennedy's work. According to Frank Meriwether, Jupiter is "a preposterous coxcomb" who must be appeased with little gifts—including a worn *chapeau de bras* that signals his superiority over the other slaves (*SB*, 452). Hafen Bok is first introduced as a possible antagonist in "The Goblin Swamp" episode, but is rendered harmless once we realize his true social function: to play fiddle and sing tunes about "the days of knighthood and minstrelsy" to the masters of Swallow Barn (380). Jupiter and Hafen Bok are repressed agents of social disorder: as long as they are kept within the roles prescribed to them by the Old Dominion's semifeudal order, they are more or less harmless to the dominant class. "The Devil in the Belfry" dramatizes what happens when those agents are unleashed—and when they collaborate.

Both "King Pest" and "The Devil and the Belfry" are satires of sitting U.S. Presidents, Andrew Jackson and Martin Van Buren, respectively. Their critique is similar: democracy without aristocratic order paves the way for anarchy and social dissolution. As Poe moved away from the southern publishing context and attempted to establish a career in the North, his overtly racialist and pro-southern tendencies began to take a backseat to the general cultivation of a pro-aristocratic thesis that at first seems radically disconnected from the immediate political context of his times. Poe's later works do not represent a break from his southern regionalist roots, but are instead refined iterations of the themes and narrative dynamics he had begun to flesh out in Richmond.

POE'S LATER FICTION: PLANTATIONS OUT OF TIME

The works of Poe's "plantation romance period" are not the source of his continuing fame. Later tales—"The Masque of the Red Death," "The Pit and the Pendulum," "The Tell-Tale Heart," and the tales of ratiocination—have had a much greater influence on world literature than the early works we have discussed so far. It is be tempting to read Poe's later works as having escaped the gravitational pull of the proslavery literary market Poe courted in his Richmond period. Poe was, after all, in the North and courting Northern capital at the end of his life; and the magazines he worked with (New York's *New-York Mirror* and *Broadway Journal*, and Philadelphia's *Graham's Magazine*), while not abolitionist publications, were not primarily organs for southern nationalism, either. But the essence of proslavery thought—rigid belief in relationships of dominance and subordination, valorization of the perfectly maintained estate, and veneration of the great man of genius and his foil, the tragic woman of endless virtue—persists in Poe despite shifts in the accidents of presentation.

"The Masque of the Red Death" provides a strong case study in the endurance of plantation romance tropes in Poe's later fiction. Published in *Graham's* in May 1842—only one month after Poe's first review of Hawthorne in that same magazine, which I discussed in relation to "The Domain of Arnheim"—"The Masque of the Red Death" functions precisely according to Poe's philosophy of the short tale. Prince Prospero expresses Poe's view of the creative writer as author of a unique, totalizing world; his palace, an "extensive and magnificent structure," is, like Ellison's Arnheim, a "creation of the prince's own eccentric yet august taste," a taste described in terms that could easily be ascribed to Poe himself. In Prospero's creations, "there was much of the beautiful, much of the wanton, much of the bizarre, something of the terrible, and not a little of that which might have excited disgust."[63] Paul Haspel points out that "Prince Prospero . . . is named for one of the few characters in William Shakespeare's work who is specifically described as a slaveholder."[64] The artist, landowner, aristocrat, and slaveholder are thus all constellated in Poe's aristocratic architect.

The "novel effect" produced by Prospero's creations is not disinterested aesthetic appreciation or the overwhelming power of the sublime, but an intimate, bodily terror: the last of his seven "imperial" apartments, "the western or black chamber," is "ghastly in the extreme, and produced so wild a look upon the countenances of those who entered, that there were few of the company bold enough to set foot within its precincts at all" ("MRD," 486–487). The description of the western chamber's "blood-tinted" windowpanes forces the reader to associate the room with the first paragraph's description of the Red Death, thus foreshadowing the tale's denouement, Prospero's murder and the mob's assault on the mummer. As long as Prospero can contain blood within the frame of a window—or, as long as blood can be maintained within the capillaries of a healthy denizen of Prospero's kingdom—the blood may remain the motor force of the estate's vitality. Unleashed through the Red Death, blood becomes an agent of destruction.

Prospero's seventh chamber represents the implicit threat of violence that haunts the otherwise idyllic feudal estate. If Prospero's estate were only a playful masquerade—if there was no repressive apparatus strictly maintaining its borders—then why would the Red Death masquerader have to sneak into the ball? Poe signals the extent of Prospero's control over his estate through the large "ebony clock" that, like the clock tower in "The Devil in the Belfry," maintains order in the court. The clock's "brazen lungs" emit "a sound which was clear and loud and deep and exceedingly musical, but of so peculiar a note and emphasis that, at each lapse of the hour, the musicians in the orchestra were constrained to pause." Upon hearing the ebony clock chime, Prospero's guests express feelings of "disapprobation and surprise—then, finally, of terror, of horror, and of disgust" ("MRD," 488–489). Prospero's autocratic rule allows for an enchanting atmosphere, but one that is, like a plantation, shot through with intimations of menace, subordination, and punishment.

The mummer's pursuit of Prospero through the seven apartments culminates in the prince-artist's execution in the western chamber. As in "The Devil in the Belfry," Poe ends his tale with an attempt to quash the intruder: "Then, summoning the wild courage of despair, a throng of revelers at once threw themselves into the black apartment, and, seizing the mummer, whose tall figure stood erect and motionless within the shadow of the ebony clock, gasped in unutterable horror at finding the grave-cerements and corpse-like mask which they handled with so violent a rudeness, untenanted by any tangible form." The uprising ends in the replacement of one absolute authority, Prospero's aesthetic-political regime, with another, the Red Death's "illimitable dominion" of "Darkness and Decay" (490). Despite the intimations of control and exclusion at work in Poe's earlier descriptions of the western chamber and the ebony clock, Prospero's estate can now be understood as a safe space for the "well-educated man peculiarly without prejudice" (to recall Poe's description of southern and western planters) to enact his dream world. Excluding and/or subduing the Red (or, as it ends up by the end of the story, Ebony) Death allows Prospero's estate to flourish and his imagination to soar. But, once the powers latent in the respective colors are unleashed, his world collapses.

While "The Masque of the Red Death" is pro-aristocratic, Prospero is both a cruel lord who revels in excess while his subjects suffer and the ingenious architect of Poe's most elaborate manor. That Poe punishes his aristocrats in such a brutal way is strange and has led some to read "The Masque of the Red Death" as an "anti-aristocratic" allegory.[65] The often-tortuous close readings that those who would recuperate Poe's political reputation are forced to undertake ought to show us that these readings are historically and thematically inconsistent with what is evident on the page and in the archive. The act of reintroducing history to Poe's ahistorical worlds—whether it be the history of the national debate over slavery or the more mundane history of the comings and goings of the nineteenth-century southern literati—helps us make legible aspects of the tales that remain foreclosed to seemingly more "theoretical" arguments.

"Hop-Frog, or the Eight-Chained Orangutans," first published in 1849 in Boston's popular weekly newspaper the *Flag of Our Union*, makes explicit the political fears that "The Mask of the Red Death" intimates. It is also, like the earlier "King Pest," a Poe tale with a concretely medieval provenance; Poe's primary source for "Hop-Frog" was a similar episode of court revenge drawn from Jean Froissart's *Chroniques* (1322–1400).[66] Even more important, several critics have demonstrated that "Hop-Frog" functions as an allegory for slavery.[67] This reading is evident in the tale itself: Hop-Frog and his companion Trippetta are "forcibly" carried off from a "barbarous region" and "sent as presents to the king," who holds them in perpetual, unpaid bondage.[68] The conflagration that caps "Hop-Frog" allows us to see the story as Poe's last and most ambitious "plantation romance," a short, hard tale that grotesquely dramatizes the fallout from a patriarch failing to maintain authority over his illusion.

To illustrate this point, I want to draw your attention to the king, Hop-Frog's master, rather than Hop-Frog himself. Like "The Masque of the Red Death," "Hop-Frog" is set during a masquerade: a celebration that brings to mind artifice and artistry. Poe's King loses control of his estate when, in a drunken reverie, he throws a full goblet of wine in Trippetta's face. This violence—an open affront to the feminine ideal we see throughout Poe's works—excites Hop-Frog's anger and is the sole impetus behind Hop-Frog's revenge. At the end of the tale, Hop-Frog addresses a horrified crowd of onlookers before setting fire to his victims: "I now see *distinctly* . . . what manner of people these maskers are. They are a great king and his seven privy-councilors—a king who does not scruple to strike a defence-less girl, and his seven councilors who abet him in the outrage" ("HF," 908). The King is not burned alive for the crime of holding Hop-Frog and Trippetta as slaves, and Hop-Frog's rebellion is a far cry from that of Nat Turner. This is a personal revenge, not a political one. Hop-Frog is offended by the violation of the key tenet of the South's mock chivalry: its idealization of an abstract femininity.

For Poe, the crime the king commits is not abusing and enslaving his wards, but allowing them to wrest control of his narrative. In the opening scenes of the tale, the king and his councilors petition Hop-Frog to give them "the benefit of [his] invention," to give them "*characters*, man—something novel—out of the way" ("HF," 901). After being forced to drink a glass of wine, Hop-Frog fumes and repeats the king's request, in the king's words: "I am endeavoring to think of something *novel*" (902). Recall, from Poe's two reviews of Hawthorne's tales, the special stress placed on the power of the novel as opposed to that of the tale: the novel as chaos, disjointed time, a distracted readership; the tale as focus, totality, an enthralled reader in the hands of an able master. By yielding his political sovereignty to Hop-Frog's narrative sovereignty, the king lays the groundwork for his own undoing.[69] But Hop-Frog's authority proceeds according to the anarchic logic of the novel, not the mannered and measured logic of the tale. The King and his men are "saturated with tar," chained, and suspended from a chandelier; or, they are made black, enslaved, and naturalized into the architecture of his estate (904–905).

Hop-Frog executes his revenge in the palace's "grand saloon," "a circular room, very lofty," whose sole source of light is "a large chandelier, depending by a chain from the centre of the sky-light, and lowered, or elevated, by means of a counter-balance" (905). Dressed in hyperrealistic "ourang-outang" outfits—made apes, and thus made similar to Hop-Frog himself, who is described earlier as looking like "a small monkey"—the disguised nobles inspire terror in the revelers. Remember, too, that the troupe of false beasts is chained together; in Hop-Frog's telling, this is so that the partygoers will believe the king and his men have "escaped, *en masse*, from [their] keepers" (904). Shades of the plantation romance's fear of slave escape and insurrection are not hard to find here.

The plan works as intended: the partygoers panic, and chaos ensues. Hop-Frog takes advantage of the mob's fear of the beastly intruders, connecting the chains binding them together to the chain holding up the grand saloon's sole source of light. Poe describes the chaining in detail. The men

> found themselves ... in immediate contact with the chain. While they were thus situated, the dwarf, who had followed closely at their heels, inciting them to keep up the commotion, took hold of their own chain at the intersection of the two portions which crosses the circle diametrically and at right angles. Here, with the rapidity of thought, he inserted the hook from which the chandelier had been wont to depend; and, in an instant, by some unseen agency, the chandelier-chain was drawn so far upward as to

take the hook out of reach, and, as an inevitable consequence, to drag the ourang-outangs together in close connection, face to face. (906)

Like the chambers described so carefully in "The Masque of the Red Death," the king's "grand saloon" is an allegorical space. It is hard not to see in the chain that raises and lifts the chandelier an echo of the slave coffle, which Edward Baptist usefully notes served as "a machine" that "forced the black people inside [the coffle] to do exactly what entrepreneurial enslavers, and investors far distant from slavery's frontier, needed them to do."[70] When used by the king, the chain elevates a luxurious item—the chandelier—that offers light to the room, the self-containment circularity of which implies autarky and continuity. In Hop-Frog's hands, the coffle-machine becomes a weapon of insurrection. It allows Hop-Frog to force the king and his men to "do what he needed them to do": die.

Hop-Frog next lights the chained men on fire. Poe describes the resulting substance as "a fetid, blackened, hideous, and indistinguishable mass" (908). This passage is role reversal as body horror, and the reversal upsets Poe's emphasis on distinction, control, and order within his tales.[71] White bodies—distinct and total before Hop-Frog sets them ablaze—are reduced to a single black mass, one without features, with no self-control. Feudalism—its pageantry and the myth of its noblesse oblige, its luxurious accouterments—is the only safeguard against the destabilization of social form that slave insurrection institutes. As in "The Masque of the Red Death," "Hop-Frog" concludes with a master class being racialized into a horror that, in Poe's view, a well-managed fiefdom ought to contain.

"THE FALL OF THE HOUSE OF USHER" AND THE REACTIONARY IMAGINATION

As I have characterized it in this chapter, Poe's short fiction contains some of American literature's most powerful demonstrations of "the reactionary mind" at work. The phrase, which I borrow from political theorist and historian of conservatism Corey Robin, offers a convenient exit point for this chapter's discussion of Poe's interpenetrating constructions of social order, race, beauty, and decline. For Robin, the conservative reaction to social upheavals such as the French and Haitian revolutions, U.S. slave revolts, and nascent labor movements is "about power besieged and power protected.

It is an activist doctrine for an activist time. It waxes in response to movements from below and wanes in response to their disappearance."[72] Robin's characterization of conservatism as an "activist" doctrine is of special interest considering the history of U.S. conservatism's reception in literary studies. Whereas F. O. Matthiessen famously insists in *American Renaissance* that Poe's "[hostility] to democracy" means that the "chief interest in treating his work would be to examine the effect of his narrow but intense theories of poetry and the short story" and how those theories influenced developments in European letters, a formula that separates Poe's aestheticism from his instinctual hatred of mass politics, an emphasis of broader patterns of conservative reaction to social change allows us to see the connection between Poe's politics and his aesthetic theories. If proslavery novelists such as Kennedy, Hentz, Simms, and Tucker warned that the South's supposedly feudal plantation life was threatened by abolitionist meddling, Poe imagined what life on plantations would look like after restrained slave energies were freed. A landscape of crumbling battlements where declining lords are harassed by forces they can no longer control—in a phrase, "American carnage"—is the recurrent nightmare of the reactionary imagination and its paranoid view of social change and mass politics in the United States.

Beauty—that evergreen preoccupation of so many conservatives, from Burke through Trump—is key here. Beauty represents both the decadence and futility of the crumbling old regime, whose turgid luxuriousness and hereditary lines of ascension allowed the rabble to overrun the battlements, and the aspirations of the new-old regime, who will construct a new and greater beauty on different, more durable foundations. Robin traces this idea back to Burke, for whom the greatest enemy of ancient hierarchies is "the old regime itself or, to be more precise, the defenders of the old regime. They simply lack the ideological wherewithal to press the cause of the old regime with the requisite vigor, clarity, and purpose."[73] In order to overcome social carnage and ongoing threats to hierarchies of gender, race, class, and (in Poe's case) artistic talent, the conservative must engage in something like leftist "criticism/self-criticism," sorting out those elements in his system that ennoble power from those that enervate it. At the base of this criticism/self-criticism is an understanding that the mere prettiness of old regimes has been or will be washed away by the sublime, all-dashing moment of revolution. In order to reestablish beauty on new premises, the conservative must likewise tap into the revolutionary sublimity unleashed during times of mass political upheaval. A conservative aesthetics, therefore, does not shy away from the grotesque; on the contrary, it embraces the grotesque as a means by which the author may inspire his reader to action in the present. The charred bodies in "Hop-Frog," the dental mutilation that caps "Berenice," the plague that overwhelms the court in "The Masque of the Red Death": these grotesqueries function as warnings to Poe's conservative readership. Maintain your hierarchies, Poe warns, or you and your civilization will collapse.

No element of the waning old regime's power seemed to obsess Poe more than its emphasis on hereditary wealth. Born to bohemian parents in Boston but raised as an outsider in a Virginia plantation home, Poe was at both the center and the margins of the slave power, and this vexed relationship plays out again and again in his stories. Poe's fixation on family lines and incest has traditionally been read through Sigmund Freud, a tradition inaugurated by Freud's associate Marie Bonaparte.[74] But reorienting our understanding of Poe's fixation on heredity and incest through the lens of Robin's explanation of activist conservatism's quarrel with the old regime allows us to better understand how Poe's aesthetic and political tendencies animate his most famous works. Robin locates the conservative critique of old regimes not in the internal logics of those regimes—their methods of social control and the ways in which they manage a nation's political life—but instead in their failure to circulate and redistribute power at the upper echelons of rule. The closed system of feudal law and its self-recursive systems of inheritance leave the old regimes open to assault from those who live on the outside of that incestuous economy. A new world, as Robin observes, will require new rules to maintain old hierarchies: "Unlike the feudal past, where power was presumed and privilege inherited, the conservative future envisions a world where power is demonstrated and privilege earned."[75]

"The Fall of the House of Usher" (1839) allegorizes this conservative critique. "The House of Usher" refers both to the physical building that will be destroyed by the story's end and the Usher family line, which has declined into hypochondria and incestuous obsession. The title of the story, the family decline it chronicles, and the physical space that Poe describes in exacting detail therefore stand as monuments to the greatest aspirations of the old regime and its decadence in the present moment. For the narrator, approaching the Usher ruin breeds "an iciness, a sinking, a sickening of the heart—and unredeemed dreariness of thought which no goading of the imagination could torture into aught of the sublime."[76] While the Usher home is undoubtedly in disrepair, the narrator does not see the rot as having compromised the building's architectural integrity:

> Its principal features seemed to be that of an excessive antiquity. The discoloration of ages had been great. Minute fungi overspread the whole exterior, hanging in a fine tangled web-work from the eaves. Yet all this was apart from any extraordinary dilapidation. No portion of the masonry had fallen; and there appeared to be a wild inconsistency between its still perfect adaptation of parts, and the crumbling condition of the individual stones. In this there was much that reminded me of the specious totality of old woodwork which has rotted for long years in some neglected vault, with no disturbance from the breath of the external air. ("Usher," 319–320).

While the Usher manse is of an "excessive antiquity" that has been discolored by time and neglect, it nevertheless remains a monumental structure—albeit one whose consistency can be chalked up to "specious totality." But the decay is not irreparable. Earlier, the narrator observes that the soul-deadening effect of the estate's decline could be corrected by "a mere different arrangement of the particulars of the scene, of the details of the picture" (317–318). Locked away in its "neglected vault" of arbitrary privilege, the Usher home may be renovated by "the breath of the external air," a breath granted by "a mere different arrangement... of the details of the picture." Given Poe's views of the artist as laid out explicitly in his literary theory and implicitly in the landscape fictions in "The Landscape Garden," "The Domain of Arnheim," and "Landor's Cottage," the narrator's call for an *aesthetic* rearrangement of the Usher lands becomes a telling political allegory for Poe's view of social redemption. The old regime's decadence has allowed the beautiful edifice of its institutions to decline, but the artist-genius's power may eventually redeem the whole system.

That redemption never arrives. Instead, the narrator witnesses the house's collapse, which is produced by Roderick Usher's incestuous desires for his sister, Madeline. Roderick admits "that much of the peculiar gloom which thus afflicted him could be traced . . . to the evidently approaching dissolution—of a tenderly beloved sister—his sole companion for long years—his last and only relative on earth" ("Usher," 323). Like the French ancien régime, which was as Burke claims in *Reflections on the Revolution in France* (1790) symbolically smashed by the capture and eventual execution of Marie Antoinette by the Jacobins, Usher's sovereignty cannot withstand the loss of its feminine antipode.

While the most dramatic expression of this collapse comes in the story's conclusion, Poe foreshadows both the narrative action and political meaning of the estate's collapse in Roderick Usher's poem "The Haunted Castle." "Tenanted" by "good angels," the "radiant palace" is a realm of aesthetic perfection, where "Spirits [move] musically / To a lute's well-tunèd law" ("Usher," 325–326). The "ruler of the realm" is surrounded by "a troop of Echoes whose sweet duty / Was but to sing / In voices of surpassing beauty, / The wit and wisdom of their king" (326). "The Haunted Castle" is an estate ruled entirely by internal logics of control and replication, each tenant reinforcing the "wit and wisdom" of the sovereign's "well-tunèd law." Yoking together aesthetics and government, beauty and social order, Poe dreams of a world where beauty, law, and order constitute a closed system of benign despotism.

Like Roderick and Madeline, between whom the author notes a "striking similitude" ("Usher," 329), the monarch's power derives from a self-replicating and self-reinforcing arrangement. And it is, finally, the palace's closed, incestuous structure of power that lead to its collapse:

> But evil things, in robes of sorrow,
>   Assailed the monarch's high estate;
> (Ah, let us mourn, for never morrow
>   Shall dawn upon him, desolate!)
> And, round about his home, the glory
>   That blushed and bloomed
> Is but a dim-remembered story
>   Of the old time entombed. ("Usher," 326–327)

"Entombed" in the monuments of its former glory—much like the Usher manor, which was itself described as having "rotted for long years in some neglected vault"—feudal power cannot prepare defenses for assaults from the outside, whether those assaults come from Jacobins, rebelling peasants, upset laborers, or insurrectionist slaves. The two characteristics of the "glory" around the castle—it "blooms," or grows, and "blushes," or demurs—indicates both the power and fragility of an old regime helpless against the oncoming tides of modernity and democracy. Like Madeline and her brother, the monarch and his Echoes are helpless to stem the assault of the amorphous "evil things" that, like the fungi clinging to Usher's mansion, threaten to drag his kingdom into perfidy.

While the Ushers are unable to save their home and family line, the narrator offers Roderick an "activist doctrine" in the form of another frame story told just before the mansion's collapse. The narrator seeks to calm Roderick by reading one of his "favorite romances": the story of Ethelred and the dragon, by the invented author Sir Launcelot Canning. An obsolete definition of "canning" as being or ability, along with canning's possible pun on "cunning," may help us understand why Poe places this fictive romance so close to the climax of his own tale. The narrator seeks to calm his friend's nerves by reminding him of the ability of his ancestors by teaching him about a Saxon with "ability" and the cunning to exercise that ability to overcome his foes.[77] Facing "a dragon of a scaly and prodigious demeanor, and of a fiery tongue, which sate in guard before a palace of gold, with a floor of silver," Ethelred acts quickly, striking the beast down with his mace ("Usher," 333). But there's a tint of Poe's characteristic irony here. Ethelred seems to refer to the Saxon king Æthelred (966–1016), who in later years would receive the unflattering nickname "Æthelred the Unready" due to his mismanagement of military affairs during repeated conflicts with the Danes. The narrator's poem poses a challenge to Roderick Usher: Will you be "unready" to rule, as your ancestor was, or will you follow the example of the poem's Ethelred, who slays the dragon and secures his domain?

As Poe's narrator reaches the romance's climax, he hears a shriek in the Usher home that foreshadows the home's coming collapse: "I did actually hear . . . a low and apparently distant, but harsh, protracted, and most unusual screaming or grating sound—the exact counterpart of what my fancy had already conjured up for the dragon's unnatural shriek as described by the romancer" ("Usher," 333). Poe here forces us to consider the action of the "Mad Trist" alongside that of "The Fall of the House of Usher." Ethelred, a Saxon man of action, faces down his adversary and is able to claim the "palace of gold, with a floor of silver" as his own; in the tradition of the Grail quests, Ethelred faces a blasted land and redeems it by virtue of his unthinking courage. Usher, on the other hand, rushes back to the specter of his dead sister, avatar of the closed system of feudal inheritance, and his domain implodes in a frenzied collapse scored by "a long tumultuous shouting sound like the voice of a thousand waters" ("Usher," 336). Ethelred is an avatar of elective aristocracy, the "superior man" whom Mabie, in the speech on Poe that opened this chapter, encourages us to "recognize and honor." Roderick Usher, on the other hand, stands helpless in the face of oncoming social change; the "thousand waters" of revolution and upheaval wash him, his home, and his family away.

The majority of Poe's stories present a tragic world in which feudal aristocracy is unable, in its current configuration, to withstand the emergence of democratic movements. He is the most conservative figure we'll meet in this book, a man for whom the world represented nothing but a charnel house of dead ages and the dross of old modes of power. Unlike Cooper, whom we will turn to next, Poe does not see hope for elites in a traditional conservative platform of reform and gradual renovation. Poe's imagination tends more toward the apocalyptic conservatism that would eventually characterize fascism (or, indeed, southern separatism that precipitated the Civil War) than it does the staid conservatism of an Alexander Hamilton or John Quincy Adams. In order for the artist-genius to flourish in his creative revels, the world must be made anew, and old aristocracies must be instantiated on different terms. The inventiveness evidenced by Poe's works—and their continuing influence on modernist and postmodernist literary cultures and theories—thus shields from view a notion central to eighteenth- and nineteenth-century conservative social thought: the impulse to restore ancient regimes of power and influence on new, firmer ground.

⊗ CHAPTER TWO ⊗

Melodrama of Primitive Accumulation
Cooper's Feudal Claims

> Resurgences of biological determinism correlate with episodes of political retrenchment . . . or at times of fear among ruling elites, when disadvantaged groups sow serious social unrest or even threaten to usurp power. What argument against social change could be more chillingly effective than the claim that established orders, with some groups on top and others at the bottom, exist as an accurate reflection of the innate and unchangeable intellectual capacities of people so ranked?
>
> —Stephen Jay Gould, *The Mismeasure of Man* (1981/1996)

In the opening passages of James Fenimore Cooper's late novel *Satanstoe* (1845), narrator Cornelius Littlepage worries over the trajectory of U.S. history. Littlepage sees that the United States, in the wake of its victory against British colonial authority, "is destined to undergo great and rapid changes," but is concerned that his generation of New Yorkers will not produce a body of work that can express "household life" as it was. Cornelius admits that "history will doubtless attempt to record, and probably with the questionable veracity and prejudice that are apt to influence the labours of that particular muse," the important political events of his era. But, due to the nation's lack of a flourishing literary culture, he can "see scarcely a mode by which the next generation can preserve" the "manners and the opinions" that to him constitute the true story of any given historical moment.[1]

Cornelius's desire for a synchronic narration of U.S. history, one that emphasizes the passing habits and manners of a given historical moment over that moment's major political and economic events, leads him to undertake an ambitious literary project: a multigenerational historical novel that will offer "the feelings, incidents, and interests of what is purely private life" without (he claims) recourse to any broader historical issues. Cornelius goes so far as to make the intellectual property of the memorial project part of the real property that will be passed to his heirs: "I have made a solemn request in my will, that those who come after me will consent to continue this narrative ... down as low at least as my grandson, if I ever have one" (*S*, 1:10). By placing the duty of narrating national history in the hands of an elect, literate, and mannered few—a few that will be drawn, he hopes, from his own family line—Cornelius Littlepage undermines the democratic and egalitarian impulses for which the first generation of Americans claimed to have fought. Literary talent, social influence, and the power to accurately represent history are heritable traits for Cooper's paterfamilias, as legitimate a birthright as a parcel of land or the contents of a bank account.

While Cooper casts the founder of the feudal estate that is threatened by rebellious tenants in *The Chainbearer* and *The Redskins* as a dutiful citizen whose patriotism compels him to make an honest record of daily colonial life, Cornelius's humble desire to archive his generation's "manners and opinions" belies Cooper's stated purpose in his own prologue to *Satanstoe* to offer a three-book attack on "the great New York question of the day, ANTI-RENTISM" (*S*, 1:v). Cooper refers here to the violent struggle between Mohawk Valley landlords and their long-aggrieved tenants that occupied New York politics throughout the late 1830s into the 1840s. Landlords such as Stephen Van Rensselaer administered estates based on ancient feudal titles. They defended their claims with centuries-old common law precedents, using their dependent tenantry to marshal political influence in a manner that stood in open opposition to free elections and the democratic political institutions these elections were meant to staff. Swaying renters' votes to purchase political power became increasingly untenable in the populist atmosphere of the Jacksonian era, leading Whig politicians who had once sided with the Mohawk Valley "patroons" to align themselves with the tenants' cause.[2]

But the limit of Whig allegiance to the anti-rent agitators was drawn along class lines. The rioting tenants posed questions about land ownership and governmental authority that seemed radical even by the standards of the most sympathetic observer. Progressive newspaperman Horace Greely, for example, pegged anti-rent agitation on popular misinterpretations of "the pregnant language of the Declaration of Independence," and many observers worried that anti-rent agitation threatened the sanctity of private property.[3] As the struggle wore on, however, more and more observers became outraged by the continuation of feudal claims on U.S. soil. In the end, Van Rensselaer and his cohort were defeated in a series of court decisions, and their land titles were gradually modernized.

The Anti-Rent War was a moment of "political retrenchment" for Mohawk Valley landlords, to use Stephen Jay Gould's phrase from the epigraph to this chapter. As rioting tenants and Whig reformers threatened their material interests, this small landholding class sought new ways to justify their claims. Cooper's Littlepage novels were part of this process. But Cooper significantly extends the arguments put forward by the patroons, using the anti-rent protests as an opportunity to reevaluate Anglo-America's increasing rejection of social (if not economic) hierarchies and the damage he feared this leveling impulse would do to the national character. Throughout the Littlepage novels, Cooper draws a connection between a private history tied to private property (Cornelius's estate and the multigenerational literary project itself), and a public history tied to broader arcs of national development. Against historians "who aspire to enroll their names among the Tacituses of former ages" (*S*, 1:10), the Littlepage family will (Cornelius hopes) contribute to the establishment of a national literary culture, one he believes will present a more honest portrait of the interests and motives of his landowning class.

The class interests of feudal Mohawk Valley landlords are therefore tied directly to literary production, which itself is taken as a more realistic record of national development than "mere" history. By favoring a personal mode of historical narration that focuses on rupture and generational change over a longer, diachronic historical narration that would demonstrate the continuity of landed power in the republic, the Littlepage family skirts the immediate political question at the center of Cooper's narrative. In this way, the Littlepage family naturalizes their claim to the land, thereby making hereditary hierarchies seem like the inevitable results of natural law.[4] If you only take the time to get to know the "first families" of the Mohawk Valley, Cooper implies, you will find that they are the true owners of the land—more so than the tenants who have labored to make that land of use to the emerging markets, or the indigenous peoples who continue to walk its old growth forests.

FEUDALISM AND LAND LAW IN THE EARLY REPUBLIC

While singular in its scale and intensity, the Anti-Rent War was not a unique political occurrence. The persistence of feudal land titles had long plagued U.S. politics, representing a serious challenge to the ideological and legal thrust of the Revolutionary Generation's earliest land reform efforts. Unlike slavery or the oppression of women, both of which could be justified (albeit tenuously) by Enlightenment notions of natural order, feudal titles as protected by common law precedent carried the historical weight of the deposed British crown and its absolute claim to allodial titles for colonial lands.[5] By democratizing the allodial title—allowing any person (as legally defined by a state's constitution) of sufficient capital to purchase or receive land as a freeholder—the Revolutionary Generation sought to disperse sovereign power into the hands of the white men who constituted "the people" of the newly formed United States.

Land law thus followed an "every man a king" ethos, vesting each landholder with rights that had traditionally been held only by the sovereign. The proliferation of these individualized domains encouraged white men of the laboring and middle classes both to strive toward the aristocracy and to support those aristocrats who already held privilege and power. If some men were able, through luck or superior talents, to amass more property than other men, then so be it.

Because land ownership was connected to political participation, it became imperative for the Revolutionary Generation to look at English land law in a new light. The principle of the freehold was so central to the ideological development of the United States that John Adams, in his "Dissertation on Canon and Feudal Law" (1765), suggests that a "great struggle" between the defenders of "ecclesiastical and civil tyranny" (i.e., the state/church alliance and the feudal land system) was the key factor in the peopling of Anglo-America.[6] "It was not religion alone, as is commonly supposed," Adams writes, "but it was a love of universal liberty, and a hatred, a dread, a horror, of the infernal confederacy [of church and state], that projected, conducted, and accomplished the settlement of America" (213). Only through a system wherein lands are held "allodially," and "every man ... [is] the sovereign lord and proprietor of the ground he occupie[s]" can a "commonwealth" be established (217).

Thomas Jefferson likewise insists in his *Autobiography* that, by eradicating primogeniture and entail in Virginia, his generation had "removed the feudal and unnatural distinction which made one member of every family rich, and all the rest poor, substituting equal partition, the best of all Agrarian laws."[7] By abolishing feudal inheritance, which he calls a "religion of the rich," Jefferson and his fellow Virginia planters restored "the rights of conscience" and created conditions for the emergence of a class "qualified to understand their rights, to maintain them, and to exercise with intelligence their parts in self-government."⁸ But none of this meant that Adams and Jefferson advocated the abolishment of inheritance, let alone landed power. In order to show that their estates were not the same as the estates that had, in their estimation, strangled freedom in the Old World, America's new landed gentry had to separate private property from its legal history and establish a transcendental basis for the right of one person to extract rents and labor from his subordinates.

There was only one problem: the vision of a political sovereignty rooted in small freeholds was a movement backward from developments in English land law. The social upheavals in Europe over the early modern period had slowly severed land title from sovereignty, placing the power to shape social institutions in the hands of centralized state governments. The crown as sovereign—the era of the absolute monarchs—stood opposed to the feudal conception of small landholds as discrete sovereignties with their own laws and cultures. The model of small landholders with more or less absolute authority over their domains championed by Adams and Jefferson, then, is *closer to the medieval notion of "parcelized sovereignty" than it is to the modern idea of a "civic corporation" as an agency of social control.*

The process of articulating a new, popular sovereignty within the legal framework of an English political culture that had carefully balanced monarchical power with landed aristocratic power proved to be one of frustration and compromise. Despite Jefferson's pugnacious rhetoric, the land reforms he pursued during the 1770s did little to disestablish the hereditary power structure of Virginia.⁹ Land, as both Jefferson and his English contemporary Edmund Burke understood, was essential in maintaining the continuity of hereditary political power as the colonies formed into a nascent bourgeois federation.¹⁰ By allowing political power to remain in the hands of a landed aristocracy, colonial power structures were largely maintained in the new republic. Without the influence of a strong, centralized political authority, America stood ready to lapse back into the complex fragmentation of power that characterized medieval political culture. America's superstructural synthesis of "parcelized sovereignty" with a popular sovereignty based in the primacy of the civic corporation leads us to a strange impasse: even in states where the most evident outrages of feudalism were dismantled, property law was still based on centuries-old English precedent.¹¹ While English law had been slowly working away from its feudal past since the sixteenth century, U.S. law relied on increasingly outdated decisions and statutes.

What does this legal tendency mean in a cultural context? If each state is able to establish regulations concerning something as essential to human life as where one lives on legacy decisions from premodern law, then what do we make of the Revolutionary Generation's impassioned arguments against the legal and cultural institutions of the English past? It is not within the scope of this book to sort through the dense history of U.S. land law on a state-by-state—or, worse yet, case-by-case—basis. I likewise do not want to commit the familiar and widespread fallacy of mistaking one representative court case for a watershed moment in this or that institution or this or that mentality. Instead, I would like you to consider how shocking and anachronistic it must have been for a small tenant to face legal precedents such as *Quai Emptores*, a thirteenth-century statute that prevented tenants from "subinfeudating" (subleasing) land they did not own allodially, in courtrooms that their Fourth of July orations told them were wholly modern, wholly "American," and wholly based on their sovereign power as "the people" of the new republic. The dialectic between tenant and landlord is a microcosm of the broader dialectic between on the one hand the ideal of a civic corporation underwritten by "the people" and their consent to be governed, and on the other the reality of a byzantine legal system arbitrated by a small, well-educated elite working in their own class interests. This, in turn, asks us to consider and question the relationship between the early republic's understanding of how its political present related to the English past, or of how the "new country" would approach history.

The struggle between feudal land law and democratic sovereignty reached a bloody climax in New York's Anti-Rent War.[12] Between 1839 and 1845, tenants in the Mohawk Valley mobilized into well-trained militia units that blocked the collection of rents, disseminated propaganda in the form of newspapers and broadsides, staged wide-scale theatrical protests, and successfully pushed New York politics away from its cozy relationship with wealthy "patroons" who used ancient Dutch land titles and English common law precedent to defend their manors. The rights afforded to Mohawk Valley patroons were considerable: profits from rent were free from taxation, and landlords could demand extravagant and often bizarre tributes from their tenants, including the ceremonial presentation of "four fat fowl" on New Year's Day, an ancient provision that rightly struck nineteenth-century tenants as a reminder of late feudalism's most absurd abuses.[13] The social graces and mannerisms of the English aristocracy were likewise maintained.

Stephen Van Rensselaer, for instance, only deigned to extend his forefinger when greeting his subordinates.[14]

More important, Mohawk Valley landlords claimed absolute right to all improvements on tenants' lands, including mills and barns. Robert Livingston, whose family controlled a 150,000-acre estate, demanded that his tenants "sow at least twelve bushels of winter wheat and plant an orchard of one hundred apple and pear trees within seven years of moving onto the premises," "build a barn of forty-five by twenty feet and a barrack to preserve corn crops," and "erect and maintain fences" in order to keep their lease.[15] In the case of eviction, tenants stood to lose generations' worth of such improvements, leaving them destitute. In the words of an 1844 document produced by the anti-renters for their annual convention, the Mohawk Valley patroons were "'highly privileged above any other class of citizens' and subjected tenants to 'feudal slavery . . . inconsistent with a code of equal laws.'"[16] It is not unreasonable to say that despite Adams's and Jefferson's claims to the contrary, "the spirit of feudal aristocracy" survived the American Revolution.[17]

Wealthy patroons hoped to maintain their manors as permanent autonomous zones. Like the southern slaveholders we saw in chapter 1, the Mohawk Valley landlords argued that their loyalty to the colonies during the Revolutionary War made them true Americans, and that their civil liberties were being infringed upon by rioting tenants. The landlords were not entirely wrong in this: prominent families such as the Van Rensselaers had indeed sided with the colonies, and the continuation of their leases was considered a just reward for that loyalty. In the wake of the Revolution, Loyalist landlords were "hounded and humiliated by revolutionary committees" and saw their lands confiscated by state legislatures.[18] Even families that had sided with the colonies sold off lands to their tenants in an attempt to avoid expropriation of their lands. By the 1830s, feudal tenures such as those on Rensselaerswyck, the Van Rensselaer family manor, were rare, making their continuation an even more evident outrage to tenants. But the Rensselaers, their fellow landlords, and the political supporters of both remained intransigent, insisting that their leasehold estates were protected by both law and the natural order of creation.

Before violence broke out in 1845, New York tenants argued for their rights using rhetoric and legal ideas drawn from the heady days of declaration and constitution writing of the 1770s and 1780s, language that had been renewed during the populist fervor of the Jacksonian era.[19] Anti-rent protesters in Delaware County argued, with words that could be taken directly from Jefferson's works, that a people "cannot be free unless independent. . . . To be completely sovereign, they must individually be the lords of the soil they occupy."[20] The Delaware County anti-rent agitators and their fellow protesters in Mohawk County were neither a proto-Marxist political faction nor a protoanarchist collective, but instead a populist settler movement that aimed to secure allodial titles to their lands and better access to agricultural markets. They wanted, in short, to hold Jeffersonianism to its word. In this sense, the tenants sought to replicate "autonomous, small-holding, patriarchal households," a goal that Huston believes their agitation achieved.[21] Their methods were not unlike those of the recent Occupy movements: theatrical protests segued into direct, targeted action against specific institutions and individuals who supported the landlords. The anti-renters dressed as Indians, a tradition of protest that predates the Revolution. In 1761, aggrieved tenants in Maine dressed as "White Indians" to attack the home of a local owner; similar costumed attacks occurred from the 1780s to the early 1800s in Maine, New York, Pennsylvania, and, most famously, at 1773's Boston Tea Party.[22] Rural whites adopted Indian costume to make a point about their newfound liberties; then as now, Indians held a near-mythological status in the white imaginary, signaling absolute freedom and organic connection to the land.[23] Even as settlers deprived the Northeast's first people of their own rights, they performed a burlesque of indigenous sovereignty to press their claims to private property. In the words of Sioux scholar and political organizer Vine Deloria Jr., white dissenters who assume Indian dress (and, oftentimes, claim Indian heritage) "need some blood tie with the frontier and its dangers in order to experience what it means to be American."[24]

Despite white tenants' justifiable grievances against overreaching landlords, the ideological lines dividing the groups was thin: both parties agreed on natural hierarchies of race and nationality, and both sought to hold allodial title to their properties. The quarrel between anti-renters and landlords was finally a class issue, the latter party believing that only certain exceptional family lines ought to have the right to property, and the former holding that all white men deserve a chance to become the sovereigns of their own small estates.[25]

When put in these terms, James Fenimore Cooper's support of the landlords—an unpopular position in New York politics by the 1840s—begins to make sense. As we will see, Cooper came to believe more and more that greatness and social position were heritable traits—and, of course, that his own family line possessed the genetic stuff of a U.S. aristocracy.[26] William Cooper, a shrewd businessman who used the liberties and mobility afforded by the relative chaos of the period after the Revolutionary War to secure his own fiefdom in New York State, provided James Fenimore Cooper with an at-hand example of liberal energies being harnessed to buttress feudal pretensions.[27]

Biographical context aside, the long form defense of feudal rights that Cooper takes up in the Littlepage novels may best be understood as a practical application of the political doctrines Cooper puts forward in his most substantial piece of social analysis, *The American Democrat* (1838). The work is a complex political treatise that finds its author "in the situation of a foreigner in his own country."[28] Already in this introductory qualification we begin to see the delicate rhetorical task Cooper is setting for himself. If the earlier *Notions of the Americans* (1830) found Cooper attempting to justify his nation's democratic impulses to a hostile European audience, then *The American Democrat* is Cooper attempting to justify his aristocratic tendencies to a U.S. audience. Cooper structures his argument around three theoretical categories: "despotisms," "limited monarchies," and "republicks" (369). Immediately after establishing and defining his terms, Cooper sets about showing how these categories are imperfect through general analyses of Prussia, England, and France. Prussia, technically a despotic state, offers (in Cooper's view) more political freedoms than France, a limited, constitutional monarchy. England, the most vexing of the three, is putatively a monarchy, but in practice "a complicated but efficient aristocracy" managed by a parliament that defends the class interests of landed nobles (371). Cooper concludes, "The institutions of no country are rigidly respected in practice, owing to the cupidity and passions of men" (373). Cooper here pegs the tendency of governments to fail in their mandates on human nature, thus framing the synthesis of democracy and aristocracy he attempts in the chapters that follow in post-Enlightenment terms of natural law.

There is a tacit rejection of history and historical development in this stance. In order to make political systems coherent and free from contradiction, Cooper ignores the role that history has in their institutional heterodoxy, focusing instead on how this heterodoxy mirrors innate human tendencies. Cooper is no defender of strict hereditary monarchies, nor does he approach aristocracy without addressing its problems and abuses. The historical monarchies and aristocracies of Europe provide plenty of fodder for Cooper, who routinely demonstrates their inferiority when compared to U.S. institutions. However, Cooper is doing something much more subtle—and dangerous—in *The American Democrat* than celebrating the splendor of lost European nobilities. He is arguing, through the language of U.S. democracy, for a perpetual and natural aristocracy, one founded in an equality of civil and political rights that has no relation to "equality of condition."

Following Rousseau, Cooper asserts that "equality of condition is incompatible with civilization, and is found only to exist in those communities that are but slightly removed from the savage state" (392). Cooper's arguments against "equality of condition" are blunt: "One man must labor, while another may live luxuriously on his means.... Men are not born equals, physically, since one has a good constitution, another a bad; one is handsome, another ugly; one white, another black" (394–395). Cooper later frames this claim in the language of divine order—"That one man is not deemed as good as another in the grand moral system of providence, is revealed to us in Holy Writ" (417)—somewhat obviating his earlier claim that the ideal American democrat rejects jus divinum as the basis for political power (417). Finally, the great American innovation for Cooper is not in initiating a leveling process through a world-historical redistribution of wealth, but instead in laying bare the true nature of political power. "All that the great American proposition, therefore, can mean," he writes, "is to set up new and juster notions of natural rights than those which existed previously, by asserting, in substance, that God has not instituted political inequalities" (396). Human biological difference—the supposed superiority of this creature over that one—is for Cooper the basis for political and social power.

This aspect of Cooper's argument comes further into focus in his detailed defense of private property. Once again, Cooper reifies the right to private property through a recourse to Enlightenment-tinged political economy: "Even insects, reptiles, beasts and birds, have their several possessions, in their nests, dens and supplies. So completely is animal exertion, in general, whether in man or beast, dependent on the enjoyment of this right ... that we may infer that the rights of property, to a certain extent, are founded in nature" (456). Despite this, Cooper admits that, as civilization expands, "the rights of property become artificial and extended." Property holders should therefore not be allowed "constitutional privileges" that would strengthen their inevitable political influence (456, 458). (It is interesting to consider this claim against Cooper's defense of the Mohawk Valley patroons, who by all accounts sought precisely to cement their privilege in constitutional law.) Even still, Cooper falls on the side of the landed aristocrat against the democratic mob, asserting that a "consciousness of inferiority" leads the democrat to declaim "against [the aristocrat] for holding himself aloof from general association" (456, 458). This distinction between the aristocrat and the democrat is vital for Cooper's political vision: for Cooper, "the purest democrat" is one who "maintains his rights" against all potential violators, including the democrat mob who would rob the aristocrat through "unseasonable invasions on his time, by the coarse-minded and ignorant" (430). It's a slippery line of reasoning, one that manages to celebrate the most important aspects of U.S. democracy while at the same time naturalizing aristocracy and proving, counterintuitively, that this aristocratic impulse is indeed the lifeblood of the nation's democratic institutions.

The American Democrat is a keen, if underread, intervention into political debates concerning sovereignty, the Constitution, and property, and theoretical debates concerning history, heredity, and natural order. Cooper's analysis of U.S. political life predicts conservative "strict construction" schools of constitutional law, a point underscored by the fact that the most recent scholarly edition of his political writings was produced by two scholars from Hillsdale College (nicknamed "the conservative Harvard" by the *National Review*) and issued as part of a Conservative Leadership Series by Regnery Publishing.[29] Cooper's strict constructionist view of U.S. political institutions depends on a dynamic between aristocracy (or feudalism) and democracy (or liberalism) that was likewise understood by the framers of the Constitution. In *Federalist* no. 17, Hamilton, Madison, and Jay claim that "the separate governments in a confederacy may aptly be compared with feudal baronies," and, in *Federalist* no. 45, they further argue that feudalism provides a sound model for the U.S. polity because it favors "local sovereigns in the rivalship for encroachments" against the federal authority. For the authors of the *Federalist*, the feudal-confederate system represents an organic compromise between absolute local sovereignty and national "tyranny": under the feudal confederacies, "component parts were pressed together . . . and consequently less powerful ligaments within would be sufficient to bind the members to the head, and to each other."[30] Cooper's political thought binds U.S. constitutional thinking to a natural hereditary order in order to justify the class position of aristocratic gentlemen in a country whose basis of political power was slowly shifting away from landed gentlemen and toward smaller, freeholding patriarchs with starkly differing views on society, literature, and manners. In the Littlepage novels, Cooper attempts to demonstrate the social and familial implications of his political vision.

LITTLEPAGE AND LEATHERSTOCKING AMONG THE PATROONS

In an 1848 letter, Cooper offers a concise rationale for the political and social notions that influenced his later career:

> There is a growing and most dangerous disposition in the people to take from those who have, and to give to those who have not; and this without any other motive than that basest of human passions—envy. How far this downward tendency will go, I do not pretend to say; but I think it quite clear that, unless arrested, it must lead to revolution and bloodshed. This State of things has long been predicted, and he who can look back for half a century, must see that a fearful progress has been made towards anarchy and its successor tyranny, in that period. Another such half-century will, in my judgment, bring the whole country under the bayonet.[31]

Written two years after Cooper completed the final novel in his Littlepage novels sequence, and just as the land titles held by the Mohawk Valley patroons he defended were being modernized by New York's Whig establishment, Cooper's letter could well serve in place of the Littlepage novels as his summary defense of feudal titles and attack on anti-rent agitation. Cooper charts a "downward tendency," or devolution, in American moral character, one that will inevitably slide toward "anarchy and tyranny" as the century progresses. Against the optimism of his *Leatherstocking Tales* sequence, which depicts the steady rise of frontier families even as it paints the decline of native peoples in florid romantic colors, the older Cooper sees only waste and bloodshed in America's future.

In this way, Cooper's attitude is not unlike that of Poe and other southern slaveocrats who saw the erosion of patriarchal authority and landed power as symptomatic of a rot at the root of the U.S. polity. But, unlike the southerners, whose assaults on the present wasteland of U.S. life forced them into ahistorical claims concerning the eternal verity of their plantation system, Cooper grounds his critique in careful examinations of America's political institutions. Packed discretely within Cooper's declensionist view of U.S. social development is an assumption about the history of the United States. So long as the right families hold property, history may be said to progress toward a republican apotheosis. But, as soon as that right is threatened, the tenor of U.S. history modulates from triumph to a tragedy.

It's this narrative of decline that Cooper charts in the Littlepage novels. It's tempting to say that this apocalypticism contradicts Cooper's earlier view of settler sovereignty as expressed in the *Leatherstocking Tales*.[32] There is a clear difference between the tone of the younger Cooper and the Cooper of the Littlepage novels; however, I am not so certain that we can claim that the one is "democratic" while the other is "aristocratic." As I argue above, Cooper's political thought, inasmuch as it was a product of mainstream political thought among the landed gentry of the Early Republic, had always emphasized the synthesis between aristocratic/feudal and democratic/liberal values. And, as I will demonstrate in the conclusion to this chapter, even an early work such as *The Pioneers* (1823) evidences the same ideological impulses as the later, supposedly more "antidemocratic" novels that I am concerned with here. The Littlepage novels, then, serve as a revision of Cooper's social vision, but not a complete *reversal* of it. By renarrating the time period covered by the *Leatherstocking Tales*, the Littlepage novels put forward a new vision of U.S. social order and social decline.

Satanstoe, the first novel in the sequence, opens on the eve of the French and Indian War (1754–1763). Despite Cornelius Littlepage's attempt to privilege national history over personal history, the war drives Cooper's narrative, just as the Revolutionary War animates the action of *The Chainbearer* and the anti-rent protests of the 1830s–1840s structure of *The Redskins*. In an 1845 letter to his London publisher Richard Bentley, Cooper explains the rationale behind his organizational plan: "I divide the subjects into the 'Colony,' 'Revolution,' and 'Republic,' carrying the same family, the same localities, and same *things* generally through the three different books, but exhibiting the changes produced by time &c."[33] Despite Corny Littlepage's claim that he will only focus on individual manners and opinions, Cooper's plan for the Littlepage novels aims to narrate the first three phases of U.S. social life through the eyes of the aristocracy.

Without national history driving events, the action described in *Satanstoe* would be far too thin to sustain a two-volume, Walter Scott–style historical novel. Even against this backdrop, the plot is simplistic: "Corny" Littlepage and his friend Dirck Follock set out to claim a patent purchased by their fathers, are delayed for several months by the war, and, finally, with the help of the Onondanga tracker Susquesus, claim their lands and repel an attack by Cooper's perennial villains, the Mingoes. Along the way Corny falls in love with the daughter of an old-fashioned patriarch and landlord, Anneke Mordaunt; is harangued by the wily New Englander Jason Newcome; and interacts with several colorful local characters, from bawdy innkeepers to slaves celebrating the neo-pagan festival of Pinkster. *Satanstoe* is more concerned with offering readers a sense of place and establishing the premises of Cooper's argument concerning the nature of property, individual sovereignty, and family than it is with conveying a plot. Despite his emphasis on the narration of manners and opinions among the colonial elite, the characters in *Satanstoe* serve as stand-ins for political and historical tendencies—they are allegorical types, symbols of social relations, not "characters" in any recognizable, modern sense of the word. It's a singularly chatty epic. The Littlepages, Mordaunts, Newcomes, Follocks, and the indigenous peoples who help or hinder them develop their properties and stump for their respective class interests with such passion that *Satanstoe* often feels less like a novel meant for casual enjoyment than it does a philosophical dialogue concerning property and history.

Unlike the authors of southern plantation romances we considered in chapter 1, Cooper is refreshingly honest about his class allegiances and how his narrative will champion them. As editor of the fictional Manuscripts, Cooper believes the Littlepage family's multigenerational autobiography will help in "putting down, wholly, absolutely, and unqualifiedly, the false and dishonest theories and statements that have been boldly advanced" by anti-rent partisans. In doing so, the manuscripts will help promote "the existence of true liberty amongst us, the perpetuity of the institutions, and the safety of public morals" (*S*1:vi). Compared to the deceptive pseudofeudalism championed by the southern plantation romance, Cooper's defense of the Mohawk Valley patents and the "patroons" who held them is couched in positive arguments about the absolute moral right of a certain kind of private property and the superstructural effects that follow from that understanding. Southern feudalism sought to misrepresent slaveholding as the modern expression of harmonious medieval social interactions; Cooper and the patroons championed actual social and economic practices carried over from the Middle Ages and therefore sought to demonstrate that feudal privilege was, in reality, perfectly in line with nascent U.S. republican ideology. Cooper states this plainly in his polemical introduction to *The Chainbearer*: while anti-rent Whigs in New York have "pronounced the tenure of a durable lease to be opposed to the spirit of the institutions" of a democratic nation, "these tenures existed when the institutions were formed, and one of the provisions of the institutions guarantees the observance of the covenants under which the tenures exist."[34]

Cooper is not a rank reactionary calling for the immediate suppression of the democratic impulses that animated anti-rentism, but instead a moderately conservative bourgeois partisan arguing for what he views as the spirit of the Revolutionary Generation's compromise between republican innovation and traditional, hierarchical social arrangements. Jason Newcome, the Yankee usurper whose family will haunt the Littlepages and Mordaunts over the next century, is to be distrusted because he is "ultra leveling in his notions of social intercourse," and unused to the strong "distinctions of classes" in New York (*S*1:47). Newcome's unwillingness to bend to the manners of New York's strict class structure is a symptom of a broader social ill: the inability of Americans to establish a proper national identity. Speaking in one of the bitter editorial asides that will come to dominate the narrative as the series progresses, Cooper describes the American of his century as

> a jumble of the same senseless contradictions in his social habits, as he is fast getting to be in his political creeds and political practices; a being that is *in transitu*, pressed by circumstances on one side, and by the habit of imitation on the other; unwilling, almost unable, to think and act for himself. The only American who is temporarily independent in such things, is the unfledged provincial, fresh from his village conceit and village practices, who, until corrected by communion with the world, fancies the south-east corner of the north-west parish, in the town of Hebron, in the county of Jericho, and the State of Connecticut, to be the only portion of this globe that is perfection. (*S*1:68)

Cooper's narrative implies that the "manners and opinions" leading from an aristocratic class structure can, if judiciously democratized for new republican conditions, set the "jumble of . . . senseless contradictions" that is U.S. identity to right. Neither the "leveling" provincialism of a Jason Newcome nor the stalwart Europeanism of the most conservative New York patroon can produce a fitting national identity. Rather, Cooper's ideal is the gradual refinement of manners through art, literature, and the stage, paired with an economic base that favors a self-evident and "moral" basis for private property.

Satanstoe must thus prove that the Littlepage and Mordaunt families are above moral reproach. Anneke Mordaunt is a two-dimensional paragon of virtue, offended by even the suggestion of a crude or off-color remark; Corny Littlepage is faultlessly brave and honest, even saving his ladylove from the jaws of a lion (yes, a lion, in New York, at a public carnival) during the early Pinkster sequences; and Herman Mordaunt is a fair-minded patriarch, allowing his daughter to marry beneath her station for love. In this sense, "Corny" Littlepage's marriage to Anneke Mordaunt—whose father at first wishes her to marry Major Bulstrode, a titled English gentleman—is symbolic of a détente between the "lower" and "upper" aristocracy.

Cooper sees this compromise as the genius of New York's supposed social harmony. In an editorial aside, Cooper formulates a tripartite moral division for the young nation: "New England, or puritan-morals; middle colonies, or liberal morals; and southern colonies, or latitudinarian morals" (2:33). "Liberal morals," according to Cooper's scheme, represent a compromise between the unforgiving Calvinist moral universe of New England and the do-what-you-will moral anarchy of the southern slavocracy. Defining the New York patroon against the southern slavocrat is essential for Cooper here. The "latitudinarian" South adheres to the accidents of feudal hierarchy (political ceremony, class division, gentility) without embracing its essence (landed wealth as the basis of social position), whereas the Mohawk Valley upholds feudalism both in essence and accident.

To demonstrate the necessity of his liberal feudalism, Cooper makes the establishment of feudal estates essential to the development of the market economy in the region. Just before Corny heads north with Dirck to lay claim to his lands, Herman explains the difficulties he has faced establishing an estate at Ravensnest. Mordaunt describes "the cost and trouble he had been at . . . in getting the ten or fifteen families who were on his property, in the first place, to the spot itself; and, in the second place, to induce them to remain there" (2:74). Mordaunt induces the settlers to stay by offering extraordinarily liberal leases—"leases for three lives, or, in some cases, for thirty or forty years, at rents that were merely nominal"—and by building the rudiments of a material infrastructure for his settlers, including roads (2:75). Whereas under "classical" feudalism tenants were offered military protection (and therefore owed their landlord military allegiance), the liberal feudalism of U.S. enclosure obliges the landlord to serve as a federative power that establishes a rudimentary market of commodities imported from the cities.

Corny explains the unique situation of Mohawk Valley settlement in the language of political economy: "People were scarce, while land was superabundant. In such a condition of society, the tenant had the choice of his farm, instead of the landlord's having a selection of his tenants" (2:75). Given the "renter's market" of the Early Republic, Cooper's argument goes, it became necessary for landlords to entice settlers with favorable leases and a regular supply of amenities from urban centers. Why, given the extraordinary effort and capital outlay required to establish an estate like Ravensnest, would a landlord undertake such a project? Herman Mordaunt's response looks toward the future: "A century hence, indeed, my descendants may benefit from all this outlay of money and trouble; but it is not probable that either I or Anneke will ever see the principal and interest of the sums that will be expended in the way of roads, bridges, mills, and other things of that sort. Years must go by, before the light rents which will only begin to be paid a year or two hence, and then only by a very few tenants, can amount to a sufficient sum to meet the expenses of keeping up the settlement" (2:75–76). There is dramatic irony at work in Mordaunt's forecast. An educated reader in the 1840s would know that these leases were in fact in peril. Cooper employs irony here to make the Mordaunt and Littlepage families sympathetic to readers; their desire to provide comfort and safety for their progeny seems biologically and morally self-evident, not a political matter at all. Their desire is so pure that they are in fact willing to issue unfavorable leases on the chance that the leases will one day yield a marginal profit. Mordaunt offers just such a lease to Jason Newcome, whom Corny knows will never make good on his obligations to the patroon: "Jason was a very happy man, the moment he got his lease. . . it made him a sort of land-holder on the spot, and one who had nothing to pay for ten years to come. . . . from the first, I had a suspicion that Jason trusted to fortune to prevent any pay-day from ever coming at all"(2:94). Newcome signs his lease in order to establish a precedent for his eventual claim to an allodial title to Mordaunt's land. To underscore the supposedly corrupt moral premises on which anti-rentism is based, in the subsequent installments of the Littlepage trilogy Newcome and his descendants become leaders of the anti-rent movement.

Herman Mordaunt's conversation with Corny regarding the landlord's sacrifices, as much as any other passage in the Littlepage novels, makes the thesis of Cooper's trilogy clear. For Cooper, colonial landlords, owing to their surplus wealth and secure social positions, were the only class wealthy enough to bring civilization to the American wilderness. Their immediate rewards were minimal, but they persevered through a sense of commitment to future generations and an evangelical belief in civilization. Their homes were simple and republican when compared to the great estates of the Old World, and yet they also (as Corny writes of the Mordaunt compound at Lilacsbush, on the northern tip of Manhattan) offer "a certain indescribable air of comfort, gentility, and neatness about the whole" (S1:133). Order in wilderness and a patriarchal obligation to future generations are the intertwined virtues Cooper celebrates and defends here. This view of American social development defines ownership in terms of initial capital outlay and feudal order, and thereby minimalizes the material improvements (e.g., mills, barns, houses, churches) made by tenants on the land. "In America," Cooper notes in an editorial aside, "everything is 'built.' The priest 'builds up' a flock; the speculator, a fortune; the lawyer, a reputation; and the landlord, a settlement; sometimes, with sufficient accuracy in language, he even builds a town" (S, 2:93). That the Littlepage and Follock confederacy "build up" their communities with the help of Susquesus, the native tracker, is important: Susquesus's loyalty to the landlords and their offspring, along with his practical assistance in defending the patent, naturalizes their feudal claim to the land.

Cooper fully realizes his association of native nobility with feudal sovereignty in *The Chainbearer*. Mordaunt Littlepage, son of Cornelius Littlepage, who became a hero of the Revolution and so was able to hold his land titles, sets off to complete the job of mapping the estates laid out by his father and Dirck Follock in *Satanstoe*. At his side is Andries Coejemans, the chainbearer of the novel's title. The plot centers on a struggle between Mordaunt and the squatter Aaron "Thousandacres" Timberman, whose family, with the Yankee Newcome's blessing, has established a profitable mill on the Littlepage/Follock patent. While less accomplished as a work of fiction than *Satanstoe*, *The Chainbearer* presents a much more nuanced argument, one that sees Cooper set four warring sovereignties—that of the Yankee democrat (Newcome), the squatter (Thousandacres), the aristocracy (Littlepage and Coejemans), and the native (Susquesus)—against one another. In the end, Cooper must rationalize the aristocracy's claim to the land without dismissing out of hand the claims made by the three other groups.

Cooper handles the question of the native claim first. Mordaunt finds an aging Susquesus in the woods near Ravensnest. Though Susquesus has entered *"red* old age," his form retains an "indurated, solid look" that Cooper attributes to Susquesus's refusal to drink rum (*C*, 1:102). It is important for Cooper to make Susquesus an exemplary Indian; if Susquesus were dissipated by alcoholism, or if he had become bitter and vicious in his old age, then the tracker's allegiance with the Littlepage clan would lose its symbolic power. Susquesus, the best and last of the Onondaga, aligns himself with the Littlepages, the best of the landlords, in a partnership that reflects Cooper's ongoing emphasis on the hereditary excellence of great American types.

After briefly discussing the Revolution, Susquesus and Mordaunt turn to the question of Susquesus's future. The tracker is isolated—"No tribe—no squaw—no pappoose!"—and facing death. Mordaunt offers Susquesus a free parcel of land as a reward for his years of service to the Littlepage clan, but Susquesus refuses: "Tankee—bird plenty; fish plenty; message plenty, now; and don't want land" (1:104). Susquesus asks Mordaunt when the landlord last saw his patent, and is shocked when Mordaunt reveals that he has never laid eyes on it. "Dat queer!" Susquesus exclaims, "How you own land, when nebber see him?" Susquesus's keen observation—it is, in fact, a very strange aspect of western property conventions that a person may hold and extract rents from lands he has never seen—is met with disdain by Littlepage. Mordaunt explains that "pale-faces" use paper titles to maintain their land, and that the abundance of land in the United States has created a situation where "any man can have a farm who will pay a very moderate price for it," if not from a landlord then from the State (1:107).

What follows is surely among the strangest passages in Cooper's work, if not in nineteenth-century U.S. literature: an extended rewriting of Smith's *The Wealth of Nations* in the style of a Socratic dialogue between a U.S. aristocrat and the aging native, a passage that hinges on the question of movable versus landed property. Susquesus compares land titles to hunting pelts, asking why the former should be held by an individual when land cannot be carried on a person's body. Littlepage explains that "the riches of you red-men are confined to movable property," whereas the riches of the "pale-faces" are diverse (*C*, 1:108). Littlepage then asks Susquesus to consider the fortunes of the "red-man" versus those of the "pale-face." Cooper has the tracker reduce native genocide to a set of triumphalist dichotomies: "Be sure, differ: one strong, t'oder weak—one rich, t'oder poor—one great, t'oder little—one drive 'way, t'oder haf to go—one get all, t'oder keep nuttin'" (*C*, 1:108). Littlepage explains that the Indian's lack of gunpowder led to the white man's victory, and that the white man was only able to develop this technology because of his emphasis on private property:

> All the knowledge, and all the arts of life that the white man enjoys and turns to his profit, come from the rights of property. No man would build a wigwam to make rifles in, if he thought he could not keep it as long as he wished, sell it when he pleased, and leave it to his son when he went to the land of spirits. Without these rights of property, no people could be civilized; for no people would do their utmost, unless each man were permitted to be master of what he can acquire, subject to the great and common laws that are necessary to regulate such matters.... On this necessity is founded the rights of property; the gain being civilization; the loss ignorance, and poverty, and weakness. It is for this reason, then, that we buy and sell land, as well as clothes and arms, and beads. (109–110)

As in *The American Democrat* and his other political writings, Cooper espouses a similarly liberal view of property and social development drawn from his reading in eighteenth-century political economy. Littlepage's logic is perfectly in line with the notions of ownership and rights that motivated the landed intellectuals who led the American Revolution and shaped U.S. political institutions in its aftermath. What makes the passage interesting is the historical context of the Anti-Rent War. Cooper signals to his readers that rioting squatters and tenants undermine the core principle of Western civilization—private property—and that in doing so they have reduced themselves to the level of the native. This is at base a chauvinistic, racialist appeal to readers: if you disagree with Littlepage, Cooper implies, you are no better learned than Susquesus.

Cooper moves past Susquesus's objections without considering the complex relationship that the Five Nations Indian tribes held to the land. The Iroquois tribes held a communitarian and matrilineal view of property, one that was regulated by complex public rituals in which "sachems" were named as "trustees but not the owners of the land."[35] Land titles were finally held by women, who bequeathed the property to elder tribesmen in a perpetual trust on behalf of the entire body of the tribe. This complex understanding of property led to an equally complex polity, one made up of a hierarchy of chiefs and other persons of rank (*agoianders*), a political system that effected peace among the Five Nations until the phase of French and English accumulation of land that displaced the tribes throughout the seventeenth and eighteenth centuries.[36]

Susquesus's people would have been more than aware of the importance property arrangements have on social arrangements: their property laws, which defended personal property without a Western conception of private property, had fostered a politically sophisticated form of tribal communism before European contact.[37] Marx sees the Iroquois model of common property and matrilineal inheritance as prefiguring communist society. While tainted by the stadial racialism of his source, Lewis Henry Morgan's *Ancient Society* (1877), these readings in Morgan provided Marx with a path toward communism that would not necessarily pass through capitalism, a point he developed at some length in his 1881 letter to Vera Zasulich on Russian peasant communes. Manuel Yang argues that Marx's studies in Iroquois society indicate that Marxian historical materialism "refused to assume 'a general historical-philosophical theory' that placed itself beyond history"; instead, "each sequence and content of stages were specific to the historical and geographical conditions of the region under study, hence never generalizable to other areas without a careful study of the conditions of those areas on their own terms."[38]

It would be foolhardy to mention Marx in this context without recognizing the deep hostility toward Marxist class analysis put forward by indigenous thinkers such as Ward Churchill, Vine Deloria Jr., Russell Means, and Leslie Marmon Silko.[39] Recent scholarship by Jodi Byrd, Glenn Coulthard, and Nick Estes has attempted to bring indigenous scholarship and Marxist class analysis into dialogue, rejecting the out-of-hand association of Marxism with imperialism and racism put forward by Churchill, Deloria, Means, and Silko's generation.[40]

But *Satanstoe* is neither a Marxist polemic nor a contemporary indigenous studies monograph, and so Susquesus concedes the argument to Mordaunt. He then leads the young landlord to view his estate for the first time: "I examined the view with the interest which ownership is apt to create in us all. The earth is very beautiful in itself; but it is most beautiful in the eyes of those who have the largest stake in it, I fear" (*C*, 1:112). Littlepage's gaze obviates the physical features of the land: the description that follows considers Ravensnest's practical and economic features, not the scene in and of itself.

Littlepage's cool analysis of his holdings leads to the next warring sovereignty that Cooper must displace in order to naturalize the landlord's claim to property: that of the Yankee settler. Littlepage admits that "the millions of Yankees that are spreading themselves over the land, are producing... a most salutary influence on its practical knowledge, on its enterprise, on its improvements, and consequently on its happiness," but that they have not yet brought culture and civilization to the region (1:112–113). This is the most generous Cooper will be with the Yankee settler, who as in *Satanstoe* is portrayed here as more a coarse con man than an enterprising yeoman.

Cooper satirizes the settler's democratic pretensions in two sequences: the naming of the church and the visit to the Nest. In the first sequence, the settlers gather to vote on the denomination of their new church. Newcome sways the crowd through subtle manipulations and illusions of consensus; finally, the vote goes his way, and the voters choose Congregationalism. Littlepage, who observes the proceeding unnoticed, draws out a bitter lesson about U.S. democracy: "The thing took... for popular bodies, once under control, are as easily managed as the vessel that obeys her helm; the strength of the current always giving additional power to that material portion of the ship" (1:124–125). Newcome's ability to seduce crowds into working against their own interests will become the pivotal issue in *The Redskins*, which, as we will see, collapses Cooper's critique of the native with his critique of the Yankee settler.

Cooper's second extended critique of democracy occurs near the end of volume 1, during a visit to a mountaintop pigeon roost. "Hundreds of thousands of families" of pigeons live at the roost, a fact that gives Littlepage pause: "Our presence produced no general commotion; every one of the feathered throng appearing to be so much occupied with its own concerns, as to take little heed of the visit of a party of strangers, though of a race usually so formidable to their own" (*C*, 1:192). Settled pigeons tending to themselves map well onto the settled farmers and squatters who refuse to make way for Littlepage and his "race" of landowners. Eventually the pigeons do notice Littlepage's party, and they begin to make a ruckus. Ursula "Dus" Malbone, Coejemans's ward and Littlepage's future wife, is at the scene with Littlepage, who draws her close as the birds begin to squawk and rebel (1:193). The potential of the democratic parliament of fowls rising up draws Dus Malbone and Mordaunt Littlepage together in an allegory for the consolidation of land and privilege in family lines that Cooper argues for throughout the three Littlepage novels. There is even a surprising sensuality to the scene:

"Both hands were on my arm, and I felt that, unconsciously, her form was pressing closer to mine, in a manner she would have carefully avoided in a moment of perfect self-possession" (1:193). This first presexual contact between Dus and Mordaunt is predicated on their shared revulsion at the democratic mob whose squawking threatens to overwhelm their powers. While descending the hill, Dus takes the roost scene as evidence that "numbers can change our natures. . . . Here have we been almost in contact with pigeons which would not have suffered us to come within a hundred feet of them had they been in ordinary flocks, or as single birds" (1:195). Littlepage takes Dus's observation as an occasion to once again proselytize on his notions of government, notions that directly draw out the metaphorical flattening of the mass of pigeons with the mass of common men.

Aspects of Littlepage's speech—for instance, his claim that despotic governments can be good or bad, depending on their leadership—are borrowed directly from ideas developed in *The American Democrat*. But Cooper does not end the chapter with his summary statement on U.S. politics; instead he underscores the brief erotic contact between Dus and Littlepage. As Dus talks further on democracy versus tyranny, the mob versus the few, Mordaunt admires her physique, "the rich mouth, the brilliant teeth, and the spirited and yet tender blue eyes" (*C*, 1:149)—neglecting to tell us what, precisely, Dus has to say about her political beliefs. The lesson Cooper asks us to draw from the pigeon roost is twofold: first, that large masses of common things are frightening and pose a threat to the exceptional few, and, second, that only drawing together through conjugal relations will preserve dignity and property in the face of the mob.

As in *Satanstoe*, Cooper's plot hinges on a marriage. In this case, the Vermont squatter Thousandacres attempts to marry Dus Malbone off to his son Zephaniah as a way to secure some small property and influence for himself and his family. The Thousandacres plot is full of Gothic tropes: confinement and torture, forced marriage, and unrepentant sinners. To the last, Thousandacres remains a bitter critic of landlords and their auxiliaries. As Thousandacres lies dying, his wife begs him to repent his sins and forgive Coejemans and Littlepage, both likewise injured from the novel's bloody confrontations. Thousandacres informs the men, "If 't wasn't for your writin' titles, I shouldn't be lyin' here, breathin' my last." He adds, by way of conclusion: "I hope and believe . . . that in the world we're goin' to, there'll be no law, and no attorneys" (*C*, 2:185). Coejemans dies peacefully and is interred at Ravensnest; his ward is married off to Mordaunt Littlepage and so becomes the rightful heir to the property Coejemans helped lay out. Thousandacres dies in rage, and his family is sent down river with their possessions—all movable property, no better or further advanced in Cooper's imagination than the natives. The squatter—belonging to the lowest class position of any white represented in the Littlepage novels—receives the harshest censure from Cooper. The squatter represents something far worse than the native, who can be pitied and "domesticated" as if he were a wild animal. The squatter is a white man who has betrayed the very things that Cooper sees as the secrets to white supremacy: he has given up honest titles to land, bucks all authority and hierarchy, and has no respect whatsoever for the rule of law.

The final novel in the sequence, 1846's *The Redskins*, sees Cooper abandon plot almost entirely in favor of an extended and often muddled defense of the Littlepage family's right to an aristocratic pedigree. The story begins in Europe, where Hugh Roger Littlepage (grandson of Mordaunt Littlepage) and his uncle, also called Hugh Roger Littlepage ("Uncle Ro"), discuss at length the political and social situation in the United States. Their dialogue, made up largely of the same observations we saw in the two previous Littlepage novels and *The American Democrat*, is interrupted by a servant, who delivers shocking news: the ancestral lands in New York are under siege by anti-rent protesters. Hugh and Uncle Ro, disguised as Germans, return to America to investigate the rebellion and defend their interests. What follows is an elaborate, often nonsensical travelogue through the political and social effects of anti-rent agitation. Specific episodes in the novel are much less interesting than how its narrative action sums up Cooper's long argument in the Littlepage manuscripts. The novel is poorly written and dull, but remains rich in allegorical meaning, providing contemporary readers with insights into the imagination of an embattled upper class during a period of existential crisis.

Racial and ethnic performance—whites dressed up as Indians, U.S. aristocrats masquerading as German immigrants, Indians assuming the noble airs of English gentry, whites wearing blackface to commit horrid crimes—is the primary metaphor for the chaotic, mutually constructing cultural forces that Cooper sees shaping America in the 1840s. Susquesus and Jaap, well into their hundreds and still living at the periphery of the Littlepage estate, become the standard of authenticity in the chaos of confounding identities that motivates the rest of the novel. Susquesus and Jaap's cottage, much like the slave quarters from Pendleton Kennedy's *Swallow Barn* analyzed in chapter 1, serves as a metaphor for Cooper's view of man in his natural state:

> On one side of the hut there was a hog-pen and a small stable for a cow; but on the other the trees of the virgin forest, which had never been disturbed in that glen, overshadowed the roof. This somewhat poetical arrangement was actually the consequence of a compromise between the tenants of the cabin, the negro insisting on the accessories of his rude civilization, while the Indian required the shades of the woods to reconcile him to his position. Here had these two singularly associated beings—the one deriving his descent from the debased races of Africa, and the other from the fierce but lofty-minded aboriginal inhabitant of this continent—dwelt nearly for the whole period of an ordinary human life. The cabin itself began to look really ancient, while those who dwelt in it had little altered within the memory of man![41]

"Singularly associated" by their contact with and service to three generations of the Littlepage family, Susquesus and Jaap's domestic arrangement represents what Cooper sees as the unique peacemaking power of the Mohawk Valley landlords. The cabin fuses a romantic vision of the "noble savage" with a belief that even the "debased" African may be civilized through contact with aristocracy. Unlike the anti-rent agitators who will don blackface and Indian garb to persecute the landlords, Susquesus and Jaap are thankful for the Littlepage clan's tolerance and would never rebel.

Cooper underscores this point in a conversation between Uncle Ro, still disguising himself as a German watch seller, and Tom Miller, the manager of the Littlepage farm at Ravensnest. Miller declares that he'll have no "Injins" on his farm. Uncle Ro responds that he has just seen "an olt Injin in a hut up yonder," leading Miller to clarify himself: "Oh! that is Susquesus, an Onondago; he is a true Injin, and a gentlemen; but we have a parcel of the mock gentry about, who are a pest and an eye-sore to every honest man in the country. Half on 'em are nothing but thieves in mock Injin dresses" (*R*, 1:141). Miller associates Susquesus with natural obedience to authority and the anti-rent "Injins" with false sovereignty. Tamed and comfortable, Susquesus, the "true" Indian, has accepted his lot as a tenant on Littlepage lands; motivated by envy, the anti-rent protesters attempt to upset the balance of the region and threaten to scuttle not only the law, but also the natural hierarchies that subtend civilization.

Miller's observation leads to a lengthy discussion of the position of aristocracy in the United States. Uncle Ro asks, "Vhy do dey dalk so much of noples and arisdograts?—ist der noples and arisdograts in America?" (1:141). Miller admits that he isn't quite sure, but believes that the term is used by the masses to attack men of means. Ro responds that in Europe, an aristocrat is "one of a few men dat hast all de power of de government in deir own hands" (1:143). Miller responds: "Why, we call them critturs here DIMIGOGUES! Now, young 'Squire Littlepage ... is what we call an aristocrat, and he hasn't power enough to be named town clerk, much less to anything considerable, or what is worth having" (1:143). Cooper's definition is disingenuous: Mohawk Valley landlords did, in fact, control the politics of the region by having their tenants vote in their favor. It also obviates the real source of aristocratic power, the "parcelization of sovereignty" that characterizes feudal landholding arrangements. At its base, feudal power is local, flowing from the power of a petite sovereign to dictate specific terms of tenancy to his subordinates. When enough of these small-scale sovereigns band together to influence political power in their own class interests, an aristocracy is born. Cooper unnecessarily complicates a rather simple and self-evident understanding of what an aristocracy is and how it functions in order to further muddy his already opaque argument. By the end, Cooper has Uncle Ro proclaim that anti-rent agitators—"dem ... [that] gets all der money of der pooblic, und haf all der power"—are the actual aristocrats, and that the landed gentry represents an embattled underclass (1:150).

For Cooper, anti-rent protests represent a blow against civilization itself. The anti-rent "Injins" target every major pillar of U.S. social life, from religion to property rights, in their assaults. Cooper makes it clear that religion and property are intimately connected when the Rev. Mr. Warren, rector of the town's Episcopal church, refuses to bless an anti-rent meeting, which he believes "involves a species of blasphemy." Mr. Warren's refusal leads Hugh Littlepage to the strange observation that America's democratic spirit, "which enables the legislator to stand up in his place, and unblushingly talk about feudal usages, at the very instant he is demonstrating that equal rights are denied to those he would fain stigmatize as feudal lords," has begun to erode religion itself, which is "very generally accused of being aristocratic, too!"

(1:234). The struggle between anti-renters at the church will reach a head in the second volume of the novel, when Seneca Newsome and his "Injin" band insist that the Littlepage family canopy be removed from the church grounds; it ends up being used to cover a pigpen.

Finally, the anti-rent protesters insist on not just a revision of land laws, but a revision of U.S. history itself. An anti-rent orator proposes a reading of the historical record that favors squatters and tenants over landlords:

> I do not altogether disregard antiquity, neither. No; I respect and revere pre-emption rights; for they fortify and sustain the right to the elements. Now, I do not condemn squattin', as some doos. It's actin' accordin' to natur', and natur' is right. I respect and venerate a squatter's possession; for it's held under the sacred principle of usefulness. It says, "go and make the wilderness blossom as the rose," and means "progress." That's an antiquity I respect. I respect the antiquity of your possessions here, *as tenants*; for it is a hard-working and useful antiquity—an antiquity that increases and multiplies. (1:242)

As we saw in the introduction to *Satanstoe*, Cooper as editor of the Littlepage manuscripts holds that the sequence's true value rests in what each book can tell us about the history of the nation and its development over the course of a century. Anti-rent agitation threatens not only to unmoor property from its rightful owners, but also to revise the nation's historical record. Both *Satanstoe* and *The Chainbearer* go to great lengths to demonstrate how the Littlepage men brought every refinement to the countryside, from the church to town grids to learning, and, at the same time, how squatters and tenants have failed to maintain these improvements. Taken in context, then, the orator's claim that tenants and squatters made "the wilderness blossom as the rose" is meant to be taken ironically. But the matter finally depends, as it always does for Cooper, on heredity: "If it be said that Hugh Littlepage's ancestors—your noble has his 'ancestors,' while us 'common folks' are satisfied with forefathers ... but if this Hugh's ancestors did pay anything for the land, if I was you, fellow-citizens, I'd be gin'rous, and let him have it back ag'in" (1:242). The orator associates the Littlepage's familial claim to the land with feudal ancestry and the tenants' claim with "forefathers," a clear reference to the Revolutionary Generation. The tenants are the children of the Declaration of Independence, whereas the landlords are the children of decadent noble lines. Earlier the orator demands, "What had they [the Littlepage family] ever done for the country . . . that *they* should be lords in the land?" (1:239). Of course, the good reader of the Littlepage novels knows that the Littlepages had done quite a lot "for the land": they took it from hostile natives and peopled it through lenient leases in *Satanstoe*, fought for it against the English and then mapped it out in *The Chainbearer*, and brought an air of cultivation and aristocratic grace to it throughout.

The anti-rent speech lasts over two hours, touching on everything from natural law to the original leases, before a dissenting voice is raised. The dissenting speaker, also a tenant on the Littlepage estate, readies himself to offer a rebuttal to the two-hour anti-rent oration, but is "interrupted by a sudden whooping, and the Injins came pressing into the house in a way to drive in all the'aisles before them. . . . In less time than it takes to record the fact, the audience had nearly all dispersed" (*R*, 1:249). Here Cooper pairs his earlier critiques of popular democracy, the church naming and pigeon's roost sequences in *The Chainbearer*, with the long discourse between Susquesus and Mordaunt Littlepage concerning property rights and civilization. The meeting has been peaceful, if contentious: it follows basic parliamentary forms and ought to allow for open, civilized discourse between the two dissenting parties. By the end of volume 1 of *The Redskins*, anti-renters have become no better than the Mingoes who attack Dirck Follock and Cornelius Littlepage in the final act of *Satanstoe*. The "Injins" disband the meeting with theatrical violence, and so the popular movement becomes demagogical, threatening to erode democracy itself. Cooper's reactionary imagination associates this demagoguery with a "savage" disrespect for order, religion, and, most important, the rights of ownership. He manages even to slip in an undercurrent of anti-Semitism with the character Shabbakuk (a sham Habbakuk, the Old Testament prophet who composed songs about the future of Babylon), "a far deeper rogue" than even the anti-rent "Injins," who attempts to calculate the value of Littlepage properties using complex, usurious formulas (*R*, 1:23).

This first mass assault by the anti-rent "Injins" opens up the dynamic that will occupy the final act of Cooper's massive trilogy: the battle between anti-renters masquerading as natives and landlords supported by legitimate native power. It is very much a struggle over "first rights" to the land; the native body comes to symbolize primeval claims to property (despite the fact that native societies did not possess a European concept of private landed property), and the symbolic conflict between the allied Littlepages and Iroquois and the anti-rent "Injins" becomes a battle over who has a right to call themselves the real "natives" of the Mohawk Valley. Prairiefire, the leader of the band of Indians that has come to honor Susquesus, asks Ro if there are any other tribes nearby, to which Ro responds, "There *are* Injins—a party is in the edge of the wood, there, within thirty rods of you, at this moment. . . . They are called Anti-rent Injins—a new tribe in this part of the country, and are not much esteemed . . . They are not honest enough to go in paint, but wear shirts over their faces" (2:29). This leads to a brief confrontation between the displaced natives and the anti-rent "Injins," during which Ro removes his mask and drops his German accent to name himself as the rightful heir of the Littlepage properties. Now backed by legitimate native sovereigns, Ro and Hugh are able to make an aboriginal claim to the property, one that supersedes even the tenants' and squatters' claims to "ancient" rights. A Chippewa who has come with Prairiefire to honor Susquesus snatches the wig from Ro's hands, "and in the twinkling of an eye, all the savages were gathered round it, uttering many, but low and guarded expressions of surprise" (2:33). He concludes: "Had there been any of the ignoble vulgar among them, there is little doubt that the wig would have passed from hand to hand, and been fitted to a dozen heads, already shaved to receive it" (2:33). Cooper must emphasize the native band's wonder at and rejection of Ro's theatrical deception in order to emphasize their authentic claims to sovereignty and nobility—the natives can only ever be honest, and so whomever they align themselves with must naturally be on the side of right.

Spooked by the revelation that the Littlepage heirs are in their midst, the anti-renters adopt more violent methods. Seneca Newsome, grandson of the Yankee con artist Jason Newsome and leader of the anti-rent "Injin" brigade, leads another young anti-renter to burn down the Littlepage family's kitchen. The two abandon their Indian dress and go in blackface, but are stopped by Littlepage and a party led by the native chief Manytongues. Having unmasked Newsome and his second, Littlepage launches into an invective against the Yankee's entire family line: "Trick—trick—trick—low cunning, and overreaching management, had been the family trait, from the day Jason, of that name, had rented the mill lot, down to the present hour" (2:110). The Newsomes have so debased themselves that they commit capital offenses while dressed as the two lowliest subjects on the Littlepage estates, signaling the grim hereditary determinism that informs Cooper's worldview during this period.

The action of *The Redskins* ought to escalate toward an armed confrontation between the natives and the anti-rent "Injins," but this climax never comes. Instead, Cooper has the anti-renters flee the confrontation, replacing battle narration with cool assessments of the anti-renters' cruelty and dishonesty. The novel concludes with a lengthy ceremony sequence in which the displaced native tribes led by Prairiefire honor Susquesus. In terms of construction, this sequence structurally mirrors the long Pinkster celebration that opens *Satanstoe*. In both cases, the feudal classes of New York State are shown to preserve and secure native folkways. In this way, Cooper further naturalizes the feudal claims to the land: the anti-rent "Injins" offer a burlesque of native sovereignty, whereas the feudal class protects and promotes a genuine sovereignty that will pass from the native groups to the landholding elite. For this ending to work, of course, the reader has to forget the original theft of native lands by the very feudal class who Cooper would like us to believe protects and promotes native sovereignty, just as the Pinkster sequence demands that we forget that the slaves who are celebrating their colorful festival are being held in bondage by the class that takes part in the revelry. While at least one early critic claims that Cooper's point here is to ironize the conditions under which the Littlepage family came to take possession of the lands, it is more likely that we are witnessing in both the Pinkster and native ceremonial sequences an all-too-common blind spot in Cooper's worldview.[42]

At the conclusion of the ceremony, Prairiefire invites Susquesus to join his displaced brethren in the west: "There the sun sets—here it rises; the distance is great, and many strange tribes of pale-faces live along the path . . . but we have seen our Great Father, Uncle Sam, and we have seen our Great Father, Susquesus . . . we shall travel towards the setting sun satisfied" (2:180). Prairiefire calls the white settlers in the west "tribes," intimating (in a turn familiar to any reader of Cooper) that the course of settlement of the Americas makes new natives of white populations. The tragedy underwriting Prairiefire's assertion that he and the tribes he leads will "travel towards the setting sun" paints the violence of indigenous displacement in picturesque terms, positing it as the necessary inverse of the "westward course of empire" that was rapidly becoming a major focus of Anglo-American ideology during the Jacksonian era. Nothing could be more fitting, symbolically, than for Susquesus to join the tribe in their uncertain journey. Prairiefire admits that the situation is not ideal, as "the path [to the wigwams of the red-men] has been stretched" by years of war and theft of property, but he urges Susquesus to join them nonetheless (2:204). In a surprising turn, Susquesus refuses: "I have lived with the pale-faces, until one-half of my heart is white; though the other half is red. One-half is filled with the traditions of my fathers, the other half is filled with the wisdom of the stranger. I cannot cut my heart in two pieces" (2:207). Susquesus's claim that his heart has melded white "wisdom"—it is difficult not to recall, in this moment, Mordaunt Littlepage's dialogue with Susquesus concerning property in *The Chainbearer*—with his own Onondaga ways carries with it another implication.

If Susquesus has become half white, and "tribes" of white men people the plains between Ravensnest and the "great salt lake" in the west, then white Americans have likewise become "part native." What is interesting here is *which* white men have become "part native" in Cooper's later work. Whereas the hero of Cooper's earlier, better-known cycle of novels is a white squatter who assumes native ways, the heroes of Cooper's later cycle are the feudal lords who have come to both shelter and replace the indigenous inhabitants of the land. Hugh and Uncle Ro begin the novel, we should remember, "back east," in Europe; by the novel's end, they have travel westward to claim their ancestral lands. Susquesus likewise claims that the "great salt lake" spoken of by Prairiefire is the ancestral right of the Indians: "I have heard of those hunting-grounds. Our ancient traditions told us of them. 'Towards the rising sun,' they said, 'is a great salt lake, and towards the setting sun, great lakes of sweet water'" (*R*, 2:206). The Littlepages head west from Europe to claim their lands in the Mohawk Valley; the native tribes head west from New York to claim their "happy hunting ground" at the continent's edge. The symmetry is, I believe, intentional, signaling Cooper's most complete argument against the nativist pretensions of the anti-rent "Injins."

But, of course, this is Cooper in a polemic mode—and despite the complicated allegorical pattern he establishes through the action of the narrative, Susquesus launches into a direct critique of the anti-rent rebels:

> "These men are not warriors," continued Susquesus. "They hide their faces and they carry rifles, but they frighten none but the squaws and pappooses. When they take a scalp, it is because they are a hundred, and their enemies one. They are not braves. Why do they come at all?—What do they want? They want the land of this young chief. My children, all the land, far and near, was ours. The pale-faces came with their papers, and made laws, and said, 'It is well! We want this land. There is plenty farther west for you red-

men. Go there, and hunt, and fish, and plant your corn, and leave us this land.' Our red brethren did as they were asked to do." (2:208)

The moment of contact between the young feudal class and the native inhabitants of the Mohawk Valley is characterized as a moment of exchange between two economic actors: the natives who held the land but did not develop it, and the landlords who would develop the land and become its new natives. Theft of native lands is thus recast in terms of Enlightenment political economy. This transactional moment, and not the rights of squatters, is taken as natural and inevitable. The violence of primitive accumulation—first, the large-scale displacement of native peoples and enslavement of black labor, and, second, the exploitation of white settlers on the stolen lands—are utterly obviated in this account of the founding of the Littlepage estates. In place of these more honest reckonings with the United States' past, Cooper presents us with a melodrama of primitive accumulation: a tale of masked marauders, dastardly Yankee hypocrites, and perverse squatters plotting against the noble and ennobling forces of civilization represented by the various generations of the Littlepage family.

As it must, *The Redskins* ends with the victory of the Littlepages over the "Injins" and, inevitably, a slew of marriages. The bachelor Uncle Ro, last immediate heir to the Littlepage dynasty, secures his inheritance in his nephew Hugh, who marries Mary Warren, daughter of Ravensnest's Episcopal minister. Order is reestablished, and anti-rent agitation is put down: "The 'Injin' system has been broken up, temporarily at least, but the spirit which brought it into existence survives under the hypocritical aspect of 'human rights'" (2:228). By way of conclusion, Cooper offers an editorial warning: "Oregon, Mexico, and Europe, united against us, do not threaten this nation with one-half as much real danger as that which menaces it at this moment" by uncontrollable democratic mobs (2:230). But all is not lost. Should the country go the way of the bayonet, Cooper assures us that Mr. Littlepage—we assume he is speaking of Uncle Ro, since Hugh and Mary are safely ensconced at Ravensnest—may retire to Florence, "with the advantage of being admired as a refugee from republican tyranny" (2:230). Cooper and his heroes hope this will not be the case. As historian Philip Deloria observes, the "inevitable romantic connections among the elite Ravensnest crowd" ensures "their ownership . . . will extend from the spatial to the temporal realm, from mere landholding to control of the future itself."[43] In this way, Cooper aims to allay an Anglo-American fear, succinctly diagnosed by literary critic Susan Scheckel, that the Revolution would create "a leagacy of instability and discontinuity: the threat of repeated revolution."[44]

The aristocratic futurity of the Littlepage stories seem to sit uneasily against the themes of Cooper's earlier and more famous sequence of novels, the *Leatherstocking Tales*. Natty Bumppo is precisely the type of propertyless, lower-class white man that three generations of Littlepage men square off against, and none of the *Leatherstocking Tales* contain the levels of class rancor we find in *The Redskins*. It's thus tempting to drive a wedge between "early" and "late" Cooper, to claim that, as the author aged, his views concerning settlement and expansionism shifted in favor of landlords over settlers, owners over the cultivators of land. Natty Bumppo's status as the first archetypal American hero places the hunter, the free white man who has learned his lessons from the native populations, at the heart of the U.S. cultural imaginary. As historian Richard Slotkin puts it, readers tend to view Natty Bumppo as an *isolato*, a white man who developed his pseudoindigenous character "in almost perfect solitude, far from the settlements themselves, in the physical and psychological isolation of the dreamlike forest."[45] Natty Bumppo requires undeveloped lands, precisely the sort of wilds that Cornelius Littlepage and his ancestors want to cultivate and tame, in order to reach his full spiritual and physical development. The recurrent plots into which Bumppo is drawn, from the struggle over Templeton in *The Pioneers* (1823) to the Heyward family saga covered in *The Last of the Mohicans* (1826) and *The Prairie* (1827), signal Cooper's indebtedness to European precedents, and therefore represent the "un-American" aspect of Cooper's literary imagination. Slotkin argues that "the two parts" of Cooper's work—on the one hand Natty Bumppo's development as the first truly American hero, and on the other family plots that could be drawn from Walter Scott—"interact at various points but are in many essentials independent."[46]

Perhaps owing to his Jungian methodology, Slotkin locates in Cooper's work a structural dichotomy between American and European cultural production that goes down to the base of the U.S. cultural imaginary. But the bifid structure of this reading of Cooper ignores the degree to which Natty Bumppo serves as a defender of class status—specifically, the land claims of the aristocratic frontier landholders he repeatedly defends. In *The Pioneers*, Natty's young hunting partner and apprentice, Oliver Edwards, is revealed to be the last surviving ancestor of Edward Effingham, one of Templeton's two original leaseholders. Contrary to the division that Slotkin and subsequent readers place between Bumppo's Americanness and the frontier settlers' Europeanness, the first Leatherstocking novel concludes with a synthesis of the landlord's prerogatives with indigenous sovereignty that Cooper attempts, less successfully, in the Littlepage sequence.[47] The marriage of Oliver Edwards to Elizabeth Temple sets the tangle of broken contracts, disloyalty, and furtiveness that allowed Marmaduke Temple to hold Templeton as his own to right. Having arranged this synthesis between the new and truly "American" hunter-hero and the landholder indebted to European law and custom, Natty Bumppo moves west to help another distressed family line. The *Leatherstocking Tales* are less affirmations of a uniquely American cultural identity than they are a series of careful attempts at aligning those parts of the cultural imaginary that are "new" with centuries-old structures of law, property, and inheritance. It's the education of American nobles that finally occupies Natty Bumppo's life, not the pursuit of a different way of life in a new world.

So we return to a theme touched on in chapter 1's reading of Poe that I will further elaborate in chapter 3's reading of E. D. E. N. Southworth's *The Hidden Hand* and chapter 5's analysis of the late Emerson's social doctrines: the pedagogical intent of Anglo-American culture's synthesis of the feudal residuum with emergent liberalism. As white Americans became more literate—some 90 percent of adult whites could read by 1840—novelists began to experiment with a form of novel that would both entertain and enlighten audiences.[48] Marshaling romantic pedagogical theories to articulate and defend U.S. social structures, from political institutions to new and more liberal family arrangements, authors in the Transcendentalist and post-Transcendentalist tradition aimed to create a hybrid novel form in which the romance could be made socially useful.[49] This stylistic hybridity, which allows the novel form to absorb elements drawn from primers on science, morality, history, law, and political economy, makes U.S. literature from this period a useful index of how the literate classes viewed themselves—and how they would like the hoi polloi to view them, as well. Cooper's work and others of a similar style and intent thus offer a privileged glimpse into the logic of U.S. capitalism as it began to explain its own premises to itself. Cornelius Littlepage's fear in the introduction to *Satanstoe* that no one will recall "the manners and the opinions" of his generation of landholders, those men who established the infrastructures of wealth and influence that would breed the managerial ethos of U.S. capitalism, is a warning from one landed gentleman to his equals. Finally, Cooper fears that by ignoring the lordly origins of landed wealth in the Mohawk Valley, Americans of his time risked forgetting that in the United States "feudality . . . is a part of the institutions of the State" (*R*, 1:vii).

CHAPTER THREE

Marriage, Chivalry, and Feudal Law
Harriet Jacobs and E. D. E. N. Southworth

> We urge you by your self-respect, by every consideration for the human race, to arise and take possession of your birthright to freedom and equality. Take it not as the gracious boon tendered by the chivalry of superiors, but as your *right*, on every principle of justice and equality.
> —J. Elizabeth Jones, "Of Husband and Wife" (1849)

> Why does the slave ever love? Why allow the tendrils of the heart to twine around objects which may at any moment be wrenched away by the hand of violence?
> —Harriet A. Jacobs, *Incidents in the Life of a Slave Girl* (1861)

Early in *Incidents in the Life of a Slave Girl*, Harriet Jacobs allegorizes the injustices faced by bondswomen by recalling an intimate domestic scene: a slave owner's daughter and her illegitimate slave sister embracing. Linda turns away from the embrace, distressed by "the inevitable blight that would fall on the little slave girl's heart" (29). Through marriage, the privileged sister will lead a life of circumscribed liberty, "her pathway ... blooming with flowers, and overarched by a sunny sky"; through concubinage, the slave sister will suffer abuse and moral degradation. The brief episode foreshadows the substance of Jacobs's narrative: Linda is repeatedly denied protections that southern chivalry affords to women of the upper classes, transforming what ought to be fundamental rights (to freedom from sexual violence, for instance) into privileges afforded only to a narrow caste.

The episode also inaugurates, in the language of sentimental romance and allegory, Jacob's book-length exploration of "the failures and omissions of law" and "the crisis of consent or consensual sexual relations under domination."[1] Jacobs modulates her narrative tone from autobiographical reportage into the key of sentimental allegory not only to appeal to her readers' emotions, but also to make concrete the unjust legal system she will explore throughout her narrative.

Jacobs's exploration of "the failures and omissions of law" as it concerned bondswomen reveals how class and race were bound up in the laws concerning marriage. Jacobs's focus on marriage and conjugal law is unsurprising: living in New York, Jacobs composed her biography in an atmosphere crackling with the intellectual energy of the first wave of the American women's rights movement. Through her relationship with Amy Post in Rochester, Jacobs became familiar with critiques of male hegemony produced by the Seneca Falls Convention and subsequent conventions throughout upstate New York.[2] The rhetoric of women's liberation, particularly its critique of marriage laws, was instrumental in shaping Jacobs's narrative strategy. But, while leaning on Seneca Falls rhetoric, Jacobs also troubles some of its fundamental assumptions.[3]

Emerging alongside abolitionism, the women's rights movement often equated the loss of agency suffered by women with the more brutal stripping of self-determination suffered by bondsmen. Seneca Falls rhetoric equated marriage with slavery (and both with feudalism) in order to demonstrate that both institutions were anachronistic in liberal America. Their proposed liberalization of marriage involved shifting the legal status of women from the custom and precedent-based common law, which extended conditional *privileges* to women based on the socioeconomic status of their husbands, to legislation such as the various Married Women's Property Acts (1839–1865), which sought to articulate concrete, suprahistorical *rights* for married women. In this way, the early women's rights movement in the United States sought to extend the Enlightenment principles of the Revolutionary Generation by establishing for women the same rights afforded to propertied men.

As Jacobs's allegory of the two sisters demonstrates, the slave/wife metaphor is specious: the free sister's privileges under marriage, contingent and circumscribed as they are, will ensure her more happiness and security than the slave sister's lack of legal agency. If Jones's audience sought to achieve equality with men, slave women such as Linda Brent fought to secure even the flimsy privileges afforded by the common law conception of marriage. So while early women's rights agitators correctly noted that married women suffered a "social death" not unlike that suffered by slaves, contradictions inherent in their liberalism did not allow them to fully apprehend the structural differences created by America's racial and economic caste system. The women's movement tasked itself with dismantling feudal marriage; Jacobs and her fellow slaves wondered, in the face of utter domination, whether loving union was their domain at all. Yet, as the cautious optimism of the conclusion of Jacobs's narrative indicates, this near-absolute exclusion from the law and its social protections offered the enslaved woman a more radical position from which to assess contradictions inherent in the United States' overlapping hierarchies of gender, race, and class.

The two texts I will take up in this argument—E. D. E. N. Southworth's *The Hidden Hand* (1859) and Jacob's *Incidents in the Life of a Slave Girl*— dramatize the differences between women of privilege who were afforded the limited liberties of consensual marriage and those women for whom even the most fundamental right to self-determination were denied. In *Incidents*, Dr. Flint attempts to manipulate Linda Brent with a promise of class elevation that Linda rightly disbelieves. Later, Linda's betrayal by Mr. Sands, who procrastinates in liberating the children their affair produces, underscores the lack of legal agency afforded to slave women even when in relationships with supposedly honorable courtiers. Dr. Flint can promise to "make Linda a lady" and Mr. Sands can assure her that he will protect their children, but the words carry no legal weight. Her experiences with "chivalrous" southerners, and later with friends in the North, lead Linda to develop a network of relationships with other women and supportive men, making *Incidents* at once a depiction of slavery's injustices and an experiment in elaborating systems of support and affection outside of the bounds of marriage.

Southworth's *The Hidden Hand*, whose protagonist Capitola Le Noir enjoys a startling amount of liberty up until the novel's conclusion, offers a rosier, if no less complex, portrait of chivalry, marriage, and consent in the antebellum United States. Capitola's gender experimentation is legitimized once her class position as an heir to a Virginia plantation is established. By making Capitola his ward, the slave owner Ira Warfield extends his authority to her. In effect, Capitola assumes the chivalric role traditionally held by men without pushing against chivalry's limits and failings. Economic security and the liberty to perform a subversive gender reversal are only granted through this chivalric authority, which is always mediated through the legal recognition of male sovereignty over the women in the novel. *The Hidden Hand* and *Incidents in the Life of a Slave Girl* present two conflicting models of social life for women: in Southworth's novel women achieve a circumscribed parity through reforms to the chivalric conception of gender relations, while in Jacobs's narrative women develop networks that supersede and ultimately undermine what Jacobs portrays as a hypocritical system of inequality that elevates one caste of women by denying rights to another.

My primary goal in this chapter is to demonstrate how the legal and cultural status of women was tied up in a feudal conception of marriage that was debated in Northern women's rights circles. Jacobs's and Southworth's literary productions evidence the influence of discussions pertaining to the legal personhood of women, a question necessarily yoked to broader questions of legal personhood in general and that personhood's relation to history. They likewise demonstrate how rules of courtship, which seem so transparent and natural when performed, are in reality bound up in material and cultural considerations. Against a simple one-to-one, oppressor/oppressed dynamic of analyses that highlight continued repression of all women under an amorphously defined patriarchy, reading gender through the lens of material and legal privileges afforded by residual chivalry shows the ways in which class, law, and custom combine to define women's roles in what Giorgio Agamben usefully terms "the supermundane mystery" of "the praxis of government" and the organization of economic life.[4]

LIBERAL CRITIQUES OF CHIVALRY AND COMMON LAW: E. D. E. N. SOUTHWORTH

Women in the nineteenth century were required to exist in two worlds and to serve two purposes. Law undergirded this double status. Laws pertaining to the contracts between masters and slaves, employers and employees, and husbands and wives were all classed as "domestic relations" and were therefore the domain of local courts and the common law, not the legislature.[5] At the same time, a liberal vision of marriage as a contract between two consenting parties was imagined to replicate the notion of government as a contract between another, broader consenting pair: the state and the people. Despite being an institution based in common law that used legal and cultural terms (coverture, chivalry) inherited from feudal Europe, marriage was essential in perpetuating the nation's republican virtues. Under marriage women were "civilly dead," in Elizabeth Cady Stanton's famous phrase, and yet these "civilly dead" legal subjects were tasked with the reproduction of U.S. liberal values through childbirth, moral education, and maintenance of the domestic economy.

Despite this emphasis on what Linda Kerber terms "Republican Motherhood," laws pertaining to marriage and women's rights as handed down to U.S. jurisprudence through William Blackstone's *Commentaries on the Laws of England* (1765–1769) bore the strong mark of their origin in chivalric custom and common law. The American legal theorist Tapping Reeve's *The Law of Baron and Femme*, first published in 1816, helped formalize the use of English common law as a guide for U.S. domestic relations. Beginning in 1839, the Married Women's Property Acts weakened the common law conception of marriage, but the broader culture did not shift to account for these necessary changes in married women's legal status. Nor, indeed, did the law pertaining to women's "civil death" in marriage change as radically as we might like to think. Amasa J. Parker and Charles Baldwin, who edited and updated the third edition of Reeve's *Baron and Femme*, note in their preface that "the radical changes recently made in the law of 'Baron and Femme' by the legislatures of some of the states, together with the decisions that have been made under them" may one day lead to "an entire revolution in the law affecting the rights and liabilities of married women," but, that as of 1862, "common law, generally, remains unchanged, except within the limits of judicial discretion, in applying well-established rules to new combinations of fact, and adapting them to peculiar institutions of the country."[6]

The United States' attitude toward marriage lagged behind major legal and ideological upheavals that had begun in the seventeenth century. English moral philosophers had since the Glorious Revolution of 1688 begun to sever the direct connection between political power and patriarchal authority. Against a medieval conception of authority as mirroring down from God to his legal and clerical representatives on earth and finally to the head of the household,[7] the parliamentary supporters of William III "argued that political authority did not come naturally," but instead "had to be purposely constructed by individuals' collective consent to be governed."[8] The Revolutionary Generation in the United States inherited from England a system whereby "by consenting, the citizens delegated authority to their elected representatives, and the wife gave authority to her husband."[9] Despite this ideological upheaval in England, the liberal notion of consent (not to mention domestic happiness, sexual fulfillment, and economic parity) in marriage did not become a universal standard for women in the U.S. republic. As historian Ruth Bloch argues, the widespread adoption of common law precedent undermined the liberal vision of consensual matrimony: "While partly encouraging the privatization of marriage and contributing to the scope of individual freedoms, this increasing reliance on the common law also propelled another branch of government to step into the breach of courtship.... The shift towards the common law needs to be seen as a new type of government intervention, one that largely replaced the legislative with the judicial.... What from one perspective may look like the rise of personal freedom looks from another like the reinstitutionalization of moral codes."[10]

Women in the United States were thus placed in a peculiar historical situation: even as their nation championed legislation that sought to abolish hundreds of years of legal precedent, the specific laws pertaining to their status in marriage were being imported wholesale from the most forceful expression of that legal precedent. The "reinstitutionalization of moral codes" that Bloch associates with the adoption of common law represents the modulation of marriage from the public realm to the private. Historian Carole Shammas likewise traces the failure of U.S. law to upset prevailing social arrangements in the same way that French revolutionaries would in the 1790s to contradictions in the Revolutionary Generation's ideology: "The generation of the Founding Fathers showed real irritation when parallels were drawn between the dependency of the king's colonial subjects and that of household dependents.... In fact, considering the amount of constitution writing that went on, what is most remarkable is the reluctance to rein in the powers of the household head."[11]

While the Revolutionary Generation's Enlightenment principles allowed them to disarticulate patriarchal power from monarchical sovereignty—a result of Locke's argument against Filmer's *Patriarcha, or The Natural Power of Kings* in *Two Treatises of Government* (1689)—they were not yet ready to extend their program to the conjugal family. Their reluctance to upset the basic structure of family life may be based in a belief, expressed by Aristotle in *Politics*, that household organization (*oikonomia*) serves as the basis for economic wealth and political power.[12] Maintaining the traditional organization of the household—including the patrilineal structure of inheritance—was a key concern for the early republic and the emerging aristocracy who possessed the lion's share of its wealth. Under the United States' mixed feudal-liberal system of matrimonial law, marriage functioned as an act of interpellation that split women into two contradictory subjects: on the one hand "Republican Mothers" who would reproduce and foster the nation, and on the other courtly ladies to whom privileges, but not the right of full citizenship, were afforded.

Chivalry provided a readymade cultural apparatus to help upper- and middle-class women accept their contradictory, unstable position. The nineteenth-century United States had access to a rich body of medieval and postmedieval texts, both literary and historical, that helped to shape the nation's imagination of gender and courtship. The obvious point of departure is Walter Scott, whose influence we discussed briefly in chapter one. However, influential as Scott's novels were, American chivalry was constructed from more immediately medieval sources. In "Woman, Church, and The State," liberationist and Native American rights advocate Matilda Joslyn Gage alludes to Guillaume de Lorris and Jean de Meun's *Roman de la Rose* (1230/1275) as texts that helped shape women's roles in the nineteenth century as much as they had in the thirteenth.[13] On the other side of the debate, the Confederate soldier and poet Sidney Lanier edited a "boy's editions" of Jean Froissart's *Chroniques* (1361/2–1400), ensuring his young readers that Froissart's tales of knightly virtue during the Hundred Years' War "sets the boy's mind upon manhood" and confirms "the valor, the generosity" of "boy's early ideal of man."[14] That Lanier saw fit to publish an expurgated "boy's edition" of Froissart's works indicates their appeal to other mid-nineteenth-century audiences on the eve of the Civil War. The early nineteenth century also produced several major versions of Thomas Malory's *Le Morte D'Arthur* (1485), including those edited by Walter Scott and Robert Southey, as well as popular illustrated editions for general audiences.[15] These in turn led to a resurgence in Arthurian romance that culminated in Alfred Lord Tennyson's medievalist productions, which themselves achieved widespread popularity in the United States.[16]

The interlinked legal and cultural paradox regarding the status of women in U.S. society was well understood by the Seneca Falls generation, as was the deceptive chivalry that the culture of male domination mobilized to neutralize assaults on its hegemony. The source for much of the critique of woman's feudal legal personhood, including the specific claim that marriage renders women "civilly dead," is the legal reformer Elisha P. Hurlbut's *Essays on Human Rights and Their Political Guaranties* (1845). Hurlbut argues in the essay "The Rights of Woman" for the moral, political, and physical equality of woman to man, broadly framing his argument against the patronizing chivalric treatment of women that emerges from the medieval tradition. He opens by asserting that he will neither "mock woman with fulsome adulation" nor "treat her as 'the better half' but rather the equal half of mankind," thereby undercutting the still-circulating claim that moral, submissive women are best protected and promoted by warlike, gallant men.[17] At the Seneca Falls Convention in 1848, Elizabeth Cady Stanton and her fellow liberationists would channel Hurlbut's natural rights–based critique of common law in the "Declaration of Rights and Sentiments," which plays on the language of the Declaration of Independence to point out the injustice of woman's "civil death" under Anglo-American conjugal law.

In the years following Seneca Falls, Stanton and her coliberationists would heighten their attacks on the treatment of women as feudal legal subjects. But as effective as their attacks on common law proved to be, they also point out a problem in the critique of marriage law as the basis for a broad women's rights platform. The legal protections and abuses inherited from Blackstone did not apply to most American women. For the lower classes, married life occurred, to use constitutional historian Mark Brandon's phrase, "beneath the law's radar"; in effect, only the households of the propertied classes would benefit from the Married Women's Property legislation.[18] Heroic as their struggle was, the first generation of the women's rights movement set their sights on the emancipation of bourgeois women, inaugurating a long U.S. tradition of "trickle down" or "lean in" feminism. Their antifeudal rhetoric evidences this strategy.

At 1853's Woman's Rights State Convention in Rochester, New York, liberationists, addressing both the legislature and "capitalists and industrialists of New York," used gothic imagery to characterize the unequal treatment of women under the vestiges of common law, insisting that "man, too, is impeded in his progress by the very chains which bind woman to the lifeless skeleton of feudal civilization."[19] When J. Elizabeth Jones, writing on the occasion of an 1849 women's liberation meeting in Salem, Ohio, calls for wives to reject "the boon tendered by the chivalry of superiors" and embrace their "birthright," she assumes an audience of white, middle-to-upper-class women who had historically received the feudal privilege of coverture, not women whose conjugal lives existed beyond the reach of the common law. Likewise, when social reformer Robert Dale Owen stipulates in his marriage contract with Mary Jane Robinson that the couple would reject "all relics of a feudal, despotic system," he takes as given the social power to reject these laws—he and Robinson share the privilege to reject privilege.[20] The first liberationists sought a corrective to one specific injustice in the structure of the household *oikonomia*, not a fundamental restructuring of the *oikonomia* itself.

E. D. E. N. Southworth's *The Hidden Hand* bears witness to the Seneca Falls generation's sharp critique and yet ultimately contradictory solution to the U.S. chivalric system. Elizabeth Stockton has studied the extent to which *The Hidden Hand* was influenced by Southworth's awareness of the various Married Women's Property Reforms that were instrumental in reconfiguring American marriage as a statutory as opposed to common law issue. Against earlier critics like Barbara Bardes and Susan Gossett, who take up Southworth in their influential *Declarations of Independence: Women and Political Power in Nineteenth-Century American Fiction* (1990), Stockton does not see *The Hidden Hand* as an all-out assault on the male institution of marriage.[21] Stockton more convincingly suggests that Southworth held a conflicted view of "the law's obligation to women": "Southworth seems to have consistently resisted viewing marriage as a contract, expressing anxiety about being able to sever the matrimonial bond too easily. As such, her novels support the prevailing belief that marriage was a unique arrangement—distinct from other contracts."[22] Southworth upholds the idea of marriage as a "domestic relation" based on each partner's recognition of their role in the household economy, not a liberal contract premised on the consent of two willing parties. According to Stockton's reading, the law becomes a substitute for paternal authority for women whose "organic" family units have been disrupted: the law is the father of all fathers, the highest expression of a male-dominated social order that pervades every aspect of social life. Stockton's reading helps us to better understand the function of the law within Southworth's narrative. Despite its reputation as an adventure novel, *The Hidden Hand* contains only a handful of proper "action" sequences. Courtroom scenes, depositions, and testimonies (both false and honest) constitute the real substance of Capitola's adventures. That the majority of these courtroom sequences concern domestic relations (guardian/ward relationships, right to inheritance, and other conjugal concerns) points toward Southworth's focus on inheritance and lineage.

Even the most celebrated aspect of Southworth's novel, Capitola dressing up as a young boy while living in New York, ultimately leads us back to the maintenance of domestic relations. Capitola's gender performance—the first step in her assumption of masculine power—serves a pretext for first her reclamation of her father Eugene Le Noir's vast estate, and then her marriage to Herbert Grayson.[23] Even when she is dressing up like a boy on the Bowery, Capitola is working toward fulfilling Herbert's early desire for all the characters in the novel to reach "a perfect family union" (*HH*, 99). So, while Southworth does put forward a robust critique of male hypocrisy and its legal ramifications for unprotected women, the narrative action finally reaffirms patriarchal power and its expression through chivalric discourse.

Southworth lampoons the failures of individual men—Warfield, for instance, who abandons his young wife Marah Rocke and son Traverse to a life of penury—while stopping short of a full, Seneca Falls–style critique of masculine authority as such. Read this way, Capitola's assumption of chivalric codes and behaviors traditionally associated with men does not give her in an "essentially revolutionary role" (as one critic puts it), but instead a decidedly reformist one: Capitola is a restorer of lost honor who steps into roles that the men in the novel cannot.[24] Cap embodies a new brand of chivalry; she does not dismantle the old one.

This is not to say that Southworth is unaware of contradictions in the chivalric mentality. While Capitola ultimately reinforces American chivalry, Southworth does criticize the hypocrisy of men who misuse the discourse to their sexual and financial advantage. Capitola's first meeting in the woods with Craven Le Noir, archvillain Gabriel Le Noir's son and therefore Capitola's first cousin, depicts an elaborate chivalric performance as the prelude to rape. After being warned about Black Donald and his gang's "darker crimes" by Miss Condiment, Capitola nonetheless rides into the woods alone. Craven Le Noir hails her in purposefully antique diction: "Whither away so fast, pretty one?" (113). Craven then deploys a number of mock-chivalric gestures—he lays a blanket on the ground to protect Cap's dress, worries over Cap riding alone, offers to escort Cap back to Hurricane Hall—with a repetitiveness that, when considered against Miss Condiment's earlier reference to the "darker crimes" young women may suffer, creates a sense of increasing sexual menace. Later in the novel, when Craven's abuse escalates to open harassment, he performs an equally mechanical chivalry to tease Capitola: "The first time he took occasion to meet her in her rides, he merely bowed deeply, even to the flaps of his saddle, and with a melancholy smile passed on" (351). This action is repeated several times and ultimately leads to Craven's false claim that he and Cap have had a sexual relationship. In these passages,

Craven performs, as Herbert Greyson puts it elsewhere when discussing Ira Warfield's abandonment of his young wife, a false and exploitive form of chivalry: "Such protection as vultures give to doves—covering and devouring them" (94).

Capitola provides an even more pointed critique of male hypocrisy after her benefactor Ira Warfield dresses her down for riding out alone: "I won't be treated with both kicks and half-pennies by the same person—and so I tell you. I'm not a cur to be fed with roast-beef and beaten with a stick! Nor, nor, nor a Turk's slave to be caressed and oppressed as her master likes! . . . Freedom and peace are even sweeter than wealth and honors!" (123). Here Capitola echoes rhetoric deployed by the first wave of women's liberationists when discussing the abusive and hypocritical treatment of women under U.S. law. She points to the basic contradiction in the chivalric order, which did indeed force women to submit their wills to their husbands for the limited protections afforded them by coverture under common law precedent. While Warfield is Capitola's guardian and not her husband, Capitola eroticizes their relationship (Warfield is a "Turk," Capitola a member of his harem) to place her complaint in broadly conjugal terms. Later, Cap will complain that she is "decomposing above ground" in Hurricane Hall (173), wording that cannot help but recall the "civil death" of woman under traditional matrimony. Finally, Southworth has Clara Day, the novel's "damsel in distress," offer an appeal for the dignity of women's labor: "I stand upon the broad platform of human rights, and I say I have just as good a right to work as others" (326). Clara's statement borrows from liberal, Revolutionary Generation rhetoric ("the broad platform of human rights"), recalling Stanton's approach in the Seneca Falls "Declaration."

The main objects of Southworth's critique of chivalry in *The Hidden Hand* are also the three men who determine much of the novel's narrative action: Ira "Old Hurricane" Warfield, Black Donald, and Gabriel Le Noir. Like Poe's abusive, drunken king in "Hop-Frog," each man embodies a "bad sovereignty." Black Donald has a beard that "would have made his own fortune in any city of America as a French count or a German baron. He had decidedly 'the air noble and distinguished'" (*HH*, 143). The rogue has the appearance of a nobleman, but does not act nobly: he is the gothic antipode to Capitola, Herbert, and Traverse's incorruptible gallantry. Whereas the Bowery trickster, merchant marine, and long-suffering orphan embody noble qualities but do not physically resemble the nobility, Black Donald physically resembles the nobility but does not embody noble qualities. Black Donald points toward the symbolic connection between his ignominy and Capitola's heroism while skulking around Hurricane Hall: "She is doomed to be my destruction, or I hers. Our fates are evidently connected!" (210). Capitola likewise understands that she is different from Black Donald only by degrees and not in type: "If Black Donald were only as honest and he is brave, I should quite *adore* him!" (156). Black Donald is a travesty of the chivalric virtues that Capitola, Herbert, and Traverse will come to represent.

Like Black Donald, Gabriel Le Noir, the novel's proper villain, is also a gothic travesty of the chivalric spirit. He entraps Clara Day in his cobweb-ridden mansion, the "Hidden House," not through an outlandish plot device (e.g., a cursed painting or poisoned rose), but instead through an abuse of the courts, making Clara his ward in a clear mockery of Warfield's legal adoption of Capitola. In court, Clara's representative informs Le Noir that the father's dying wish was to leave his daughter under Marah Rocke's care. Le Noir refuses: "I cannot venture to act upon any 'verbal instructions,' however well attested, but shall be guided in every respect by the will" (245). Doctor Day's authority is only as strong as the legally binding documents that are left after his death. Having made himself Clara's "protector," Le Noir attempts to take her family wealth by forcing her into marriage with his son (300). Le Noir deftly manipulates the "civic death" of women under common law in order to exercise his authority over their financial and conjugal fates. That these same mechanisms of inheritance and coverture will, ultimately, lead to Capitola and Clara's redemption through inheritance and marriage defangs what is otherwise an able dramatization of woman's feudal legal personhood.

Ira Warfield represents a waning—if not yet debased—chivalric spirit. Despite her consistent criticisms of his behavior throughout the novel, Southworth nonetheless provides Warfield with enough legal authority (and enough residual gallantry) to set the novel's action in motion. As a justice of the peace, Warfield is imbued with civic authority. When Hat, the midwife at Capitola's birth, tells Warfield her remarkable story, he reminds her over and over again that she is "on [her] oath." Hat responds: "I know that, sir, and I will tell the truth; but it must be in my own way" (17). In this moment Hat lays claim to discursive power, but only through Warfield's consent: he is, in the end, the voice and arm of the law. Hat has attempted to tell her story several times, but, in the end, Capitola's liberation from necessity in New York and reunion with patriarchal power in the South can only be set into motion through Warfield's legal agency.

That this agency is based in a decidedly medievalist worldview is evident in Southworth's epigraph to chapter 3: "Then did Sir Knight abandon dwelling,/And he rode out" (30). The lines are adapted from Samuel Butler's *Hudibras* (1674–1678). Like the knight in Butler's poem, Warfield is held up for ridicule, and his chivalric reawakening is cast in broadly comic terms. Warfield is a blustering old drunk and an irresponsible master, and the epigraph from *Hudibras* is Southworth's way of calling his authority into question. Southworth returns to Butler's work later in the novel, just before Warfield upbraids Capitola for riding alone. By setting Capitola's criticism of Warfield's hypocritical treatment of women against the figure of the mock-heroic knight, Southworth gestures toward a broad critique of Warfield's inadequate, contradictory chivalry. However, she offers us glimpses of his former chivalric glory in moments such as his impromptu *blason* of the young Marah Rocke (*HH*, 85) and Marah Rocke's own remembrance of his glory in youth: "The very perfection of manly strength, and beauty, and goodness" (93). Warfield is finally a tragic, not a comical or contemptible, figure—a great man gone to seed, irredeemably decadent and yet still able to provide the kernel of a new chivalry that will bear fruit in those people to whom he offers up the remainder of his waning authority.

Capitola herself offers the most damning take on the failures of chivalry when she complains to her cousin that none of the men in Hurricane Hall will defend her honor against Craven Le Noir's insults:

> "What would you have them do, Cap? The longer an affair of this kind is agitated, the more offensive it becomes! Besides, chivalry is out of date. The knights-errant are all dead."
>
> "The MEN are all dead! If any really lived!" cried Cap in a fury. "Heaven knows I am inclined to believe them to have been a fabulous race like that of the mastodon or the centaur! I certainly never saw a creature that deserved the name of man!" (366)

Capitola makes up for the failures of the men around her by assuming the roles traditionally held by them: she duels Craven Le Noir, rescues Clara Day, and finally becomes mistress of a grand estate. At first, Southworth seems to hold up Capitola's chivalric performance to ridicule: "Cap was a bit of a Don

Quixote," Southworth writes, inviting an inevitable comparison to Warfield's Hudibrasian bluster (269). But by the time Capitola "caps the climax" in her confrontation with Craven Le Noir, Southworth compares her to a more noble chivalric predecessor, the fifteenth-century French knight Pierre Terrail, seigneur de Bayard: "From childhood she had been inured to danger, and had never suffered harm; therefore, Cap, like the Chevalier Bayard, was 'without fear and without reproach'" (351). As Joanne Dobson points out in her introduction to her edition of the novel, Southworth alludes to "a masculine realm of legend, adventure, and heroism," and that "by placing an heroic protagonist, an adventurer who owes much to the masculine heroes of Walter Scott and Alexander Dumas, in a feminine sentimental framework, Southworth challenges the limits of genre and stretches imaginative boundaries" (*HH*, xxx).

It is less certain that, as Dobson also writes, "the politics of this maneuver are clear" (xxx). Capitola's gender performance and the equality she achieves with the men in the novel emerge from her ability to manipulate her self-representation. Economic necessity leads her to dress as a boy, a performance of masculinity that foreshadows her later performance of chivalric codes. Were Capitola to remain an orphaned girl raised by a biracial governess who, through pluck and courage, is able to win a fortune, critics' arguments that she represents a challenge to traditional social roles reserved for women would carry more weight. But, soon after being rescued from the New York slums, Capitola is the "little mistress" of Hurricane Hall—no longer a feminist rejoinder to Emerson's self-made man, but instead a free spirit who (despite the occasionally lively protest) nonetheless accepts her place in the household economy of Virginia slavocracy.

By the novel's conclusion, she is more than the "little mistress": she is the proper owner of her father's "land, negroes, coal-mines, iron-foundries, railway shares and bank-stock" (108, 149). Cap receives her inheritance in a chapter titled "Capitola a Capitalist," further underscoring the potential "newness" of this young heroine's social position. Cap's portfolio is diverse, split equally between fixed capital (bonded human labor, real estate) and two decidedly modern income streams, "railway shares and bank-stock" (149). Sari Edelstein finds the title of *The Hidden Hand*'s penultimate chapter "cryptic," in that the chapter "does not see Capitola's return to working as a newsboy or to any profession, as its title would suggest."[25] Edelstein evidences an all-too-common misunderstanding of just what a "capitalist" is, confusing one who is forced to sell her labor on the market for the purchaser of that labor. In fact, by commanding large amounts of wealth derived from a variety of sources, Capitola is a capitalist's capitalist!

Edelstein's misconception of what makes a capitalist also speaks to the dominant critical desire to read Cap's progress as a narrative of liberation, and, by extension, an argument for expanding the rights of women in the public sphere. The temptation to accept this reading is strong. Cap is a fantastic heroine, and her courage in the face of danger and her rapid-fire wit make her an appealing counterpoint to a masculinist U.S. literary canon that so often reduces female characters to adored ladies, depraved seductresses, or long-suffering mothers. But to make Cap a heroic prefiguration of the "New Woman" who would emerge in Anglo-American fiction in the 1880s—or a forerunner of postmodern gender-queer identity—ignores an essential "plot point": Capitola's embodiment of masculine chivalric power, subversive as it may at first seem, extends from her noble lineage.[26] Early in the novel, we learn that Capitola's mother is the daughter of "a French patriot," and that "her father and mother had both perished on the scaffold in the sacred cause of liberty" (*HH*, 177). This first evocation of the French Revolution is ambiguous; were Capitola's grandparents revolutionaries who were later purged, or were they members of the French aristocracy? Toward the novel's conclusion, Traverse rescues Capitola's mother from an asylum in New Orleans, where she retells the story in her own words. Capitola's mother's account removes any ambiguity: "My father was a French patriot, who suffered death in the cause of liberty, when I, his only child, was but fourteen years of age.... I was left an orphan and penniless, for our estate was confiscated" (449). Capitola's mother is flung into the web of the Le Noir family's debased, decadent chivalry because of the violent dismantling of the French aristocracy during the revolution. Cap is capable of chivalry because her French ancestors were; likewise, Traverse Rocke is great because he is the mirror of Ira Warfield's vigorous, youthful gallantry. A daughter of the aristocracy suffering momentary financial embarrassment, Capitola regains her birthright by the end of the novel, making *The Hidden Hand* more a conservative reaffirmation of the inheritability of class signifiers than a liberal critique of women's position in U.S. social life. Edmund Burke famously declared that, in the wake of the French Revolution, "the age of chivalry is gone."[27] Southworth's heroine is a response to Burke's lament. "The age of chivalry" is not gone, her narrative implies: its spirit has just moved to the Americas and has accordingly become more democratic. Cap wins her birthright and her privilege, but not her rights.

Just as it is tempting to take up Capitola as a heroic political figure, it is equally tempting to dismiss *The Hidden Hand* as gleefully apolitical, a popular novel aimed at an audience that was seeking broad adventure in a world of stark moral contrasts. Yet Southworth remains ambiguous on the social message she means to impart in *The Hidden Hand*. While emphasizing Cap's inherent sense of justice, Southworth remains silent on the question of her status as a slaveholding southerner. Capitola choosing to "liberate" Black Donald and send him off to new territories represents a moral plea aimed at southern mistresses to likewise free their own slaves. *The Hidden Hand* bolsters dangerous notions of inherent black criminality and renders abolition as an act of charity on behalf of an enlightened master class. Southworth would be a conservative abolitionist and proponent of African colonization at best.[28] Southworth's social vision is an abolitionism to be granted from above, as a "tender boon" bred from noblesse oblige to a wretched class below, not as a struggle for genuine emancipation.

The same can be said of Capitola's liberation in *The Hidden Hand*. The novel concludes with a "magnificent, old-fashioned wedding" at Hurricane Hall, a "double ceremony... performed by the bishop of the diocese" (484). Southworth is at pains to emphasize the traditionalism of it all, down to Cap and Clara's "white satin and honiton lace, pearls, and orange flowers" (484): material expressions of the conventionality of the novel's conclusion. But the final clause of the final line introduces a note of ambiguity: "I am happy to say that they all enjoy a fair amount of human felicity" (485). It would push credulity to the limit to suggest that the "double ceremony," when paired with Southworth's ambiguous and seemingly clinical description of married life as providing the women "a fair amount of human felicity" (shades of Jefferson's exhortation in the "Declaration of Independence" are surely not accidental), signals a subversive attack on traditional matrimony that Southworth can't yet express.

This ambiguous line allows us to consider how Southworth's partial critique of the culture of American chivalry and the economic and legal structures that sustained it mirrors the partial critique of women's social positions offered by the Seneca Falls generation. Southworth wasn't alone in this uncertainty surrounding marriage; other nineteenth-century feminists shared an anxiety as to women's roles in a social landscape where the legal roots of marriage were upended. Elizabeth Cady Stanton puts it succinctly in her 1890 article "Divorce versus Domestic Warfare": "As woman is the most important factor in the marriage relation, her enfranchisement is the primal step in the settlement of the basis of family life."[29] Southworth's women exist in a world where this "primal step" toward equality seems like a distant prospect, and Clara Day's desire to "stand upon the broad platform of human rights" is little more than a declaration of intent, not a positive step toward action. The culture of chivalry and the legal apparatuses that it supported could only be dismantled after universal suffrage, when women (once again to use Stanton's words) may be "heard . . . in the halls of legislation," not just the courtrooms where individual cases are deliberated. It's the inability to see beyond the individual triumphs of particular propertied women to a "broad platform of human rights" for all citizens that makes Capitola's liberation frustratingly limited, and yet at the same time predictive of more systemic changes to come.

THE SEXUAL ECONOMY OF THE SLAVE HOUSEHOLD: HARRIET JACOBS

Southworth presents us a fantasy in which the emerging U.S. bourgeoisie ("Capitola, a Capitalist") is married to the waning feudal aristocracy, assuming its cultural trappings and benefiting from its privilege. The intricate network of blood relations that sustains Southworth's narrative evidences the victory of genetic aristocracy over the plucky individualism that Capitola seems at first to represent. Jacobs's autobiography is diametrically opposed to both the narrative action and ideological framework of Southworth's romance. Whereas Capitola is integrated into the mainstream of antebellum U.S. life through marriage, Linda ultimately rejects marriage in favor of a life of political agitation and literary production. In terms of genre, Southworth plays with history to show an idealized vision of chivalry at work in the real world whereas Jacobs infuses her narrative with borrowings from the sentimental romance and the gothic novel in order to critique the representational logic of white supremacy in both the South and North. *The Hidden Hand* is a novel that borrows from and plays with history; *Incidents in the Life of a Slave Girl* is history that borrows from and subverts the novel.

The differences between Southworth's novel and Jacobs's stylized autobiography run deeper than their differing genres. Southworth falls prey to contradictions that in many ways continue to mark progressive discourse in the

United States. Most of all, she is unable to fully account for the experiences of the oppressed classes represented in her novel—thus her reliance on broad racial caricature and ultimate reaffirmation of the Virginia slaveocracy and its patriarchal authority through Capitola's inheritance plot. Southworth's exploration of the American chivalric mentality is compelling, but, like the critiques offered by Stanton and other white propertied women, it does not adequately articulate the particular struggles of enslaved women under the American chivalric system.

A more robust critique of this system was put forward by early black feminist Anna Julia Cooper, whose incendiary *A Voice From the South* (1886) gathers together lectures delivered through the mid-to-late nineteenth century. In her lecture "Womanhood: A Vital Element in the Regeneration and Progress of a Race," Cooper follows Seneca Falls rhetoric by positing premodern origins for the "noble and ennobling ideal of woman" espoused by male thinkers of her time:

> This high regard for woman, this germ of a prolific idea which in our own day is bearing such rich and varied fruit, was ingrafted into European civilization ... from two sources, the Christian Church and the Feudal System. For although the Feudal System can in no sense be said to have originated the idea, yet there can be no doubt that the habits of life and modes of thought to which Feudalism gave rise, materially fostered and developed it; for they gave us chivalry, than which no institution has more sensibly magnified and elevated woman's position in society.[30]

Cooper supports her claim by citing two academic sources: the conservative liberal French historian François Guizot (1787–1874) and American rhetorician John Bascom (1827–1911).[31] Cooper's choice of sources for her view of the Middle Ages speaks volumes to the influence historical medievalism exercised over the intellectual imagination of the nineteenth-century United States. Bascom's account of the chivalric spirit, which precedes a lengthy and insightful analysis of Chaucer, is far different from the historically uninformed rhapsodies of the southern slavocrats who influenced Poe's medievalism: "Chivalry was the deceptive bloom of unripe fruit; those who set their teeth in it, found it sharp and indigestible. Chivalry gave a tint of amethyst to a bitter winter's day. Those who looked out from castle windows, found their delight in it, but God's poor were frozen nonetheless. Later, as the expression of a sweet and gentle heart, as the dream of poetry, it has become quite another thing, a prodigality of nature that at once satisfies the mind and feeds the senses."[32]

Bascom's account captures the process by which the "ennoblement" of one class of women, which had been understood since Adam Smith as an economic expedient for the establishment of family wealth under feudalism, was transformed into a literary ideal that aestheticized certain interactions between genders while failing to account for broader social disparities.[33] His critique is centered on something like "false consciousness": feudal society told itself a story about its great respect for women of a certain class as a cover for daily crimes committed against everyone else. Cooper follows Bascom in pointing out this basic contradiction in the "noble and ennobling ideal of woman" put forward by feudalism: "Respect for woman, the much lauded chivalry of the Middle Ages, meant what I fear it still means to some men in our own day—respect for the elect few among whom they expect to consort" (55). For Cooper, chivalric discourse disguises the biological and economic desires of upper-class men; it is a way to tell a pretty story about courtship while ignoring the financial and sexual gains men receive from their superior legal and cultural position. Against this, Cooper calls for a "radical amelioration of womankind" based in what she sees as the egalitarian spirit of the Gospels.

By emphasizing the premodern origins for the nineteenth century's view of women, Cooper taps into the dominant rhetoric of the women's movement. However, her account of chivalry and its abuses incorporates a critique of class that is often missing in the accounts of Stanton and others. Cooper's argument for the "radical amelioration of womankind" is based in her own experiences under slavery: the "elect few among whom they expect to consort" are privileged women of the upper classes, while women of the subordinate classes are denied even the most basic protections. After charting the history of chivalry's détente between Christian egalitarianism and "barbaric" militarism—including a brief selection from Chaucer's "Wife of Bath's Tale"—Cooper asserts that southern black women in the nineteenth century now occupy the position that peasant women did in the Middle Ages: "I would beg to add my plea for the Colored Girls of the South:—that large, bright, promising, fatally beautiful class that stand shivering like a delicate plantlet before the fury of tempestuous elements, so full of promise and possibilities, yet so sure of destruction."[34] Like the peasant, who in both Bascom and Cooper's accounts stands out in the "bitter winter's day" of inequality, black women are disbarred from the "tint of amethyst" afforded by the romance of chivalry. Without a fundamental realignment of the black woman's social standing, Cooper argues, the entirety of the race will continue to be kept in a subordinate position: "Only the BLACK WOMAN can say 'when and where I enter, in the quiet, undisputed dignity of my womanhood, without violence and without suing or special patronage, then and there the whole Negro race enters with me.'"[35] Cooper's rejection of "suing and special privilege" is important. Neither minute reforms in the byzantine system of common law precedent nor privileges doled out to a select caste of women will guarantee the fundamental realignment of social roles that constitutes a "radical amelioration": only social reorganization will do.

Like Ann Julia Cooper, who would have been around the age of Jacobs's daughter Ellen during the timeframe of *Incidents*, Jacobs is careful to note the exceptional nature of black women's suffering under the American chivalric order. Harriet Jacobs is—to use a medieval figure who would not have been unfamiliar to nineteenth-century readers like Cooper—a southern Christine de Pizan, exposing the reality of male domination and celebrating the resourcefulness of women who dared to resist it. Jacobs's main tool for exploring this reality is the subversion of conventional literary tropes. Through her collaboration with Lydia Marie Child, Jacobs is able to at once issue a series of blows against her specific oppressors and the whole national system of white supremacy, and to interrogate the representational apparatuses that sustain the dehumanization of enslaved women. Jacobs gives the lie to the "ennoblement" of women under chivalric culture, emphasizing how male domination over women is sustained through abuses of law and physical violence.

Jacobs also evidences a complex understanding of the ways in which law and custom were used to limit the agency of upper-class white women. In *Incidents*, slaves' lives are bound up in decisions made not only by their mistresses, but also by a wider network of blood and legal relations. Jacobs addresses the effect of the common law enactment of the wife's "civil death" on slaves in the brief story of a slaved named Harry. Treated kindly by his mistress, Harry faces an uncertain future after she marries: "I can do nothing for you now, Harry," his mistress informs him after Harry asks about freeing his children, "I no longer have the power I had a week ago" (43–44). Jacobs acknowledges the white woman's civil death in marriage, but is not willing to go quite as far as Stanton and others in claiming that the married woman is equal to the slave. Harry's mistress lacks the power to free Harry's children, but she is nonetheless sustained (admittedly, in an unhappy marriage) by the labor supplied by Harry and his fellow bondsmen.

Later, when Linda attempts to marry her free black suitor, she laments that "the marriage would give him no power to protect me from my master," a stark reminder of the precariousness of the slave woman's life under southern law (37). The *coverture* offered to the married women is only as good as the sovereignty granted to the spouse offering her that cover. White women may suffer the moral pangs of their husband's bad behavior, but their class status remains fixed. Harry's mistress must relent some power in marriage, and Mrs. Flint must suffer repeated cuckolding by her husband; however, neither woman's rights are trampled as brutally as those of Linda and her fellow slaves, for whom "there [is] no protecting arm of the law... to invoke" (109). By contrast, Mrs. Flint's marriage vows afford her the privilege of her husband's authority, a bitter dynamic Jacobs highlights by recounting Mrs. Flint's request to have Aunt Nancy buried at her feet, bound to her mistress even in death. Law and custom do not prevent Mrs. Flint from making this gruesome request, and only an uncharacteristic act of noblesse oblige prevents Nancy from suffering this final indignity.

Jacobs uses her grandmother's first conflict with the Flint family to illustrate the material ramifications of the feudal conception of marriage on slave women. After the death of her mistress's husband, Martha's youngest son, Benjamin, is sold for seven hundred dollars. The mistress retains Martha to work in a hotel. Jacobs calls the hotel the widow's "dower," underscoring how slave labor is tied up in the political economy of premodern legal codes that dictated women's property under marriage. Shortly after Benjamin's sale, the mistress borrows three hundred dollars from Martha, a loan Jacobs qualifies with a blunt reminder: "The reader probably knows that no promise or writing given to a slave is legally binding... a slave, *being* property, can *hold* no property" (10). The idea that a slave could issue a loan that would be honored is an evident absurdity; however, the fiction is allowed to stand. Jacobs invests this moment with symbolic power: the story of a literal loan from a slave to her mistress represents the labor and value stolen under the system of chattel bondage. Jacobs's resolution to this episode underscores that value flows from slave to master on a one-way street.

After the mistress's death, Dr. Flint refuses to repay the debt owed Martha, and we learn that the money was spent on a silver candelabra, which Linda presumes "will be handed down in the family, from generation to generation" (13). In bare economic terms—the terms are crude, but then so is the system—Martha is down a thousand dollars in addition to the years of labor that have been wrenched from her. That the mistress used Martha's capital for a piece of ornament, the price of which soon becomes richly symbolic for Jacobs, is all the more cruel. In a final indignity, Flint attempts to sell Martha, a betrayal that is prevented by an act of charity at her auction.

Benjamin's sale, the price of the candelabra, and Martha's lack of recourse to gallant southerner's storied integrity merge in "The Slave Who Dared to Feel Like a Man." When Benjamin is imprisoned after an escape attempt, Jacobs uses gothic imagery to draw a familiar association between slavery and the worst abuses of feudal Europe: "There was a jingle of chains. The moon had just risen, and cast an uncertain light through the bars of the window" (*I*, 21–22). Benjamin emerged from imprisonment wasted away, and Jacobs describes him with phrases that could come from the pages of Ann Radcliffe or Horace Walpole. The vengeful master decides to sell Benjamin to a slave trader heading South, but his decision carries a significant financial loss. Jacobs employs direct address to bring concrete cash transactions into the reader's imagination: "You remember, I told you what price [Benjamin] brought when ten years of age. Now he was more than twenty years old, and sold for three hundred dollars. The master had been blind to his own interest" (23). Jacobs ironically reproaches the master to underscore the maddening economics of the slave trade. Broken by imprisonment, Benjamin is now worth as much as the candelabra purchased with Martha's stolen capital, and, like the candelabra, Benjamin's fate is tied up in the financial and emotional caprices of the Flint family. Finally, Martha is able to buy Benjamin from the trader for $900—triple his stated value and $200 above his initial price—bringing Martha's total loss to $1,900, or roughly $50,000 in 2017 dollars.

Of course the other losses Martha and Benjamin incur—of dignity, agency, and familial peace—cannot be measured in terms of cash. But that is the subtext of Jacob's argument: the crimes committed against slaves are both spiritual (thus her literary appeals to sentiment and sensation) and material. Unlike abolitionist authors who used figures from the gothic and sentimental romance to win readers through emotional appeal and "moral suasion," Jacobs takes the opportunity to pair the familiar aspects of representations of slavery (sensationalized suffering, macabre detail) with the more mundane economic realities of its day-to-day functioning.

Flint's deceptions in the Benjamin/candelabra episode foreshadow the confidence games and assaults that he will perpetrate against Linda and her family throughout the narrative. In her retelling of these events, Jacobs emphasizes the ways in which Flint's "false representations" are wedded to physical violence to demonstrate the structural connection between the material and discursive abuses committed against slaves. Flint's abuses begin with language: "My master began to whisper foul words in my ears... He peopled my mind with unclean images, such as only a vile monster could think of" (26). After the gallery of "unclean images" of sexual and physical degradation in "Sketches of Neighboring Plantations," Jacobs's description of Flint's first act of sexual abuse take on extra weight, signifying both a specific crime committed by one master and the broader system of crimes that constitute the slave system. Jacobs hastens to remind readers that "no shadow of law" protects the slave "from insult, violence, or even death" (26). Associating "insult" with violence and death allows Jacobs to articulate a critique of the law's inability to manage the manifold abuses suffered by slaves.

As her narrative progresses, Jacobs continues to draw connections between Flint's "false representations" and the physical outrages that go hand in hand with them. Flint's abuses progress from the aural to the manual (Flint miming his intentions to Linda), and finally to letters (28). Once Flint learns that Linda is teaching herself to write, his abuse becomes a perversion of a literary education: "One day he caught me teaching myself to write. He frowned, as if he was not well pleased; but I suppose he came to the conclusion that such an accomplishment might help to advance his favorite scheme. Before long, notes were often slipped into my hand. I would return them, saying, 'I can't read them, sir.' 'Can't you?' he replied; 'then I must read them to you.' He always finished the reading by asking, 'Do you understand?'" (28–29). In this passage Flint repurposes Linda's literary education, which will end up being the tool of her liberation, for the goal of sexual exploitation. Flint acts a tutor, and through his instruction intends to further inaugurate Linda in the complex physical and linguistic "scheme" that underwrites his domination of her. Coupled with this open manipulation is a subtler one that relates back to Jacobs's ongoing critique of southern chivalry.

Flint describes to Linda "the happiness [she] was so foolishly throwing away" (29) by denying his advances, mischaracterizing her concubinage as a form of consensual marriage. "Happiness" is, of course, a loaded word in U.S. discourse, exceeding its colloquial, affective meaning to constellate rights and privileges relating to property, self-determination, and freedom from harm. Flint thus vacillates between two opposing strategies in his attempted seduction. First, he verbally and physically abuses Linda, then attempts to place her in the United States' chivalric gender hierarchy with false promises of coverture. Linda understands that Flint's promises are empty. When Jacobs notes that Mrs. Flint feels her "marriage vows were desecrated, her dignity insulted," she highlights the irony in a man like Flint promising conjugal happiness to anyone at all (30). Jacobs also subtly reveals that claims of coverture belie the white woman's ultimate powerlessness in traditional marriage. After Mrs. Flint begins to openly accuse her husband of sleeping with Linda, naming Linda "as the author of the accusation," Flint responds that Linda must have been "tortured" into a false confession. Linda responds: "I understood his object in making this false representation. It was to show me that I gained nothing by seeking the protection of my mistress; that the power was still all in his own hands" (31). Flint denies both his wife and Linda the ability to "author" representations of their life experience.

When Flint's representational powers are threatened, he inevitably resorts to violence. Flint menaces Linda with a razor to prevent her avoiding his advances, and threatens to "grind [her] bones to powder" when he learns she is pregnant with Sands's child (50). Flint's cruelest punishment—sending Linda to his plantation, where she will be worked and whipped at his capricious son's will—is the climax of his physical domination.

Tellingly, Flint's most vividly described act of violence occurs in the library, where (we can assume) he produces the obscene letters with which he torments Linda and manages the daily operations of both his medical practice and plantation. Linda objects to Flint calling her fiancé "a puppy," and Flint flies into a rage: "He sprang upon me like a tiger, and gave me a stunning blow. It was the first time he had ever struck me" (35). Linda responds to Flint's bestial metaphor (she and her lover are "puppies") with her own (Flint is a "tiger"), signaling a key moment in her education in the manipulation of signs. Later, Linda refuses to admit that she has been caught up in "an intrigue" regarding Sands's attempts to purchase her, and Flint once again responds with violence: "'Do you tell me I lie?' exclaimed he, dragging me from my chair. 'Will you say again that you never saw that man?'" (67). Of course, Linda is misrepresenting herself: she is well aware of the conspiracy to purchase her and her children and lies on purpose in order to prevent the "intrigue" from unraveling. Flint is less threatened by the implication that he is a liar—he must of course know this, unless he is a much more profound sociopath than *Incidents* lets on—than he is by Linda's growing ability to manipulate representations to her own ends. In this passage, *Incidents in the Life of a Slave Girl* becomes a competition in cunning between Linda and Flint, representing a broader representational and political struggle between slaves and masters in the South and, ultimately, black and white across the nation.

As an autobiography, *Incidents* is an exhaustive chronicle of the legal and moral implications of an actual struggle with the Norcum family over Jacobs's life. In its symbolic valence, Linda's conflict with and victory over Flint represents the dismantling of the artist-master figure we saw Poe and other southern writers developing in chapter 1. Like the artist-master, Flint is well educated, adept at manipulating letters, and willing to use violence to achieve his ends. Linda creates the conditions that make her liberty possible by learning how to manipulate appearances with even greater skill than the artist-master, as evidenced by the letter-writing scheme she runs while in hiding (102). During her trip to England, Jacobs even critiques the slave/serf metaphor that did so much political work for southern slavocrats: "The people I saw around me were, many of them, among the poorest of the poor. But when I visited them in their little thatched cottages, I felt that the condition of even the meanest and most ignorant among them was vastly superior to the condition of the most favored slaves in America" (143). Against the aristocratic pretensions and outright fabrications of the southern slaveholding class, Jacobs posits the reality of the slave's social position. That she does so through a representational apparatus every bit as sophisticated as that deployed by her oppressors is an inspired, and politically efficacious, authorial decision.

The formal heterodoxy of Jacobs's work—its deft navigation of popular literary forms, autobiographical reportage, legal analysis, and historical narration—does not just represent Lydia Marie Childs's editorial intervention or Jacobs's capitulation to her audiences' generic expectations.[36] While these must certainly be considered as factors, I prefer to see Jacobs (filtered through a collaboration with Child that admittedly left Jacobs in a dependent position regarding reception and publication) as playing with generic codes in order to affect a multifront siege on the nationwide system of racial caste domination. Childs's insistence on pseudonyms, a decision Jacobs's initially resisted, offers us a compelling (and certainly unintended) metaphor for the interpenetration of the factual and the representative, the material and the linguistic, and the often-conflicting arenas of social praxis and legal theory. Jacobs's narrative expropriates the ideological tools used to produce the subordinate subject position to which slave women have been regulated. If one answer to exploitation is to smash the machinery used by the master class to engineer its representations (literary Ludditism, with the artisan's mentality the term implies), another is to seize that machinery in order to produce representations that do oppositional political work. When Jacobs confesses that the "system of violence and wrong" to which she has been subjected "left [her] no alternative but to enact a falsehood" (130), she both laments the moral compromises slaves must make in order to survive and offers a sly wink to the reader: How else but through dissimulation can the slave trump a system that is at its base a tessellation of falsehoods and crimes? The long struggle with Flint therefore represents both the factual recounting of Harriet Jacobs's difficult liberation and her avatar Linda Brent's education in the engineering of representations.

The literary borrowings in *Incidents* are rich and varied. Jacobs's early critics note the similarities between Flint's failed seduction of Linda and the familiar seduction plot of sentimental romances such as Samuel Richardson's *Pamela* (1740) and *Clarissa* (1747–1748), in which a feudal aristocrat relentlessly pursues the virtuous woman who resists his advances, some derisively calling Linda Brent "the Pamela of the slave narratives" (Doherty, 79). Against these dismissive early readings, Thomas Doherty notes that Jacobs exploits "the propagandistic possibilities" of the sentimental romance in order to "appropriate its popularity while undercutting its presumptions."[37] Jennifer Rae Greeson likewise argues that Jacobs uses "fallen woman" tropes borrowed from sensationalistic urban gothic fiction, particularly in the sequences concerning Ellen's struggles as a domestic laborer in New York City.[38] Both of these readings work off of assumptions regarding Jacobs's class position. For Doherty, Jacobs posits "personal autonomy," the endgame of classical liberalism, as Jacobs's goal, thereby mapping her political strategy onto the hegemonic rhetoric of U.S. culture that continues to pervade U.S. thought.[39] Doherty's reading makes Linda Brent a Capitola Black in reverse; whereas Capitola moves south to gain authority, Linda moves north to gain autonomy. Greeson's reading similarly emphasizes the middle-class, liberal aspects of Jacobs's narrative. For Greeson, Jacobs opens *Incidents* with an emphasis on her father's position as a free artisan both to mirror the generic conventions of the "fallen woman" narrative and to present "a certain class of southern slaves to Northern readers as the last repositories of republican virtue."[40]

By equating the romantic American novel to bourgeois social values, Doherty and Greeson channel Leslie Fiedler's influential reading of the sentimental and the gothic in *Love and Death in the American Novel*. Fiedler asserts that the popularity of the genres in the early United States can be attributed to their portrayals of a symbolic struggle between the emerging middle class (Pamela, Clarissa, or any of the "pursued women" in the gothic narratives) and the creaking remnants of the feudal aristocracy (Mr. B., Lovelace, or the lustful baron from central casting). In America no less than England, "the appeal of the seduction novel rested surely on its presentation of the conflict of aristocracy and bourgeoisie within the confines of the boudoir."[41] In Fiedler's reading of the sentimental and gothic romance, the romantic heroine's victory (through marriage, heavenly reward, or escape from sexual violence) symbolizes the bourgeoisie's victory over feudal aristocracy. But Fiedler couches his reading in disavowals of a U.S. feudal past that, as I demonstrated in the introduction, have structured liberal historiography since the nineteenth century. Fiedler declares that there is "no real tradition of gallantry in America, no debased aristocratic codes against which the bourgeois belief can define itself," and that the country's lack of "inherited Aristocratic privilege" leads the American romance toward "feminism and anti-intellectualism" instead of a critique of class relations.[42] There is reason to Fiedler's assertion—to claim that the United States had as strict an aristocratic order as England or Spain is historically inaccurate. But to claim that we absolutely lacked the feudal element is, as is hopefully becoming clear, equally untenable. The excluded middle in the stark binary created by "liberalism" and "feudalism" is the ways in which U.S. law and culture democratized inherited feudal privilege for propertied men (and, by extension, their wives), while simultaneously instating an intricate racial caste system that disbarred others from these privileges. If we accept this reading, then the continued popularity of "feudal" literary forms in the United States may have owed just as much to a sense that premodern legal, economic, and political forces continued to shape U.S. social life as much as it did a cultural victory lap around feudalism's crumbling battlements.

In Jacobs's case, borrowings from the sentimental and gothic romance are tools that help her to break down readers' potentially racist assumptions regarding her sexual virtue. These borrowings are not put to the service of reaffirming a conservative, or even bourgeois, social order. There is no stark opposition in Jacobs between romance on the one hand and political agitation on the other. Instead, sentimental romance supplies Jacobs a language through which to enact her book-length critique of the "civil death" of the white woman under common law, and the gothic supplies her with a language to translate slavery's horrors to her audience.

The novel's influence on Jacobs's narrative is evident, but Jacobs's political stance is less clear. Linda's progress troubles the idea that Jacobs returns to the moderate social values she expresses at the beginning. As Linda famously asserts, "My story ends with freedom; not in the usual way, with marriage" (156). With this statement, Jacobs escapes the orbit of bourgeois sentimentalism and heads toward a new political constellation. Freedom may be read in its conservative liberal meaning—as freedom to own profit-yielding property and to purchase labor from others—or in another, more communal sense. It is this second sense, I want to argue, to which Jacobs's narrative leads. Linda expropriates the representational logic of the master class in order to articulate a new vision of family life that exceeds the one afforded by moderate-conservative U.S. marriage laws, and even the openly contractual, liberal conception championed by the Seneca Falls generation.

Jacobs hints at the failure of traditional family units to black foster women's social development through the story of her artisan father. While Jacobs's portrayal of him is loving and sympathetic, Linda's father does not fully understand the nature of the U.S. racial caste system that slavery has bred. Unlike Martha, who like Linda demonstrates a keen ability to negotiate slavery's web of "false representations," Linda's father attempts to assert his own will over that of the slaveocracy. When Linda's brother William admits that he does not know whether he should respond to his father or his master's call, his father thunders, "You are *my* child . . . and when I call you, you should come immediately, if you have to pass through fire and water" (12). But this recourse to patriarchal authority cannot exceed the limits placed on parental authority by slavery. Jacobs's highlights this after her father's death: "I spent the day gathering flowers and weaving them into festoons, while the dead body of my father was lying within a mile of me. What cared my owners for that? He was merely a piece of property. Moreover, they thought he had spoiled his children, teaching them to feel that they were human beings" (13). Just as Benjamin's suffering is connected to the exchange of the candelabra, the father's death is placed against the festoons Linda is forced to weave. The passage is touched with an ineffable sadness, one that emerges from its bare statement of the facts of domination, facts Jacobs's father cannot quite comprehend. The tragedy of this episode is double, encompassing the failures of loving but finally ineffectual efforts by the aging patriarch, and the degradation of a living human subject to an insensible thing. Jacobs recalls her father's attempts with pity in the narrative's conclusion: "I remembered how my poor father had tried to buy me, when I was a small child, and how he had been disappointed. I hoped his spirit was rejoicing over me now" (156).

Law prevents men like Jacobs's father from providing coverture to the women they wish to protect. But, instead of offering a conservative lament of waning patriarchal authority, Jacobs formulates a new vision of family and support. The bonds that Jacobs forms in the North—including the bond with Mrs. Bruce, which will ultimately lead to her final liberation from the Flint family's influence—provide an alternative to the traditional patriarchal family that her father represents. As historian Sharon Block puts it, although "enslaved women ordinarily did not have access to the protection offered by a patriarchal figure," Jacobs was able to find supporters outside her master's household who were "crucial to her limited redress."[43] This network included her grandmother and the many women in the North (especially Amy Post and her amanuensis Lydia Maria Child) who assisted Jacobs in her flight and in the recording of her experiences in *Incidents*. Christina Accomando connects the new family units Jacobs presents with her "reformulation of the domestic novel": Jacobs "subverts the marriage plot of domestic fiction, the expectation that the story will end with male-female domestic union. Family is privileged, but husband is not; motherhood is valued, but marriage specifically is omitted."[44] Jacobs's multifront attack on slavery encompasses a critique of the laws, representational apparatuses, and finally social practices that shore up white supremacy in the South and the North.

DISCOURSE, LAW, AND/OR CULTURE

While a whole network of discursive practices emerged from the paradox of woman's feudal legal personhood in the United States, the question was finally an economic one: Do women have the right to their own property, including possession of their own bodies, or do they lose those rights once the marriage vows are enacted? U.S. law, fragmented by the system of "state's rights" that continues to make substantive change in the United States difficult, met this quandary by developing a system of "trickle-down feminism" wherein discrete changes in legal discourse were expected to lead inexorably toward a realignment of women's material social existences. Yet, as we have seen, this liberal discourse had the contrary effect of reaffirming class divisions between women. Common law had never applied, in a serious way, to women of the lower classes; thus, by taking up the critique of common law as the basis for America's first feminist movement, the Seneca Falls generation effectively guaranteed that their program would be for and by women of the propertied classes. The lives of lower-class women, especially those of slaves, did not receive the same treatment as did the lives of the class of men and women who produced discourse in the Seneca Falls generation. And the class that makes the discourses often makes itself appear to be the prime mover of social progress.

Because of their class's ability to produce legal and philosophical discourse, liberal critics of marriage held a semimessianic faith in the ability of their discourse to create new social subjects. In "The Rights of Woman," Hurlbut demonstrates the law's ability to create new subjects through the figure of the "spinster." He asserts that, by institutionalizing a series of legal protections for single women, U.S. law has effectively created a new social subject: "She becomes most emphatically a new creature after this event—a being of the law's own creation—a monster, (pardon the word,) whom nature disowns—a fictitious being, breathing a legal, not a moral atmosphere."[45] Hurlbut believes that the "spinster" is created by the law, leaving open the possibility that legal discourse could, in theory, produce new human subjects. Legal reform, Hurlbut seems to imply, will lead to material change in women's social positions; change the way we discuss, categorize, and theorize human subjects, and we will change the subjects themselves. One response to these classical liberal assessments of law is deceptively simple: politics and economy do, in fact, exist, inasmuch as the words signify really existing systems of governance and production that constitute the material basis for all human interactions, *including* the production of a society's various discourses. Juridical power does not "produce what it seeks to represent"; instead, it enshrines in literary discourse no less than in legal discourse the dominant party's material interests in the struggle over the right to self-determination to which the subordinate party has been denied.

The study of discursive practice—whether in literature, art, or law—and the study of the material conditions that allow these discourses to emerge are necessarily imbricated. And yet the bridge between these two seemingly opposed islands of critical engagement is always at peril of collapsing, leaving each disconnected from the currents of history and representation in which we're all anchored. For the critic or historian of literature, the problem can be thought of methodologically: How can we best square political commitments with literary exegesis? This chapter's readings of Southworth and Jacobs leads to a difficult answer: representations are political, but politics is not (strictly speaking) representational. One may, as Cap does in *The Hidden Hand*, seize the representative apparatuses of a master class only to find oneself recapitulating logics of domination and exclusion. However, one may also, like Linda Brent, learn the master's tricks in order to break free of his orbit of influence and strive toward new, fairer social relations.

The meaning of this double lesson is, to my mind, precisely what Harriet Jacobs, in different words and at a very different time in U.S. history, leaves her readers to sort out at the end of *Incidents in the Life of a Slave Girl*. Jacobs's network of friends, powerful as it proved to be, could only do so much for her social position. Despite finally being freed from Flint's influence, Linda's liberation is frustratingly incomplete. As a single mother in a culture that evidences little tolerance for either unmarried women or free blacks, she hopes for a security that she fears may prove elusive: "The dream of my life is not yet realized. I do not sit with my children in a home of my own. I still long for a hearthstone of my own, however humble" (156). Jacobs asserts twice that she longs for a home *of her own*: not a bourgeois marriage, necessarily, but a place to live, a small parcel of personal property. Jacobs's desire is not a capitulation to prevailing social norms, but instead a quiet assertion of her right to dignity and self-determination. Flint is both master of his estate and of *representations* of that estate; his social position affords him the power to produce discourse that in turn reaffirms his social position. Linda has received a partial parity with Flint: she can produce discourse, but she cannot yet inhabit a social position that offers her legal and domestic protection. Flint dreams and realizes those dreams through his subject position; Linda dreams but remains in subjection.

The cause of Linda's incomplete liberation is the impossibility of breaking from the national economy that fosters the slave trade: "We are as free from the power of slaveholders as are the white people of the north; and though that, according to my ideas, is not saying a great deal, it is a vast improvement in *my* condition" (156, emphasis in original). Like her uncle Benjamin, who resisted a system that turns humans into "foot-balls, cattle, every thing that's mean," or her brother William, who declares that "he [does] not intend to *buy* his freedom" (21, 13), Linda comes to resent the economic system that benefits from slavery as much as she does the institution itself.

The threat of being pulled back into the economics of the slave trade is ever-present for Linda. After Dr. Flint's death, Emily Flint's new husband, Mr. Dodge, attempts to trap Linda in another "false representation": "Tell me where she is," Dodge tells Linda's friend, "and I will give her a chance to buy her freedom" (153). Like Flint before him, Dodge exploits his wife's "civil death" to claim her property as his own, potentially renewing the decades-long struggle Linda is so close to ending. Against Linda's wishes, her friend Mrs. Bruce purchases her from Dodge—for the sum of three hundred dollars the same amount Flint refused to repay Martha. Linda learns that Mrs. Bruce has acquired her bill of sale, and her reaction is ambiguous:

> "The bill of sale!" Those words struck me like a blow. So I was *sold* at last! A human being *sold* in the free city of New York! The bill of sale is on record, and future generations will learn from it that women were articles of traffic in New York, late in the nineteenth century of the Christian religion. It may hereafter prove a useful document to antiquaries, who are seeking to measure the progress of civilization in the United States. I well know the value of that bit of paper; but much as I love freedom, I do not to look upon it. I am deeply grateful to the generous friend who procured it, but I despise the miscreant who demanded payment for what never rightfully belong to him or his. (155)

In those last lines, Jacobs questions both Dodge's presumption that a human being can be bought and sold like "foot-balls or cattle" and the equal absurdity that, were she property, her fate could be decided by a man she had never met simply because he married her mistress. This double critique of both slavery and Emily Flint's "civil death" recalls Harry and his mistress's plight in "Sketches of Neighboring Plantations" and cements Jacobs's total critique of the intertwined dominations of women and slaves under the feudal structure of U.S. conjugal law.

More than this, the passage signals Jacobs's awareness of a future audience that will recoil in disgust at the hypocrisy of a human being bought and sold in such a manner. No less than Flint's "stunning blow" against Linda in the library, it is a marker of her subordinate position in the U.S. race-caste system. The bill of sale represents the broader economic forces to which Jacobs is subjected. Benjamin, valued at three hundred dollars, is correlated to the candelabra; Linda, valued at three hundred dollars, is correlated to her free papers. The difference between the two transactions is one of degree, not type. Until humans are free of a system that equates them with commodities, Jacobs suggests, she will not cease to feel conflicted about the status of her freedom.

In the existing text of *Incidents*, Jacobs concludes with the sentimental image of her grandmother as a way to remind her readers of the cruelties women suffer under bondage. The complexity of Linda Brent's position as both a living witness to the horrors of the slave trade and a figure of brave resistance to slavery's systems of domination is resolved in the image of her grandmother, whose memory appears to her as "light, fleecy clouds floating over a dark and troubled sea" (158). But the original ending to Jacobs's text, a now-lost encomium to John Brown, points to a starkly different resolution. Bruce Mills observes that Lydia Maria Child felt that the original John Brown conclusion did not "'naturally' fit the story... because it is not as 'appropriate' a conclusion as the grandmother's death."[46] While there is some logic to Child's editorial decision, Child's assertion that Brown's revolutionary actions at Harper's Ferry constitute an "unnatural" conclusion to Jacobs's tale of suffering and exploitation is a telling metaphor for liberal approaches to social change. Child's insistence that *Incidents* conclude with a sentimental image situates Jacobs's narrative firmly in a feminine novelistic tradition. It also insists on a liberal solution to the problems sketched out in Jacobs's tale: the memory of Linda's grandmother makes the disjunction between the "dark and troubled sea" of slavery and the "light, fleecy clouds" of familial contentment bearable, but does not seek to resolve the disjunction.

Jacobs's original ending would likely have made a different argument: the disunities produced by the slave system, not to mention the rigid class structures bred by America's mixed feudal-liberal system, would not disappear through "moral suasion" alone. In the next chapter, I will turn to two authors who, like Jacobs, sensed that the contradictions inherent in U.S. liberalism may only be resolved through violence. Whereas the gendered generic expectations of Jacobs's prose forms led Child to conclude that the John Brown ending would be "unnatural," Herman Melville and John Rollin Ridge take advantage of their masculine subject positions and the generic liberties it affords them to imagine the violent revolt of figures living outside of America's feudal-liberal synthesis.

CHAPTER FOUR

Resistance to the Feudal-Liberal Alliance

Ridge's *The Life and Adventures of Joaquín Murieta* and Melville's *Benito Cereno*

> Then I did perceive how God, who seeth the end from the beginning, had prepared the West to be mighty, and still wieldable, that the moral energy of his word and spirit might take it up as a very little thing.
>
> —Lyman Beecher, *A Plea for the West* (1835)

In the quote above, Presbyterian preacher Lyman Beecher prophesizes a continental destiny for the United States. Like so many thinkers of his time, Beecher views the lands west of the Mississippi as a second Garden of Eden where Adamic man will regenerate his Protestant faith and promulgate the institutions he believes will follow from this system. The line between Beecher's religious agitation for westward conquest and political arguments for the same was often indistinguishable. In an open statement to pro-expansion Kentuckians in 1845, the plantation owner Robert John Walker argued that America's divine right to the west was part and parcel of creation itself. "If the Creator had separated Texas from the Union by mountain barriers, the Alps or the Andes," then antiexpansionist forces may have an argument for leaving the territory with Mexico, Walker writes. God, however, has designed the landscape with a different end in mind: "He has planed down the whole valley, including Texas, and united every atom of the soil and every drop of the waters of the mighty whole.... Texas is a part of Kentucky, a portion of the same great valley. It is a part of New York and Pennsylvania, a part of Maryland and Virginia, and Ohio, and of all the western states, whilst the Tennessee unites with it the waters of Georgia, Alabama, and Carolina." Walker goes on to exhort his readers to witness "the young eagle of America ... [refix] her gaze upon our former limits, and [replume] her pinions for her returning flight."[1] Walker's image is martial and imperial, the American eagle staring down its prey and preparing for flight, ready (as the possible pun in the last clause indicates) to pinion its opponents.

A decade after the publication of Beecher's *A Plea for the West*, politicians such as Walker actualized the book's Protestant millennial call with a war that would come to define U.S. foreign policy over the next century. The impact of the war was felt around the globe. Friedrich Engels, writing on "The Movements of 1847" for the *Deutsche-Brüsseler-Zeitung* in 1848, connects U.S. westward expansion with similarly massive social upheavals in Europe: "An unexpectedly rapid awakening in political life and a general arming against Austria in Italy; a civil war in Switzerland; a new Parliament of pronounced radical complexion in Britain; in France scandals and Reform banquets; in America the conquest of Mexico by the United States—that is a series of changes and movements such as no other recent year can show." He later ironically cheers the bourgeoisie's victories: "So just fight bravely on, most gracious masters of capital! We need you for the present; here and there we even need you as rulers. You have to clear the vestiges of the Middle Ages and of absolute monarchy out of our path."[2] Though speaking from a radically different political perspective, Engels's mock-heroic exhortation of the transnational capitalist class shares the belief in American progress and power expressed by Beecher, Walker, and other war boosters.

But the triumphalist narrative sketched by these men could not withstand the reality of an imperialist war. Abolitionists feared that westward expansion would embolden the slaveholding classes, undercutting their efforts to replace the semifeudal plantation regime with capitalist settlements and labor relations. At the same time, Whigs, nativists, and Democrats worried that by annexing Mexican lands, the United States would invite subversive elements that might undercut the nation's republican project. Furthermore, Spain's feudal rancho laws and the racial heterogeneity of Mexico's landed class vexed the nation as it sought to forge national political consensus around Anglo-Saxon homogeneity.[3]

These various tensions received legal and political expression in the Treaty of Guadalupe Hidalgo (1848) that ended the U.S.-Mexico War and in the court battles concerning violations of the treaty's provisions that occupied western courts over the second half of the nineteenth century. The 1845 Texas State Constitution, for instance, barred Tejanos from owning property or serving in government—a direct affront to the spirit of the 1848 Treaty.[4]

Similarly, California was admitted to the union as an ethnostate in which, according to its 1849 constitution, "every white male citizen of the United States, and every white male citizen of Mexico who shall have elected to become a citizen of the United States" was afforded the right to vote.[5] California's constitution thus left large swathes of the racially indeterminate Mexican populace—not to mention indigenous peoples who fared better under Spanish than U.S. rule—in a political limbo that would end with an 1870 legislative decision recognizing the rights of all Mexican Americans to full citizenship.[6]

While law and policy dictated the terms of assimilation or exclusion for people who lived in former Mexican territories, prose fiction offered a way to imagine how social life in an expanding U.S. would play out. As literary critic Shelly Streeby has argued, popular fiction "establish[ed] a new subgenre of mass entertainment that focused on Mexico as a space that was potentially like the United States—and therefore not entirely 'savage'—but that was still viewed as alien, largely because of the mixtures of multiple 'races' and the persistence of feudal and colonial institutions."[7] The two works I'll focus on in this chapter, Herman Melville's *Benito Cereno* (1855) and John Rollin Ridge's *The Life and Adventures of Joaquín Murieta: The Celebrated California Bandit* (1854), evidence the discord produced when the United States encountered decadent empires and colonized peoples. This chapter locates Ridge and Melville's texts within centuries-long political and ideological traditions that reached a head in the U.S.-Mexico War. Authors writing for readers in the colonial metropole faced serious difficulties as they attempted to explore non-European sovereignty, not to mention the anarchic political energies whipped up among the settlers and soldiers who represented "hard power" on the frontier. To properly understand how Melville and Ridge approached the problem of emergent liberal polity, residual feudal order, and existing indigenous sovereignty therefore requires both a thoroughgoing historical analysis of westward expansion and a literary analysis of the discourses produced around these issues.

This methodological heterodoxy mirrors the formal heterodoxy of Ridge's and Melville's works. Ridge and Melville could only investigate the problems their texts take up by freely mixing the sensation story, gothic romance, high literature, poetry, history, legal discourse, and the sensationalistic language of the news press. More troubling, they could give voice to their views on indigenous sovereignty only by stripping indigenous groups of their particularity and viewing them within the dialectic of "civilization" and "savagery" that, as Lumbee legal scholar Robert A. Williams argues, had structured Europe's historical imagination from the ancient Greeks forward.[8] The instability of this dialectic allows us to find a crucial interstice in the dense pattern of competing constructions of sovereignty and liberty we have charted so far. Taken as a political and economic regime on the order of feudalism and liberalism, indigeneity demands that we consider the history of U.S. cultural development from outside our usual European frames of reference. Mexico, imagined as a borderland where liberal democracy, feudal law, and indigenous sovereignty may clash and meld, forced nineteenth-century thinkers to explore the deep structures of their own ideologies more fully. That *Benito Cereno* and *The Life and Adventures of Joaquín Murieta* both end in the failure of their respective rebellions points toward the horizon of the nineteenth-century U.S. political imaginary.

SPAIN AND MEXICO IN THE ANGLO-AMERICAN IMAGINARY

James K. Polk's Third Annual Message to the U.S. Senate and House of Representatives in December 1847 concerning the results of the U.S.-Mexico War captures many of the issues regarding Anglo-American attitudes toward Mexico that I will outline in the following pages.[9] Delivered to Congress in the wake of General Winfield Scott's march on Mexico City in September 1847, Polk's Third Annual Message is a forceful argument for U.S. hegemony over Mexico's territories in the west, and a telling indicator of the political effects of decades of rhetoric that posited America as the liberal antitype to feudal Spain.

Polk opens his address by celebrating the United States as a thoroughly modern political entity. "The success of our admirable system," he argues, "is a conclusive refutation of the theories of those in other countries who maintain that a 'favored few' are born to rule and that the mass of mankind must be governed by force." In a direct rebuff of feudal order, Polk reminds his audience that Americans are "subject to no arbitrary or hereditary authority." Mexico, by contrast, is a weak and declining feudal state—"too feeble a power" to hold and cultivate Texas and Upper California. Polk ends by stoking his audience's fears of indigenous rebellion. Speaking of New Mexico, he warns that "numerous bands of fierce and warlike savages wander over it and upon its borders," and that "Mexico has been and must continue to be too feeble to restrain them from committing depredations, robberies, and murders, not only upon the inhabitants of New Mexico itself, but upon those of the northern States of Mexico."[10] In Polk's imagination of hemispheric history, Spain abused indigenous peoples but could not control them. As Polk's previous statements regarding the state of manufactures in the Spanish-speaking west indicates, even if Spain had controlled these indigenous populations, it would have been to stoke Spanish vanity and greed, not to introduce nineteenth-century civilization as Polk's audience understood it. The United States, on the other hand, will subdue native groups with an eye toward industry, bringing enlightenment and economic development to a benighted land.

Polk did not invent the rhetoric he used as a blunt instrument in his Third Annual Message. Anglo-America's exceptionalist historiography had long held that the United States stood to inherit the mantle of imperial dominance once worn by the decadent European powers. But, unlike those earlier empires, the United States would not be beholden to the past and could therefore avoid the narrative arc of rise, dominance, and decline that structured Western historiography in the nineteenth century. The classic expression of this argument is John O'Sullivan's "The Great Nation of Futurity" (1839), where O'Sullivan asserts that America "[has], in reality, but little connection with the past history of any of [other nations], and still less with all antiquity, its glories, or its crimes."[11] O'Sullivan's reference to "glories" and "crimes" would have immediately brought Spain to mind. In his 1845 article "Annexation," O'Sullivan moves from vague historical disavowals of "glories" and "crimes" to ad hominem attack. "Imbecile and distracted, Mexico never can exert any real governmental authority" over the west, a claim O'Sullivan supports with words that recall his earlier and more famous work: "Anglo-Saxons" in the west will join the United States "without agency of our government, without responsibility of our people—in the natural flow of events, the spontaneous working of principles, and the adaptation of the tendencies and wants of the human race to the elemental circumstances in the midst of which they find themselves placed."[12] The march of humanity, destined to be led by the United States—which was in turn destined to be led by Anglo-Americans—demanded a new kind of continental empire led by a regenerated race of white men.

The Spanish Americas offered an at-hand example of the European past that "the land of futurity" was eager to overcome. Throughout the first half of the nineteenth century, "Spain was firmly established as the antithesis of democratic, enterprising America."[13] Waddy Thompson, U.S. minister to Mexico from 1842–1844 and key player in the southern "nullification crisis" of the 1830s that paved the way for the coming Civil War, asserts in *Recollections of Mexico* (1846) that Spain is a "bye-word [sic] amongst the nations; whilst other countries have been moving on in constant career of improvements in every way . . . she has of necessity retrograded, for nations cannot long remain stationary."[14] The anonymous author of "Spain in the Fifteenth Century," a short historical essay published in the March 1841 issue of the *Southern Literary Messenger*, is no less harsh than Thompson: "The brightest jewel in the monarchical diadem is robbed of its splendor. Her chivalry and daring have departed; her knights are no longer celebrated in the tournament for brilliancy of exploits. The fearless hero has degenerated into the admirer of dark-eyed maidens, and he has forgotten the glory of his ancestors."[15] Interestingly, in the July 1841 edition of the same magazine, lawyer and future northern prisoner of war Severn Teackle Wallis would pin such declensionist views of Spanish history on English prejudice:

> England, our good mother, with a common language, has indoctrinated us after her own fashion. . . . Those who are disposed to think the best, recall to mind the glorious romance of [Spain's] past history; and suffering their imaginations to roam through the deserted halls of the Alhambra, dwell only on the time when the peninsula was the battle-ground of Christendom and Paynimrie [pagandom; i.e., Islam]—forgetting, all the while, that the same soil is trodden by a living, existing nation, modern, civilized, and Christian. The rest of us, forming the great mass, seem to be aware of her existence, only for the purposes of disparaging illustration, and have set up certain conventional commonplaces of opprobrium, which appear to be suggested, on all occasions, by the simple mention of her name. Where other nations would pass without commentary or epithet, we have always at hand some term of gentle endearment, such as "bigoted," "benighted," "degraded," "miserable," and "blood-thirsty," to grace poor Spain withal. Our idea of her religion is typified by an *auto-da-fe*—of her refinement and humanity, by a bull-fight.[16]

Wallis's allusion to men whose "imaginations roam through the deserted halls of the Alhambra" may be a reference to Washington Irving, whose *Tales of the Alhambra* (1832–1851) is a classic literary expression of the romantic/

declensionist view of Spanish history. In Irving's tales, the Moorish palace, once a testament to Islamic industry and Iberian grandeur, is by the 1830s "desolate," "a farcical termination to the drama of human pride."[17] Whether defending or attacking Spain, Irving and his contemporaries emphasized the gothic and tragic elements in the nation's history.

Contrary to Wallis's claim, this disparaging view of Spain was not held exclusively by people of English descent. In fact, Mexican patriots and their supporters relied on anti-Spanish rhetoric to further their cause during and after Mexico's war for independence. The author of *Xicoténcatl* (1826) argues that a "monarchical vertigo . . . has stultified Europe" and led its historians to "cloak the black infamy" of Hernán Cortés's conquest of Mexico.[18] "Monarchical vertigo" implies woozy stultification, an inability to move beyond the old modes of social life toward new, more robust ones. We likewise find Lorenzo de Zavala, who helped lead the newly formed Mexican government after the ratification of the Constitución Federal de Los Estados Unidos Mexicanos de 1824, exhort his countrymen to "mend [their] ways," "get rid of those eighty-seven holidays during the year that you dedicate to play, drunkenness and pleasure," "save up capital for the decent support of yourself and your families," and "give guarantees of [their] concern for the preservation of the social order."[19] Later in the work, Zavala concludes that the liberated Mexican people will witness the making of a new historical epoch: "Over the Gothic rubble of untenable privileges will rise a new, glorious, and enlightened generation."[20] Neither were such assessments the exclusive domain of liberal thinkers; as the Engels passage cited earlier demonstrates, similar claims became commonplace across the nineteenth-century political spectrum, from socialist to monarchist. Owing to a racial historiography that emphasized the potential for U.S. institutions to realize tendencies inherent in different European ethnic groups, what was said to be true of Spain was invariably said to also be true of its former colonies.[21] This was despite the fact that many white U.S. citizens, increasingly unable to secure employment and land in the United States, converted to Catholicism, learned Spanish, and emigrated to Mexican Texas in the first two decades of the nineteenth century, seeking (in the words of historian Brian DeLay) "a better life under a different flag."[22]

But, as the century progressed and U.S. politics took on an increasingly nativist tinge, Anglo-American attitudes toward Mexico began to shift. The corruption and stultification that characterized Mexican social life in the

U.S. imaginary was no longer blamed only on colonial inheritances from Old Europe. Anglo-American thinkers on the nativist spectrum—from prowar Democrats to Know-Nothings—began to posit both spiritual and racial causes for Mexican inferiority.

Anti-Catholicism was a readymade explanation for perceived Mexican backwardness. For anti-Catholic religious luminaries, the global project of spiritual and social purification that began with the Reformation and continued with the establishment of the Puritan theocracy in New England would climax in the victory of Protestant forces against the "priest-ridden" Spanish colonies in the west.[23] Such anti-Catholic ideas helped forge national consensus around shared Anglo-Saxon, Protestant origins.[24] Popular serialized novels played a particularly important role in defining the United States as "a nation of brothers united against an incestuous usurper from another time and place," thereby offering "'national homogeneity' to a country threatened by sectionalism and facing growing religious diversity and disaffection."[25]

Anti-Catholicism cut across both "high" and "low" culture, influencing everyone from prominent literary authors and Protestant religious lights to writers of popular novels and songs. A telling example can be found in Philip Young and George C. Furber's *History of Mexico* (1847).[26] In their long chapter "Church Revenues," the authors write that the "Mexican hierarchy during the Spanish domination was probably the most opulent and splendid in the world," staffed by "a swarm of monks, friars, inquisitors, and their familiars, who crossed the sea in pursuit of the objects of their own ambition, rather than to do the holy cause they had enlisted in." Young and Furber associate Church wealth with indigenous displacement. "Living among themselves, apart from the white population," the Aztec descendant continues to "cherish the vindictive feelings inherited from his ancestors" as he walks "in melancholy silence among the gigantic ruins of pyramid and temple, consecrated to the religion of his fathers."[27] In *History of Mexico*, Catholic malfeasance was the motive force of indigenous displacement in the hemisphere; Cortés and his men's material drives are secondary. The book in fact implies that Cortés's actions weren't inspired by greed at all, but by faith: "Fortunately, however, the policy of the prince did not conflict with that of the priest; the political system of the former, and the theological one of the latter, were alike based upon the same pedestal of intellectual degradation."[28]

While anti-Catholicism was instrumental in stoking the United States' fear of waning Spanish power, the racial intermixture that characterized the Spanish Americas presented an even more immediate threat to Anglo-American hegemony. As literary scholar Maria DeGuzmán puts it, by the mid-nineteenth century "'Spain' and 'Spaniards' meant African, Asian, Middle Eastern, and 'Indian.'"²⁹ The Moor, the Indian, the *indio*—"Spanish" (and, more specifically, "Mexican") became a term of approbation that bundled diverse identities together. William H. Prescott, for instance, worried that an annexed Mexico "will be a heavy drag on our republican car, and the Creole blood will not mix well with the Anglo-Saxon."³⁰ As Prescott's use of the word "creole" suggests, what most troubled Anglo-America was not the idea of intermixing with "pure-blooded" Spaniards, but instead with the mestizos who occupied all social levels in the Spanish American colonies.

In February 1846, three months before Gen. Zachary Taylor's army clashed with Gen. Mariano Arista's forces at the Nueces Strip, beginning the U.S.-Mexico War in earnest, Swedish-born lawyer Gustavus Schmidt would use this same fear of racial heterogeneity as an argument in support of American aggression against Mexico. Writing in the proslavery journal *Debow's Review*, Schmidt narrates a series of arguments about Spanish depravity and superstition that would have been very familiar to his audience.³¹ He then leaps three hundred years to the nineteenth century, where he finds precisely the same forces at work in postindependence Mexico. Added to Schmidt's critique of residual feudal structures is a portrait of racial degeneration. Under Spanish rule, Mexico has become overwhelmingly mixed-race: "The whole population of Mexico may be stated in round numbers at seven millions; of which four millions are Indians, two millions mestizoes, mulattoes, zamboes, &c., usually denominated *castes*, and the remaining million are whites."³² After this demographic assessment, Schmidt—citing, of all people, the Mexican patriot Lorenzo de Zavala—insists that Mexico is "not yet ready for the establishment of republican institutions." Racial diversity and ancient feudal privilege have left Mexican citizens unable to "[suppress] and [control] . . . individual passions," making it impossible for each citizen to "sustain his part in the administration of the affairs of the nation."³³ Under such social conditions, Schmidt concludes, it will be impossible for Mexicans to produce "professional men, merchants, mechanics, farmers and planters," those classes that have allowed the United States to "[advance] with giant strides in the path of knowledge and civilization."³⁴

Prescott and Schmidt were not alone in their fears of the mysterious, dormant racial forces Polk's war might awaken. In the wake of postromantic thought that bundled race, nation, and historical destiny together with the "scientific racism" of Philadelphian Samuel George Morton and South Carolinian Josiah C. Nott, connecting racial intermixture to national decline would have struck readers as a clever application of cutting edge scientific thought.[35] Lingering behind these scientific claims is, as is so often the case, an unspoken set of economic assumptions, however. The effect of arguments such as Prescott and Schmidt's was to support northern European superiority with an eye toward positing industrial, not colonial, origins for Western capitalism.[36] The businessmen, planters, and professionals that Schmidt calls the catalysts of U.S. progress share no connection to the feudal aristocracy in Spain's former colonies. And yet the gold they extracted from Mexico's first peoples was still there, waiting for industrious Americans to make good on its wasted potential.

The idea that Spain had no role in the development capitalist modernity denies a crucial historical fact: the New World gold that flowed out of Spain during the sixteenth and seventeenth centuries led to a "price revolution" in the rest of Europe, paving the way for the birth of modern capitalism in the Protestant countries.[37] During capitalism's childhood in the fifteenth century, gold was just one of many commodities accepted as payment for services and goods; its exceptional status as the basis of capitalist exchange was not inevitable or natural. Pierre Vilar notes that, before the sixteenth century, "gold was a commodity, and another commodity was Tabasco pepper (*mereghera, manegata*). Payment was sometimes denominated 'in gold and Tabasco.'"[38] Gold became the commodity of commodities because there was so much of it, a direct effect of colonial activity in the Americas and Africa. Economic and political history therefore lend some credence to the declensionist view of Spanish history "M.R." channels: Spain *was* barbarous in its treatment of native people, and the Spanish monarchy *did* struggle to enter the kind of political modernity we find in other European nations—hence the series of abdications that characterized Carlos V's rule and fed the image of the king as an enfeebled madman. Nevertheless, the story that a combination of Dutch mercantilism, English technical ingenuity, and U.S. entrepreneurship led to the growth of global capitalism ignores the importance of Spanish gold, as well as the feudal hierarchies that made the extraction of that gold possible in the colonies.[39] Capitalism is, from its very origins, bound up with indigenous displacement, genocide, and enslavement. This is the "secret of primitive accumulation" with which Marx ends the first volume of *Capital*. It's a historical actuality that nineteenth-century writing often ignores and that many still find difficult to admit.[40] Spain was a reliable scapegoat for western and northern European nations and their progeny in the United States. Having done the dirty work of extracting the gold that led to the "price revolution," Spain could now be written out of the history of the enlightened world, and the gold mined by indigenous Americans that was so crucial to capitalist development could be reimagined as the deferred birthright of America's lowly volunteer soldiers.

No less than their Old World counterparts, Americans sought to distance their tactics from those of fifteenth- and sixteenth-century Spain, even as the nation replicated many of those methods (conquest, indigenous genocide, rapacious mineral extraction) in western and southern North America. The aforementioned liberal myth of capitalist development was a key factor in this regard. As I've demonstrated, nineteenth-century Americans—historians, literary lights, and politicians alike—were on the whole loath to admit that their founders, no less than those of French and Spanish colonies, relied on feudal hierarchies and land laws in the New World.

An example from Prescott's *History of the Conquest of Mexico* will demonstrate this point. In a long footnote to his brief account of the papal Bulls of Donation (1493) that Spain used to justify conquest, Prescott contrasts the first Puritan colonies with Spain's through the language of political economy. The Puritans did not avail themselves of legal trickery as the Spanish did, but, according to Prescott, "established their title to the soil by fair purchase of the Aborigines; thus forming an honorable contrast to the policy pursued by too many of the settlers on the American continents."[41] Prescott's story of the founding of Anglo-America renders devious land grabs and outright wars as reasonable capitalist exchanges of currency for Indian lands. Waddy Thompson lays out a similar juxtaposition in *Recollections of Mexico*, arguing that while Mexico's first settlers were "the nobles spirits of Spain in her Augustan age" and Massachusetts's first settlers were "poor pilgrims... who carried with them nothing but their own hardy virtues," the former colony has languished while the latter stands triumphant: "In everything which makes a people great, there is not in the world, and there never was in the world, such a commonwealth as Massachusetts. 'There she is! look at her!'—'and Mexico.'"[42]

"And Mexico." It's as if Thompson is cussing; I imagine him spitting out the nation's name in disgust. Rendering a whole nation and its people a by-word was essential in laying an ideological groundwork for the conquest of western lands. If the enemy is of a foreign faith, a citizen of a foreign land, and of indeterminate racial origin to boot, then any violence against them can be imagined as a march forward, not a retrenchment in well-worn modes of conquest and exploitation.

The unique histories of Mexican and South American indigenous groups made the problem even more difficult. Whereas North American indigenous communities were written out of history books as having not yet attained civilization as the West understood it, the Aztec in Nueva España and Inca in Peru were viewed as rival sovereignties that threatened the supposed legitimacy of European expansion. Prescott is again useful here: in his *History of the Conquest of Mexico*, he helps readers distinguish civilized Mesoamericans from their tribal North American counterparts. In the Aztec, he writes, "we find no resemblance to the other races of North American Indians."[43] The Aztec and Inca empires developed complex legal and religious systems; built infrastructure, including roads and ceremonial sites; and maintained strong hereditary monarchies with centralizing tendencies not unlike those of early modern Europe. Gustavus Schmidt, who wrote with such force against supposed Spanish backwardness, offers qualified praise of Aztec ingenuity: "The knowledge we possess of the ancient Aztecs . . . proves, beyond the possibility of a doubt, that they had made considerable progress not only in agriculture and the mechanical arts, but that they cultivated successfully some of the fine arts, and were acquainted with the science of government."[44] Prescott's and Schmidt's assessments of the Aztec sum up American and European thought on indigenous people in the Americas: South American and Mesoamerican *indios* were believed to have civilization, while North American Indians were not.[45]

Anglo-Americans therefore found in Mexico a double declension: the motive force behind Spanish decline was greed and violence against indigenous groups, and these indigenous groups had likewise declined into rootless agents in the west. This double declension has everything to do with race. Spain's colonial policy had encouraged hundreds of years of racial intermixture between Spanish aristocrats and native leaders, making Mexicans a people with "Creole blood" that men such as Prescott feared would corrupt U.S. racial harmony. Despite efforts by the eighteenth-century Bourbon government to regulate colonial bloodlines, Spanish America remained startlingly diverse.[46] For many white Americans of the nineteenth century, no less than for many white Americans of this century, victory for Mexico would have represented a belated victory of brown peoples over white power.

The two types at the heart of this chapter's conclusion—the African slave and the displaced indigenous Mexican—emerge, conjoined, from the imbricated histories of conquest, capital accumulation, and social organization sketched above. Literary scholar Joselyn Almeida-Beveridge usefully describes a series of "symbolic doublings between enslaved Amerindians and Africans" that plays out across American literature.[47] This is both a historical and theoretical observation. Historically, Spain expanded the transatlantic slave trade after the condemnation of indigenous bondage laid down in Las Casa's *Brevísima relación* (1852), a fact Las Casas himself came to regret in his later life.[48] Theoretically, the African slave and the Amerindian both trouble the Enlightenment ideas that were used to justify the continental empire of the United States. As Chickasaw cultural theorist Jodi Byrd puts it, there is a black irony at play in America's self-conception as the telos of Western history, an irony that breeds "the syllogistic traps of participatory democracy born out of the violent occupation of lands."[49] Political historian J. G. A. Pocock likewise asserts that the Enlightenment's fixation on differentiating the "savage" from the "civilized" bred a "deeply reactionary" modernity, one "aimed at relegating half of the planet to an alien and alienated universe."[50]

Yet, try as they might, white Europeans could never entirely abrogate the sovereignty of slaves and first peoples. Byrd notes that recognizing indigenous subject's survival in the face of genocide upsets the systems of thought and governance derived from Europe's expansionist projects: when a settler project such as that championed by U.S.-Mexican War boosters "confronts, approaches, touches, or encounters Indianness, it also confronts the colonialist project that has made that flow possible.... Not being prepared to disrupt the logics of settler colonialism necessary for the terra nullius through which to wander, the entire system either freezes or reboots."[51] Byrd's formula makes plain the logic of Ridge and Melville's novellas. In both works, the presence of the non-European—the Amerindian and African slave, taken as "symbolic doubles" of one another—"disrupts the logics of settler colonialism, forcing readers to reconsider their nation's origins and expansion.

As we've seen, Anglo-American political thinkers, poets, authors, and journalists deflected the structural inequalities and acts of force that led to their nation's founding and expansion by projecting these crimes onto Spain and its colonies. This created a binary scheme wherein a white, Anglo-Saxon,

Protestant, and capitalist United States stood against a miscegenated, Catholic, and feudal Spain. Melville and Ridge register the hypocrisy of Anglo-American views of Spanish empire in their fiction, but they also take the argument further, imagining how resistance to European power might play out in the mid-nineteenth century.

In *The Life and Adventures of Joaquín Murieta*, Ridge "indigenizes" the Mexican bandit by linking his band with Aztec nobles and North American Indians. Melville likewise transforms the Senegalese insurgent Babo and his crew of rebellious slaves (whose ancestries are diverse and largely unidentified) into hybrid figures of African and Amerindian indigeneity. Both Melville and Ridge take creative liberties with the reality of indigenous politics and kinship structures; the facts of indigenous life are subordinated to the literary necessities of each author's allegory. Some of this hybridization is a product of the authors' incomplete knowledge of Native groups in the west. But the slippages also signal a broader problem of imperial knowledge. Simile (e.g., claiming this group of slaves is like that group of Indians, or that the mestizo rancher is a reminder of the Aztec noble) allows Ridge and Melville to describe societies for which their Anglo-American literary context had a rather poor vocabulary. Both texts are thus best understood as structural explorations of the authors' respective views of the relationship between Western civilization and indigenous civilizations. That Babo and Joaquín both fail—and fail spectacularly—in their insurgent enterprises shows us how, only seventy-some years after declaring independence from the Old World, America's political vision had already begun to ossify around a set of assumptions that made imagining resistance to Anglo-American dominance difficult.

THE LIFE AND ADVENTURES OF JOAQUÍN MURIETA: ARISTOCRATIC REVOLT

The Life and Adventures of Joaquín Murieta questions the optimistic, liberal vision of U.S. imperialism. Ridge's Yankees are not reasonable men who barter with indigenous peoples or the old Mexican landholders but claim jumpers and murderers. Describing California, Ridge writes, "The country was then full of lawless and desperate men, who bore the name of Americans but failed to support the honor and dignity of the title" (*JM*, 9). The Mexicans in California are "no better than conquered subjects of the United States, having no rights which could stand before a haughtier and superior race" (9).

These assessments precede the graphic description of the murder of Murieta's family and the rape of his wife, acts Murieta is forced to watch while "tied . . . hand and foot" (10). Ridge draws the reader's attention to Murieta's finer qualities—the "old chivalrous spirit of his Spanish ancestry," his admirable treatment of women ("I have a higher purpose in view than to torture innocent females"), and his leadership skills (at one point Murieta boasts that he is "at the head of an organization . . . of two thousand men")—in order to highlight the comparative baseness of his Yankee tormentors (10, 105, 74). The exceptional depravity of Murieta's American attackers and the list of political abuses that precede the rape would have struck many nineteenth-century readers as a repudiation of rhetoric that posited the United States as a beacon of industry and order. The violent conquest portrayed in *Joaquín Murieta* offers a counternarrative to manifest destiny in that it asks readers to consider whether democracy, enlightenment, and economic development can truly bring peace when they are enforced at the barrel of a gun.

Murieta spends the bulk of Ridge's short novel in a Dantean mode, inflicting contrapuntal punishments against any and all Yankees. If his people are to be displaced, abused, and murdered—the "original sins" of manifest destiny and westward expansion—then Murieta will give back as good as he gets. But Ridge is uncomfortable following this line of thought too far down the road to revolutionary action. Instead of upending the economic and social status quo, Murieta aims to secure a comfortable life for himself: "I intend to kill the Americans by 'wholesale,' burn their ranchos, and run off their property at one single swoop so rapidly that they will not have time to collect an opposing force before I will have finished the work and found safety in the mountains of Sonora. When I do this, I shall wind up my career. My brothers, we will then be revenged for our wrongs, and some little, too, for the wrongs of our poor, bleeding country. We will divide up our substance and spend the rest of our days in peace" (*JM*, 75). Like a feudal lord, Murieta gathers men around him, plunders and occupies territory, and then rewards his vassals with riches and protection. As much as Murieta may represent the resurgence of a defiant indigenous spirit, he also represents the survival of the feudal, chivalric tradition in the capitalist west. As Rosalie reminds Murieta's Anglo captive Edward, it doesn't matter much whether Murieta "were a robber a thousand times, he is a noble man" (108). The meaning here is clearly that Murieta is a man of noble qualities and so deserves Edward's deference, but I doubt that the echo between "noble man" and "nobleman" is accidental. Joaquín is more than a protocapitalist engaged in a particularly bloody act of primitive accumulation: he is a nascent lord determined to establish a domain.

While it may seem like a stretch to compare the piratical Murieta to a feudal knight or lord, the exchange with Rosalie is not the only time Ridge connects Murieta and his band to the chivalric past. Three-Fingered Jack, for instance, is praised for his masterful equestrianism: "No one but a powerful man could have rode him; but Three-Fingered Jack, with a fine Mexican saddle (the best in the world) fastened securely with a broad girth made of horse hair as strong as a band of iron, and curbing him with a huge Spanish bit . . . managed the royal animal with ease" (84). Ridge's adjectives color his description of Three-Fingered Jack and his horse in chivalric terms. The Mexican saddle is "fine," implying refinement and aesthetic harmony; the "Spanish bit" connects both horse and rider to the chivalric tradition of the conquistadores; and, most important, the horse is "royal," suggesting both the nobility of its rider and an Aristotelian connection between a creature's biological qualities and its class status. Three-Fingered Jack and the other men who follow Murieta on his path of revenge may have noble qualities, but it is only through their leader's "brilliancy and unconquerable will" that they are formed into a political and military body: "After the death of its chief, the mighty organization which he had established was broken up. It exists now only in scattered fragments over California and Mexico" (158). Like the feudal lord, Murieta's presence and leadership give shape to an otherwise fragmentary humanity. Without the strong will of an individual leader, the subordinates sink into obscurity.

There's an inversion of Poe's formula for fiction at work in *The Life and Adventures of Joaquín Murieta*, but it is an inversion with a crucial difference. Whereas in Poe's stories the collapse of well-ordered aristocratic domains tends to unleash racialized antagonists, in Ridge's novel the preternaturally noble Joaquín himself becomes the antagonist after his own nascent fiefdom collapses. For the Yankees, Murieta is a Hop-Frog type, avenging a profound insult to his honor with sheer brutality; for Murieta, the Yankees are the imps, demonic forces that must be purged if he is to establish a harmonious, peaceful kingdom with his men. Were it not for Ridge's selective antiracism (we should remember that despite his insistence that "prejudice of color" leads to injustice, Ridge treats Chinese characters with a flippant brutality, and Ridge's prose delights in the details of Chinese victims begging for their lives and dying en masse), the dynamics of *The Life and Adventures of Joaquín Murieta* would be wholly consistent with those of Poe's work. This isn't terribly surprising when we consider some key details of Ridge's biography. It's known that he traveled west from Arkansas with a slave whom he mortgaged to fund his travels. And, in his essay on the North American Indian, Ridge notes that the Indian tribes he encountered in Arkansas—descendants, he argues, of both Mezoamerican indigenous peoples and the Appalachian Indians—are "civilized" because they hold and sell African slaves.[52]

Yet Ridge's emphasis on Joaquín's indigeneity troubles any easy readings of even this pro-aristocratic aspect of the novel. Ridge is rightly appalled by the treatment his people have received at the hands of white Americans who refused to recognize native sovereignty. By articulating indigenous sovereignty through the language of chivalry and nobility, Ridge attempts to make Joaquín not only a figure of admiration, but also a means by which to demonstrate the contradictions in Anglo-America's own chivalric self-conception. While Anglo-Americans believe themselves to be the vanguard of a new humanity who will be born on the western plains and in the western mountains, the Ridge of *The Life and Adventures of Joaquín Murieta* suggests that their nobility is sullied by rapacity and bloodthirstiness.

Elsewhere in his writings, Ridge's opinion of California settlers is much more ambiguous than it is in *Joaquín Murieta*. In the long poem "California" (1861), Ridge praises "the famed and unfamed heroes tried and true,/ Who crowded into months or days the deeds / Of year, and of young empire sow the seeds."[53] Ridge even predicts the emergence of great landowners, "the Pioneers of Pioneers," men he praises with Emersonian exuberance: "Amid the mass there here and there appears/Some reverend head, majestic as a seer's— / Around whose brow the whitening tempests break." The poem concludes with visions of excess: "Still shalt thou lavish, pour thy treasures forth, / Enriching all from thy exhaustless worth; / Still shall thy sons be brave, thy daughters fair, / And Art and Science breathe thy purer air." The lines could have been penned by any number of expansionist boosters during this period; that they come from an author whose own tribe was displaced as part of "young empire's" steady continental expansion is troubling. This is a far cry from the brutal, anarchic vision of California settlement portrayed in *Joaquín Murieta*.

While "California" concludes with the promise of future aesthetic and intellectual triumphs, Ridge's other poems on the subject of global history praise the more quotidian art of agriculture. In an untitled poem originally delivered before an audience at the Agricultural, Horticultural, and Mechanics' Society of the Northern District of California in 1860, Ridge exults agriculture as the necessary precondition for human civilization: "With Agriculture sprang whate'er in Art / Has raised the mind or purified the heart / Whate'er in Science hath exalted man."[54] Ridge here subordinates "Art and Science" to European-style cultivation, effectively writing North American Indians—whose own claims to land had so often been abrogated precisely because they had not cultivated it in a way that was legible to European settlers—out of global history. Indeed, in another untitled poem on the subject of social development Ridge dismisses native California tribes ("Diggers") as never having strived toward civilization at all: "The dream of greatness never rose / Upon his simple brain."[55] Like most thinkers of his day, Ridge is unable to decouple civilization and cultural achievement from European models.

This does not, however, mean that all the peoples of the ancient Americas have been passed over. Later in the untitled poem delivered before the Mechanics' Society of the Northern District of California, Ridge connects U.S. social development to indigenous development—not to North American Indians, but instead to the Aztec:

> As England was in Alfred's time (The Great),
> So civilized was Montezuma's state,
> And burning bright his fair and peaceful star,
> When Cortez came with red right hand of war.
> Let truth impartial say, if happier now
> Is that historic land, broad Mexico,
> Than when all greenly spread the cultured plain,
> And waved the far Cordilleras with grain,
> And rolled the deep canals, with streams that blest
> A thousand homes in Eden beauty drest,
> And all the realm from mountain slope to main,
> Was fair Montezuma's golden reign?
> Was art, that built those cities vast, less art,
> Because of Aztec genius 'twas a part?
> Was patient toil, that led thro' channels deep
> And aqueducts, and 'long the rocky steep,
> The streams a thousand fertile fields supplied,

> Less toil, because no white man's arm was tried?
> Were peace and plenty but the Spaniard's right?
> The Aztec *barbarous* because not *white?*

Ridge's call for racial equality is nested within an evolutionary social vision that praises indigenous groups only inasmuch as they have developed along lines continuous with European civilization. The evocation of Ælfræd (871–899) further complicates Ridge's view of Western historical development. In English history, Ælfræd is famed for turning back a series of Danish incursions on British soil. Connecting the Aztec to Ælfræd, Ridge likewise connects Cortez and his men to the Danes—the difference being that the Spanish were Danes who were victorious in their raid. It's a strange move for Ridge, who in his own essay on "The North American Indians" published two years later in the *Hesperian* insists that facile comparisons of indigenous Americans to other cultures would lead to "a complete mystification of the spectator" seeking information of indigenous life.[56] In that same 1862 essay, Ridge elaborates on the historical view of Mexican civilization that informs his exultation of the Aztec. Ridge praises "the indigenous antique civilization of the Mexique races" for their accomplishments "in agriculture, in weaving, in painting, in general manufactures, and in various of the arts of peace." Yet these same civilizing tendencies made the indigenous Mexicans weak in arms: "The effect of this civilization seemed to be to diminish their physical courage and to abate their warlike spirit; and they fell an easy prey to their Spanish conquerors." According to Ridge, the tribes who migrated north were reindigenized, reclaiming "their physical courage and warlike spirit" and becoming "the noblest specimens of the rude and savage man—the man nearest to nature in his deeds and aspirations."[57] Civilization emasculated the Aztec while war and migration emboldened their northern ancestors.

Mapping Ridge's idiosyncratic assessment of Aztec social development after Spanish conquest onto *The Life and Adventures of Joaquín Murieta* complicates the novel's seeming pro-aristocratic thrust. Joaquín is a racially liminal figure, "some metaphoric fusion of Mexican and native populations."[58] Ridge writes as much in his initial description of Murieta: "If the proud blood of the Castilians mounted to the cheek of a partial descendant of the Mexiques, showing that he had inherited the old chivalrous spirit of his Spanish ancestry, they looked upon it as saucy presumption" (9). Stressing Murieta's racial indeterminacy is both a moment of realism and an important symbolic turn. Like the ancestors of the "Mexique" Ridge describes in his 1862 essay, Murieta regains his "physical courage and warlike spirit" after migrating north from Mexico. Ridge may have settled on the real-life Joaquín as main character for his only work of fiction precisely because it mapped so well onto his historical vision of Aztec displacement and eventual reindigenization. Murieta's gang is, as Rifkin points out, organized along tribal lines: Murieta is "described as a 'chief' or 'chieftain,' indicating his leadership and his person. Additionally, the bandits often sound a 'loud whoop' or a 'whoop of defiance' to signal their identity to Anglos and to each other." Passing through the crucible of Yankee settler violence, Murieta and his men reclaim an indigenous spirit that has been suppressed by centuries of Spanish colonialism. The gang's rough organization allows them to gather and disperse with ease, and their comfort in "a range inhabited only by humans savages and savage beasts" guarantees their safety for a time (*JM*, 26).

Murieta is a more complicated figure, then, than he may have appeared at first blush. Ridge places Murieta—and his progenitor, the Aztec noble—in relation to the narrative arc of Anglo-American history. Murieta is "the Rinaldo Rinaldini of California," a reference to Christian August Vulpius's *Rinaldo Rinaldini, the Robber Captain* (1797), which tells the Robin Hood-like story of an Italian nobleman forced into a life of crime by circumstance (*JM*, 1). Further, Murieta himself ought by rights to be something like a feudal lord—the poet-genius who commands a small military force and establishes a domain for himself and those who pledged fealty to him. And finally he is like Ælfræd, an Anglo-Saxon, holding back an assault against his tribe, and thus of a piece with both Walter Scott's pre-Norman Invasion English romances and the dominant political and historiographical idea that Anglo-Saxons enjoyed a primitive liberty and constitutionality that stood in contraposition to Norman feudal hierarchies.

Joaquín's beheading at the end of the novel is thus loaded with symbolic meaning. In the sequences leading up to Joaquín's capture, Ridge insists that we recall the "formidable chief's" noble qualities (140). During the final pursuit, one of Murieta's captors darkly intones, "There is a Mexican above us"—a straightforward spatial description that nonetheless signals the Anglo's fear that this particular Mexican and his well-trained gang may upend the system of racial hierarchies that the new U.S. law seeks to impose (119). Once shot down by Capt. Harry Love, Joaquín is beheaded, a symbol of his group's final, bloody capitulation to Anglo law: "[Capt. Love] . . . acted as he would not otherwise have done; and I must shock the nerves of the fastidious, much against my will, by stating that he caused the head of the renowned Murieta to be cut off and to be hurried away with the utmost expedition to the nearest place, one hundred and fifty miles, at which any alcohol could be obtained in which to preserve it" (155–156).

Beheading, in literature as in life, provides an occasion to consider the nature of sovereignty, leadership, and power. Beheading is most commonly associated with English judicial practice, a longstanding tradition that began with William the Conqueror's beheading of Waltheof, Earl of Northumberland, in 1076.[59] Prior to the advent of the time-saving guillotine during the French Revolution, beheading was a highly individual form of execution: an appropriately artisanal end to the life of a nobleman. The executioner sharpens the axe, presents the victim, and severs the head from the body—it is death as the private ceremony of noble capitulation to monarchical prerogatives, not as the public snuffing out of a social problem. A Burkean element suffuses this form of execution. The nobility's instrumental role in rituals of social formation is honored by leaving the head intact, and its high station is honored by holding the execution in private, in the tower. In death by hanging the executioner strangles the breath and therefore the voice out of the criminal, whose hooded and anonymous end in front of the public is directly opposed to the private end of the nobleman's life. Two, three prisoners may be hung at once, but a nobleman's beheading is a bespoke affair.

By posthumously beheading Murieta, Love thus provides posthumous evidence of Murieta's nobility. Earlier in the novel, the American robber Peter Woodbeck and his unnamed partner are hanged, an image that warrants a rare first-person comment from Ridge's narrator: "The time-honored custom of choking a man to death was soon put into practice, and the robber stood on nothing, kicking at empty space. Bah! It is a sight that I never like to see, although I have been civilized for a good many years" (138). Ridge's ironic use of "civilized" here points to the bare violence underwriting the niceties of Anglo law: without the threat of death by hanging, the laws would not function as repressive apparatuses. Murieta is spared this ignoble fate.

Posthumous decapitation is undoubtedly a strange way of signaling nobility, implying a retroactive celebration of the dead's virtues, which were ignored or distorted into vices during conflict. But the retroactive nobility bestowed on Murieta in death is an apt metaphor for nineteenth-century Anglo-American attitudes toward Indian nations such as the Cherokee, who were treated barbarously over centuries of conquest and yet by the mid-nineteenth century had become objects of romantic fetishization for the nation's leading literary authors. The facts of the real Murieta's beheading, and the subsequent traveling display of his head around the west, are not mythical; literary critic Erica Stevens has recently undertaken exhaustive work to recover this gruesome episode in U.S. history.[60] Given that Ridge's novel is based on (loosely interpreted) historical fact, it isn't correct to say that the author "invented" the metaphor of Murieta's posthumous beheading to make a political point about indigenous sovereignty in his own time. Instead, Ridge discovered a metaphor in the historical record. He found, in the story of Murieta's criminal activities and the subsequent mythologizing of Murieta as the "Robin Hood of California," a process the novella itself takes part in. In life, Murieta poses a threat to Anglo sovereignty and settlement; in death, he is granted nobility and becomes a public spectacle, a reminder of the power Anglo authority tasked itself with upsetting in the west.

BENITO CERENO: RACE AND REVOLUTION

Babo, the insurgent at the heart of Melville's *Benito Cereno*, also suffers a beheading, but one that signals a different and, I will argue, more complex understanding of sovereignty, history, and non-European resistance to Anglo hegemony. While the major subject of *Benito Cereno* is the potential for slave insurrection in the Americas, the novella is also a palimpsest of ongoing histories of indigenous displacement and resistance in the hemisphere. By metaphorically linking Babo and his fellow slaves to Inca peoples displaced by Spanish conquistadores in the sixteenth century, Melville dramatizes the methods by which discrete populations were stripped of sovereignty, reduced to servitude, and assigned to an "alien and alienated universe" apart from enlightened civilization. Babo's beheading represents a final stripping of the slave's sovereignty, even as it points toward a messianic return of non-European power in the hemisphere.

The politics of *Benito Cereno* are best understood through Melville's career-long fascination with indigenous peoples and their social orders. Doing so helps us avoid a sort of interpretative trap Melville sets in the novella, a pervasive "*either/or* structure" that pits Spain against the United States, white against black, and history against the present.[61] Falling into this trap leads to inadvertently reductive readings of the work; *Benito Cereno* either becomes a racist proslavery fable *or* as a white author's pessimistic riff on the prospects of a slave revolution.[62] Yet recognizing the deep structural relationship between indigenous displacement and African chattel bondage that began in the Spanish Americas in the sixteenth century—and then later between the "Indian" and the "African" as discreet racial categories—can help us disentangle the knotted strands of Melville's critique of European colonialism in the novella. Despite the seeming either/or pattern of images and allusions in the novella, Melville does not take racial, national, and historical categories in isolation from one another. Instead, he views them as part of a global dialectical process, each category playing a central role in constructing the others.

Our desire to reduce *Benito Cereno* to a "Manichean allegory" of U.S. race relations, to use Dana D. Nelson's phrase, reflects a tendency for U.S. thinkers to trace racial difference along an African/Western European divide. There is a tendency to elide those elements of U.S. history that are intermixed and indeterminate in favor of moral allegories of decline, resistance, and eventual triumph that reaffirm a certain progressive view. The "either/or structure" is not just racial, but also moral, economic, and political—the central plank of a variety of U.S. exceptionalism that sees the nation as uniquely capable of cutting Gordian knots that have baffled other historic world empires. This same line in U.S. social thinking has prevented us from seeing the traces of feudal law and tradition that helped maintain liberalism as a cultural and political force. Reading *Benito Cereno* as a chronicle of failed revolt, as a text unable to escape the racist and dualistic world it portrays so vividly, or as the drama of "Young America" versus Old Spain is likewise symptomatic of this approach. We ask, "How could the great American author not come to a solution here, how could he so spectacularly fail to theorize a path toward slave revolt that would lead to eventual victory and liberation?" Our own insecurities regarding the historical failures of the U.S. political project are mapped on to Melville's novella. But this is falling right into Melville's trap; a dialectical reading of *Benito Cereno* reveals a work that does its very best to resist such pat assessments of political engagement and social change.

In terms of the broad political sweep of Melville's novella, I find Eric Sundquist's argument in *Empire and Slavery in American Literature 1820–1865* (1994) to be the most useful analysis. Sundquist argues that *Benito Cereno* was written against the backdrop of the Compromise of 1850, the legislation "which in part defined American policy in the territory acquired in the Mexican War." Read this way, the struggle onboard the *San Dominick* "anticipates

... a struggle among three forces: a Protestant, Puritan tradition of democratic liberty deriving from the American Revolution; a Hispanic, Catholic world of slaveholding and despotism based on the dying monarchical values of Europe; and a black world of rebellion driving a wedge between the others."[63] Sundquist's depiction of the social forces at work in *Benito Cereno* accurately reflects how nineteenth-century Americans viewed their errand in the post-Mexican War west. As we've seen, the Mexican War was powered by profound fears concerning the inability of the Spanish Americas to prevent racial intermixture and indigenous rebellion on the continent. While Sundquist's reading highlights the former while only hinting at the latter, his triangulation of the social forces at work in *Benito Cereno* is a useful model for understanding the deep structure of Melville's allegory.

The foundation of Melville's allegory is a stinging critique of colonialism and indigenous displacement. This should not surprise the astute reader of Melville; he ground an axe against imperialism and indigenous displacement throughout his literary career, beginning with his condemnation of the colonization of the Polynesian Islands in *Typee* (1846). There's little ambiguity in Melville's early description of "rapacious hordes of enlightened individuals who settle themselves" within "the depopulated land" of the Polynesian islands, rendering the indigenous population "an interloper in the country of [their] fathers."[64] Melville repeated this criticism throughout his brief public career. In his final novel, *The Confidence Man: His Masquerade* (1857), the only characters who can temporarily halt the herb doctor's elaborate ruse are the "dusk giant" and his "perhaps Creole, or even Camanche" daughter, spectral evocations of the human costs of imperial expansion.[65] For Melville, Western modernity's great crime was the attempted erasure of first peoples from the globe.

This theme is elaborated on at length in *Benito Cereno*. Melville signals the novella's investment in the question of indigenous displacement early on, describing the sun peeking through "low, creeping clouds" as "not unlike a Lima intriguante's one sinister eye peering across the Plaza from the Indian loop-hole of her dusk *santa-y-manta*" (36). Later, when Babo props up Don Benito after one of his many fainting spells, Melville again evokes the image of an all-seeing eye: "The black with one arm still encircled his master, at the same time keeping his eye fixed on his face, as if to watch for the first sign of complete restoration, or relapse" (44). Babo's fixed eye (singular) draws the reader back to the "Lima intriguante" of the earlier passage, both foreshadowing the revelation of Babo's own intrigue. These brief allusions, combined with the "savageness" of the slaves onboard Cereno's ship—a "savageness" that at once frightens Delano and offers him instances of "naked nature . . . pure tenderness and love" (61)—make Babo and his coconspirators represent not only West African slaves, but also the indigenous peoples of the New World. Melville explicitly identifies Babo with indigeneity later, in a brief aside between Cereno and Delano:

> "For it were strange, indeed, and not very creditable to us white-skins, if a little of our blood mixed with the African's, should, far from improving the latter's quality, have the sad effect of pouring vitriolic acid into black broth; improving the hue, perhaps, but not the wholesomeness."
>
> "Doubtless, doubtless, Señor, but"—glancing at Babo—"not to speak of negroes, your planter's remark I have heard applied to the Spanish and Indian intermixtures in our provinces. But I know nothing about the matter," he listlessly added. (76)

Melville underscores the importance of the exchange by cutting it short: "And here they entered the cabin" (76). The abrupt shift calls to mind the arbitrary lines that define the U.S. racial imaginary. The contrived, awkward transitions—their literary effect similar to that of an abrupt edit in a film—jars the reader with their artificiality, disrupting Don Benito's brief moment of dialectical insight into the nature of race in the western hemisphere. Melville's narrators cannot arrive at the multivalent understanding of race and sovereignty that Babo represents. Thus, the association of Babo with indigeneity and slavery with indigenous displacement is allegorized through the novel's action, not formal exchanges between the two men at its center. In terms of his literary craft, this is one of the *Benito Cereno*'s more quietly revolutionary and experimental moments. While not as flashy as the formal heterodoxy of the novella's second half, this syntactical hard cut demonstrates that revolutionary action by the subaltern, rather than stoic discourse between two wealthy Europeans, has the power to reveal the ideological infrastructure that upholds U.S. politics.

Melville satirizes the guileless Amasa Delano and his simplistic view of the world by putting the Yankee captain face to face with reminders of the foundational barbarity that has made his own country's progress possible. There's even a brief, telling allusion to U.S. westward expansion: in a rare reflective moment, as Delano looks out at the sea, the Yankee feels "rising a dreamy inquietude, like that of one who alone on the prairie feels unrest from the repose of the noon" (61). Looking over the ship's "carved balustrade," Delano imagines that the ship looks like "the charred ruin of some summer-house in a grand garden long running to waste," a reminder that his own nation's imperial project in the "grand garden" of the West will inevitably fall someday to ruin. Babo attempts to teach Don Benito this same lesson about imperial rise and decline at the beginning of the insurrection:

> *At sunrise, the deponent coming on deck, the negro Babo showed him a skeleton, which had been substituted for the ship's proper figure-head—the image of Christopher Colon, the discoverer of the New World; that the negro Babo asked him whose skeleton that was, and whether, from its whiteness, he should not think it a white's; that, upon discovering his face, the negro Babo, coming close, said words to this effect: "Keep faith with the blacks from here to Senegal, or you shall in spirit, as now in body, follow your leader," pointing to the prow.* (BC, 93, emphasis in original)

Babo's message is clear: Columbus may well have been successful in his efforts to depopulate the hemisphere and reduce its remaining inhabitants to slavery and dependency, but Don Benito will not do the same to Babo and his peers. Given Babo's over-the-top performance as the obsequious serf—his carefully attending to every change in Don Benito's demeanor, his endless deference and politeness to Delano, his impeccable deployment of the language of obedience—this moment is grimly comic. Babo has, to put it bluntly, "killed them with kindness." Throughout the charade leading up to the revolt, Babo "followed his leader" in body but not in spirit. Babo points to the skeleton lashed to Columbus to signal both the cleverness of his own charade and the blindness of Don Benito's—not to mention Delano's—imperial ambitions. If set at night, the scene would be plainly chilling. But setting it at sunrise offers a sense of hope and renewal, a new day of resistance against the allied imperial powers of Europe, setting Babo up as a redeemer figure who will overcome histories of displacement and brutality through organized resistance backed by the lingering threat of violence.

"Killing them with kindness" works well for a while, but, finally, force is required to wrench the new world from the cold grip of the old. Babo's masquerade ends with a sea battle that finds Melville imagining what shape an actual armed uprising of non-European actors might take. It is a living picture of Melville's ideas about sovereignty and political action. The sequence begins with a moment of temporal disjunction: "All this, with what preceded, and what followed, occurred with such involutions of rapidity, that past, present, and future seemed one" (733). The resonance between "involution" and "revolution"—the former a complication caused by an inward turn, the other a process of violent political change through a turnover of political power—complicates the action that follows. In this sentence, "involutions of rapidity" implies that the political systems represented onboard the *San Dominick* are in a process of internal struggle that will lead to an unexpected new arrangement of things. But which political system is past, which is present, and which is future? In the novella so far, Spain has stood for the decaying past (it lost control of the ship), the rebellious slaves for the present (they have taken control of this ship), and the United States for the future (soon it will have seized the ship from the slaves). There is thus a thematic resonance between Melville's *San Dominick* and the gothic U.S.-Mexico border as imagined by his contemporaries—Spanish power has ruined it, non-European power haunts it, and American power will redeem it. But, by telescoping historical time in this sentence, Melville upsets such a simple, progressive view of social development. The dominant, emergent, and residual all arise as coeval forces in the moment of political conflict. This temporal anarchy is a product of processes inherent to colonization; the "involutions of rapidity" with which conflicting timelines subsume, replace, or contain one another is produced by the on-the-ground facts of conquest and colonial struggle.

Before the battle begins, it is unclear whether Spanish feudalism or the slaves' semi-indigenous polity, both "residual" forces when compared to emergent U.S. liberalism, will claim victory. Melville thus points toward a politics whereby past modes of life may prove viable alternatives to present social arrangements. Accordingly, the battle between the allied powers of Spain and the United States and the various African tribes that Babo gathers together is not portrayed as a police action (the quashing of a civil rebellion), but instead a battle between equal forces. Melville is careful to characterize Babo's army as canny soldiers, not hasty rebels: "The negroes giving too hot a reception, the whites kept a more respectful distance. Hovering now just out of reach of the hurtling hatchets, they, with a view to the close encounter which must soon come, sought to decoy the blacks into entirely disarming themselves of their most murderous weapons in a hand-to-hand fight, by foolishly flinging them, as missiles, short of the mark, into the sea. But ere long perceiving the stratagem, the negroes desisted"(736). Melville's departure from his source here is telling. In his *Narrative*, Amasa Delano describes the slaves as having "defended themselves with a desperate courage."[66] This is the entirety of Delano's impression, and, while further details emerge in the court documents that both Delano and Melville append to the end of their narratives, Delano's curt assessment of Babo's rebellion is strikingly different from Melville's involved battle sequence. In *Benito Cereno*, the slaves are desperate to reclaim their freedom, but this desperation breeds intelligent strategic planning, not unthinking reaction. Indeed, that the battle turns toward the European powers is incidental for Melville, the product of a change in the wind and the slaves' lack of access to firearms (*BC*, 737–739).

Some of this difference is undoubtedly a product of the generic demands of the novella form. Whereas Delano's autobiography is meant to be taken as an honest record of one man's travels and his impressions of the world, Melville's novella was written to satisfy the needs of educated magazine readers who would seek both intellectual depth and narrative intrigue. To elide the sea battle in the way Delano does would have been an unwise decision for an author publishing in the popular press of the day. But how Melville describes the battle—as a clash between equal forces wherein one side has a strategic advantage, while the other has a material advantage—speaks as much to his interest in non-European resistance to European hegemony as it does the tastes of his readership.

While Melville spends time describing the sea battle, Delano focuses on its aftermath. In Delano's narrative, the slaves are tortured by the Spaniards ("some of them had part of their bowels hanging out, and some with half their backs and thighs shaved off"), an ongoing act of vengeance that Delano feels compelled to prevent: "I was obliged to be continually vigilant, to prevent them from using violence towards these wretched creatures" (*Narrative*, 328). Melville omits the graphic image presented by Delano, leaning instead on a reference to Scott's *Waverly*: he describes "their wounds—mostly inflicted by the long-edged sealing-spears—[as] resembling those shaven ones of the English at Preston Pans, made by the poled scythes of the Highlanders" (*BC*, 738). The resolutions also differ dramatically. In the *Narrative*, Delano bitterly complains about Bonito Sereno's treatment of him after the rebellion. In Lima, Sereno abuses Delano's men, going so far as to "injure [Delano's] character, so that he might not be obliged to make . . . any compensation" for their assistance (*Narrative*, 329). Delano ends the episode with a bitter statement on his fate: "When I take a retrospective view of my life, I cannot find in my soul, that I have done anything to deserve such misery and ingratitude as I have suffered... from the very persons to whom I have rendered the greatest services" (331). Symbolically, the conclusion of Delano's *Narrative* offers evidence for the declensionist view of Spanish history promulgated by Anglo writers for centuries: Bonito Sereno is untrustworthy, fundamentally corrupt, and incapable of maintaining his own crew. It is, in short, of a piece with the declensionist view of Spanish empire that circulated through nineteenth-century literature and political thought.

Melville's ending likewise leans on aspects of this myth, but does so to a different end. In *Benito Cereno*, Don Benito and Amasa Delano are equally complicit in Babo and his crew's fate, and a true friendship strikes up between them. Benito, "courteous even to the point of religion," calls Delano his "friend," and the novella ends with the two men hashing out the meaning of their recent adventure (753). Delano advises Cereno to forget the rebellion, to be thankful for the natural world and its serene beauty: "The past is passed; why moralize upon it? Forget it. See, yon bright sun has forgotten it all, and the blue sea, and the blue sky; they have turned over new leaves" (754). Delano's attempt at consolation is ironic considering the earlier association between the sun, the Lima intriguante's eye, and Babo's fixed gaze. The past is decidedly *not* passed in this story; Melville himself has chosen to "moralize upon it"; and the natural world, with its daily revolution of sunrise and sunset and the quarterly involutions of the seasons, signal the coming uprising by Babo and his crew. Delano's attempt to comfort his friend does the very opposite: it drives home the metaphor of the sun as harbinger of political change and portends its eventual ascent.

After the interminable depositions that end the novella, Babo is beheaded, and we are left to wonder what Melville means to convey through the slaves' spectacular failure. Even as Babo and his followers strike a blow against slavery, they are also enacting a symbolic revenge for indigenous peoples who were enslaved and exterminated by the Spanish during the first few hundred years of colonialism in the hemisphere. The final image of the novella—Babo's head, "that hive of subtlety," staring across the square in Lima—calls to mind legends of Túpac Amaru, the last native leader of the Inca, whose beheading in 1572 serves a central place in Spanish, U.S., and indigenous histories of the conquest of the Americas. It is also worth noting that, as a descendant of Manco Cápac, founder of the Inka empire, Túpac Amaru would have been a direct descendant of the sun god Inti, Cápac's father. Melville was familiar with this legend, opening his final novel *The Confidence-Man* with the prophetic lines, "At sunrise on the first of April, there appeared, suddenly as Manco Capac at the lake Titicaca, a man in cream-colors" (841). Melville's extended allusion to Amaru "gives voice to the victims of the *auto-da-fé*—to Babo . . . and Túpac Amaru—in the only way a voice from the empire's peaks really can: by letting their silence describe their status."[67]

For many, Babo's beheading and Murieta's beheading may well signal the same end: an assertion of the West's victories over contending social forces and social forms. But this emphasis on the tragedy of Spanish conquest or U.S. imperialism has the contrary effect of monumentalizing historical crimes, etching these crimes in stone and pointing to them as warnings of what empire has done and what it must never do again. Babo points to Columbus on the masthead and gravely intones that Cereno will "follow his leader"; we point to Babo's head on the pike and gravely intone that we must not replicate the crimes of the founders and developers of the United States. But Melville's concluding image is more complex than this. The connection to Túpac Amaru is crucial—but not necessarily for the tragic reasons one might first consider. In Peruvian legend, it is believed that Túpac Amaru will one day return as the "Inkarri," an avenging spirit who will usher in a new era of indigenous rule over the Americas. "According to this myth," writes historian Alberto Flores Galindo, "the Conquest figuratively chopped off the Inca's head and separated it from his body. When head and body are reunited, the period of disorder, confusion, and darkness that Europeans initiated will end."[68] Babo, "a black man's slave . . . who now is the white's" (*BC*, 692), is no Inkarri, but this is perhaps even more powerful: a sign that forces from below have the power to permanently arrest cycles of imperial conquest and decline.

CHAPTER FIVE

Feudalism, Individualism, and Authority in Emerson's Later Works

> Why need we copy the Doric or the Gothic model?
> —Ralph Waldo Emerson, "Self-Reliance" (1841)

> In modern Europe, the Middle Ages were called the Dark Ages. Who dares to call them so now? They are seen to be the feet on which we walk, the eyes with which we see. 'Tis one of our triumphs to have reinstated them.
> —"Progress of Culture" (1867)

The selections above dramatize a shift in the rhetoric of Emerson's Transcendentalism from a rejection of premodern European models to an embrace of them as signifiers of Northern cultural and political hegemony after the Civil War. As Emerson moved away from the liberalism of *Nature* and "Self-Reliance," the dialectical relationship he posited between society and the individual—"all society devolves on the individual, and yet the individual is a mutilated product of society," as John Peacock puts it—gave way to a doctrine of natural aristocracy theorized in *English Traits* (1856), the public addresses published as *The Conduct of Life* (1860), and the Phi Beta Kappa address "Progress of Culture."[1] Emerson found in his voyages to England and his readings in English history a means by which to resolve the central paradox of his view of the individual: a neofeudalism "derive[d] from medieval English history."[2] Emerson's neofeudal vision seeks to establish the well-ordered estate as a model for the country's future leaders. This shift is not unique to Emerson, but instead mirrors a more general trend among other Northern intellectuals at the cultural vanguard of the coming Gilded Age.

My argument concerning Emerson's "feudal turn" proceeds in three stages. First, I demonstrate how Emerson's vision of the individual's relationship to culture shifted by reading 1837's "The American Scholar" against the later

Phi Beta Kappa address "Progress of Culture" and the remaining manuscript fragments of the unpublished lecture "Chivalry." Second, I attempt to account for this shift by illustrating how *English Traits* marks the moment when Emerson shifted from a liberal social vision to one based on a mixed liberal/feudal fusion. Third, I demonstrate that *The Conduct of Life* and the late lectures collected as *The Natural History of Intellect* serve as practical applications of the neofeudalism Emerson theorized in *English Traits*.

Before tracing this neofeudalism through Emerson's texts, I want to return to Robert Ware and Henry Van Brunt's Memorial Hall at Harvard, which I mentioned in the introduction. Emerson's personal involvement in this project demonstrates just how pervasive the neofeudal spirit was in the cultural imaginary of the post–Civil War United States. In the July 18, 1865, morning edition of the *Boston Daily Advertiser*, the proposed Memorial Hall is advertised as part shrine, part auditorium, and part dining hall, a material testament to high national sentiment and Yankee pragmatism. The author of the *Advertiser* article evokes John Trumbull's neoclassical picture gallery at Yale University as an ideal model: a good Enlightenment building—Roman (but not Catholic), severe, and egalitarian.[3] Emerson's letters and journal entries from 1865 to 1870 demonstrate an active interest in all aspects of the hall's funding, development, and design. Emerson even petitions R. W. Barnwell, a Harvard classmate and Confederate champion with close personal ties to Jefferson Davis, to join the effort: "I dare not hope we shall win you this year, the time is so near; but this year completes another *lustrum*, &, as we are summoning our men, I use the occasion to say thus much."[4] Emerson strikes a conciliatory note that mirrors the forgiving tone of many Northerners toward the southern elite during Reconstruction. Emerson's outreach efforts were finally rewarded: in July 1869, John G. Palfrey, former editor of the *North American Review*, reported to the *Daily Advertiser* that Harvard had secured $398,000 toward the construction of Memorial Hall. This sum, in addition to a $40,000 influx from the estate of Harvard's recently deceased Steward, was enough to begin construction.[5]

The building Cambridge finally saw was not pragmatic and neoclassical like Yale's gallery, but instead a soaring gothic cathedral inspired by the writings of John Ruskin. In an 1899 article for the *Harvard Register*, Van Brunt ironically suggests that a more modern building would itself be an anachronism, signaling a complex understanding of how material expressions of cultural mentalities may complicate our sense of history and its uses for the present: "These drawings were made at a time when the fever of the Modern Gothic experiment was at its height.... It would have seemed almost a work of anachronism to have developed this building in any other style."⁶ As a material representation of the Northern antimodern impulse that T. J. Jackson Lears analyzes in his classic *No Place of Grace: Antimodernism and the Transformation of American Culture, 1880–1920* (1981), Memorial Hall makes perfect historical and cultural sense. Even still, it is a bizarre design choice for a memorial to a war that had so often been pitched as a struggle between progressive liberalism in the North and decadent feudalism in the South. This irony was, it seems, lost on Emerson, who in a June 1865 letter to Charles Eliot Norton promises to "assent to [his] decision" regarding the Hall's gothic design (*Letters*, 5:417). Emerson's support of Norton's architectural vision marks a strange moment in the development of U.S. liberalism's cultural imagination: a public champion of "Young America's" liberal self-image, a philosopher who once claimed (quoting Coleridge) that "a Gothic church... is a petrified religion" (*EL*, 30), fundraising for the construction of a Gothic church and arguing that "Gothic architecture... [is] the delight and tuition of [our time]" (*CW*, 7:11).

Northern culture's general drift toward antimodernism and medievalism is nearly unthinkable from the perspective of pre-Civil War Northern ideology, based as it was on assertions of a unique political and cultural destiny for the Americas. As Joyce Appleby puts it, nineteenth-century thinkers transformed the United States from "an insignificant country of several million people, three thousand miles from any major civilization" into what they saw as the vanguard of humanity's collective destiny by celebrating "their success in establishing free institutions" that starkly differed from similar institutions in Europe.⁷ To complicate the matter further, U.S. liberalism had since at least Jefferson posited tribal, Anglo-Saxon origins for its social institutions over and against tyrannical, hierarchical Norman feudalism. Even abolitionists evoked the specter of feudal Normans enslaving and selling free Anglo-Saxons as an inducement for whites to support the end of slavery.⁸ The ideological and representative apparatuses of nineteenth-century liberalism were fundamentally opposed to the "universal cult" of medievalist nostalgia that swept the Anglo world as in these decades. And yet Memorial Hall still rises over Cambridge, enshrining the world-historical victory of the Northern liberal state by casting a gothic shadow across the nation's future.

Emerson's involvement in the Memorial Hall project exemplifies the many ways that medievalism influenced his later life and thought. As with so many of his contemporaries, Emerson's medievalism was the cultural and aesthetic expression of a neofeudal economic outlook based on a volatile synthesis of biological determinist doctrines with an ossifying class structure.[9] While similar themes of authority and submission circulated through Emerson's early works, I will stay focused on the later texts as they are in themselves and within their own contexts, not as the omega to the earlier Transcendentalism's alpha.[10] I am not proposing a long-form genetic fallacy that would seek out authoritarian tendencies in the early Transcendentalist works and then forward project them onto the works of the later period, but am instead attempting to show how, of the many possible developments latent within the young Emerson's Transcendentalism, an authoritarian tendency won out.

TRANSCENDENTALIST SCHOLAR TO CORPORATE NOBLE: "THE AMERICAN SCHOLAR" AND "PROGRESS OF CULTURE"

Emerson wrote in an 1866 journal entry that he had taught "one doctrine" throughout his career: "the infinitude of the private man."[11] Emerson's readers have tended to follow the claim put forward in that journal entry, holding that the central tenet of "Emersonian self-reliance" persists unchanged in his writing well after the initial fever for his ideas during the height of what Irving Howe calls the revolutionary intellectual "newness" of the 1840s.[12] Throughout this period, Emerson articulated his vision of the "private man" through the rhetoric of self-reliance and liberal political economy.[13] During and after the Civil War, as the centers of U.S. intellectual life shifted from public lyceums to cultural review in magazines and university-based lecture series, Emerson's career evolved. This period saw Emerson's popularity peak: *English Traits* (1856) was his most successful publication in the United States, and regular articles in the *Atlantic Monthly* (beginning with its first issue in 1857) and Charles Eliot Norton's *North American Review* (beginning in 1865) kept him very much in the public spotlight.[14]

Narrating Emerson's public career in this way, we're left with a seeming contradiction. If we accept Emerson's contention in the 1866 journal entry that he consistently taught "the doctrine" of "the infinitude of the private man," then it's hard to argue that there isn't a single, overarching thrust to the development of his thought. But "the private man" in Emerson is a multifaceted figure, one that adapts to its times in some ways and resists them in others. Emerson's "private man" in the "liberal years" of *Nature*, "Self-Reliance," and "The American Scholar" is markedly different from the "private man" of what I will call Emerson's "feudal years," the period that produced *English Traits*, *The Conduct of Life*, and the other works I will take up in my argument here. As Anglo-American culture came to use medievalism and feudalism as more than dismissive terms for retrograde political beliefs, Emerson adapted his "private man" to embrace elements of feudal hierarchy.

I see this shift most clearly in two addresses delivered thirty years apart from one another: "The American Scholar" (1837) and "Progress of Culture" (1867). Emerson presented both to Harvard's Phi Beta Kappa Society, and both concern Emerson's thinking on the function of the upper classes in their respective historical moments. His audience is an elite class of New Englanders, men who in the 1840s–50s were trained for an epoch-defining victory over southern slave power and who in the 1860s–70s were tasked with reconstituting U.S. economic and ideological supremacy in an increasing industrial and transnational capitalism. The change in message that occurs between the two addresses thus mirrors similarly enormous material shifts in the nature of the Northern economy over these thirty years. In *Capital*, Marx characterizes this period as giving rise to "a finance aristocracy" who effected "a very rapid centralization of capital" in the North.[15] "The American Scholar" may thus be said to emerge from a time when knowledge, like land and finance, was diffuse and open (for some), whereas "Progress of Culture" emerges from one in which education is seen as a tool to assist the young lords of the "finance aristocracy" assume their world-historical position as architects of global economic development. Emerson accordingly revises his view of the nation's relationship to history. The self-reliant, self-authorizing "American Scholar," once a beacon of the nation's independence from what he and his audience would have viewed as the outrages of Old World feudalism, has become by "Progress of Culture" the corporate lord, sovereign in his wealth and naturally imbued with powers Emerson once reserved for the poet and religious seer.

Emerson opens "The American Scholar" with a burst of negative definitions: the elite of New England are *not* like the Greeks, *not* like Troubadours, *not* like their industry-minded "contemporaries in the British and European capitals" (*EL*, 53). His famous call for a domestic tradition of American works is couched in strategic disavowals of history and historical cultural forms. Emerson's argument culminates in the famous and frequently quoted "age of Introversion" passage, in which "Hamlet's unhappiness" is taken up as a positive virtue and model for the intellectual (68). New types will emerge from toil, trial, and despair. Who this figure will be is unclear; it is implied he will come from the literary class, but he could not solely be a scholar or educator. His motivations, beyond an all-consuming desire for knowledge, are likewise obscure. One thing is certain: Emerson in 1837 predicts that the master class for the nineteenth century will stand *in relation* to the past ("side by side"), but not in a direct line of descent from it.

The prophetic tone in "The American Scholar" positions Emerson as the wild John the Baptist to some dimly seen Christ on the horizon of his decade's horizon of possibility; he is a mystic rooting through nature for signs of a freethinking messiah and baptizing his audience in anticipation of its emergence. As the triple disavowal of the opening paragraph implies, intellectual liberty assumes a unique relation to history in order to achieve a total revolution in social and intellectual life. If the past proves usable, so be it: Emerson is implying—as his follower Friedrich Nietzsche will argue in 1873's "On The Uses and Disadvantages of History for Life"—that "the stronger the innermost roots of a man's nature, the more readily will he be able to assimilate and appropriate the things of the past."[16] As Emerson has it, only the person of discernment who can sort out "the authentic utterances" of the past and reject the rest is positioned to actualize the monumental rift between the ideas and patterns of the Old World and those of the New (*EL*, 54).[17] The United States constructs itself from the stuff of the past, but the past does not construct it.

"Progress of Culture," from 1867, seems at first to develop the historical optimism of the earlier address. "Progress of Culture" opens with a laundry list of the North's accomplishments, including the abolition of slavery, penal reform, life and health insurance, "the free-trade league," and the establishment of international congresses, "teaching nations the taking of government into their own hands, and the superseding of kings." "This country and this age," Emerson concludes, "belongs to the most liberal persuasion" (*CW*, 8:109). Totalizing liberalism, evident in every aspect of Northern social life as it emerges from the Civil War, has bred "*a new class of nobles*" in the various industries (railroads, shipping, communications, etc.) that had begun to reshape the nation's character and appearance (8:110).

Emerson's comparison of the corporate sovereign to the feudal noble opens up a series of references to medieval European art and culture. First Emerson insists that, while the United States lacks "the monumental solidity... of medieval remains in Europe," scientific developments in geology and evolutionary biology have "effaced [the] distinctions" between the Old World and the New (8:111). The macroscales of geological and evolutionary time reveal an underlying "equality between new and old countries," one that is replicated in the endurance of ideas from one epoch to another. This observation contradicts the historical disavowals that open "The American Scholar" while nonetheless remaining within the hermeneutic bounds of the earlier work: developments in the natural sciences allow the content of Emerson's message to change without disrupting the overall framework of his mode of analysis (the close reading of nature. "Progress of Culture" thus reveals a consistency in method with and an evolution in message from the earlier lecture: Emerson is still celebrating "the private man" and his unique relation to history, but in a different sphere and with different ends in mind.

Emerson's reworking of his early system allows him to collapse the old, decadent, feudal world of Europe into the new, progressive, liberal world of the United States. In a paragraph-long aside that he offers without immediate analysis, Emerson insists that the United States will produce a "romantic" literature equivalent to the Arthurian legends in Britain, *El Cid* in Spain, and the *Chanson de Roland* in France (*CW*, 8:112). He drops this line of thought and moves on to the more concrete ways in which America has fulfilled the promise of medieval England:

> In modern Europe, the Middle Ages were called the Dark Ages. Who dares to call them so now? They are seen to be the feet on which we walk, the eyes with which we see. 'Tis one of our triumphs to have reinstated them. Their Dante and Alfred and Wickliffe and Abelard and Bacon; their Magna Charta, decimal numbers, mariner's compass, gun-powder, glass, paper, and clocks; chemistry, algebra, astronomy; their Gothic architecture, their painting, are the delight and tuition of ours. Six hundred years ago Roger Bacon explained the pre-cession of the equinoxes, and the necessity of reform in the calendar; looking over how many horizons as far as into Liverpool and New York, he announced that machines can be constructed to drive ships more rapidly than a whole galley of rowers could do, nor would they need anything but a pilot to steer; carriages, to

move with incredible speed, without aid of animals; and machines to fly into the air like birds. (8:112)

"Tuition" is the key word here, especially in its implication of stewardship and education. The gothic—and, by extension, the cultural and political forces of which the gothic is the material manifestation—both tutors the age and relies on the age's tutelage. A new feudalism is the ward and the teacher of American progress, and the North is where it will flourish.

The passage closely echoes the list of liberal achievements that opens the address. The resonance between the two is not accidental: Emerson is highlighting points of similarity in order to put forward a revision of his thought on the U.S. culture's debt to European precedent. Alluding to John Wycliffe (1320–1384) reminds his Anglo-American, Protestant audience that their religious convictions stem from thirteenth-century debates about translation of the Vulgate into the vernacular; alluding to Peter Abelard (1079–1142) reminds them that their self-image as scholars and philosophers is likewise built on medieval precedent. He concludes the passage by casting the alchemist Roger Bacon (1214–1294) as the forefather of U.S. technological innovation, implying that all contemporary and future developments are realizations of his premodern vision of modernity. In "Progress of Culture," America is the direct lineal descendant of Europe: it has evolved from the primordial stew of the medieval past.

In keeping with this newfound emphasis on the emergence of the United States from feudal precedents, the "private man" of 1867 is no longer the scholar-individualist of 1837, but instead a sovereign whose innate powers and nobility make him fit to rule the new world. Culture, here defined as the inculcation of aesthetic codes and the refinement of moral character, will train him to use his power wisely: "Culture alters the political status of an individual. It raises a rival royalty in a monarchy. 'Tis king against king. It is ever the romance of history in all dynasties" (*CW*, 8:114). This is precisely the "parcelization of sovereignty" that has traditionally been associated with feudal social organization—each man is his own sovereign ruler, and the compromises reached by these "rival royalties" creates the social bond. The scholar's role is not to upset the old codes and structures of power—the implied thesis of "The American Scholar"—but instead to prepare new sovereigns for roles as communitarian businessmen with a refined sense of noblesse oblige.

Emerson highlights his audience's noble duties by dubbing Phi Beta Kappa "a great knighthood of virtue ... whose hands are strong enough to hold up the Republic" (8:123). The republican political ideals of liberalism are reconciled with the chivalric code, producing a synthesis of the medieval and the modern.

Emerson's interest in medieval literature and culture was, as I mentioned earlier, part of a broader resurgence in scholarly engagements with premodernity. The antimodern impulse that animated factions of elite educators in the post–Civil War North emerged squarely from that class's fears of decadence, moral decay, and urban unrest. The Middle Ages as these men imagined it, with its soaring yet austere architecture, strong martial culture, and settled sense of class relations, offered an anodyne to the crushing social problems that threatened to consume the industrial North. There was no doubt a reactionary valence to this line of thinking, one bred from a real anxiety over the possibility of proletarian revolution and lumpen-proletarian unrest in the Northern industrial cities. Northern medievalism in this period was in every way part of a broader process that sought to "cultivate a 'truly American'" culture through an increased "emphasis on social stratification."[18]

Yet, despite the seeming conservatism of the antimodern impulse, it was not an entirely retrograde political position. Indeed, public intellectuals used the example of the Middle Ages as a progressive tool, a means by which contradictions in industrial capitalism might be resolved without either a worker's revolution or the brutal subjection of the masses by the ruling classes. Norton, Emerson, and their like-minded colleagues at Harvard emphasized education as a means by which society could be saved from itself. Norton "gave less thought to schooling the masses than teaching the powerful: the plutocrats and their sons, the present and future opinion leaders," coming eventually to believe that only Harvard College and its graduates would "save America."[19] Norton made certain that medieval literature, art, and architecture would be central to this project.

In 1863, Norton delivered a series of lectures titled "On Some Characteristics of the Medieval Revival of Learning" at the behest of Harvard president Thomas Hill.[20] The very title of the lecture series implies that Norton looked back to the Middle Ages not nostalgically, but instead as a model for how patrician culture might be squared with a dedication to culture and social well-being through rigorous education. Even more tellingly, on January 1, 1863—the day on which Lincoln signed the Emancipation Proclamation—

Norton delivered his lecture "Emancipation in the Middle Ages" at Boston's Lowell Institute. In that lecture, Norton advises his audience that, while emancipation is an event of "transcendent import not only to ourselves but to future generations," and medieval precedent may help shed light on America's current political moment, they must not too readily collapse their historical moment into others: "events & circumstances are never reproduced in complete similarity in different ages . . . in fine the readings of history are more frequently to be drawn from analogues more or less perfect, & liable to misinterpretation."[21] Norton's scholarly engagement with the medieval past differs greatly from romanticism's emphasis on the splendor and ruin of a lost age and Walter Scott's heroic vision of knights on battlefields and ladies in peril. Against a nostalgic vision of the Middle Ages—or, worse, the perverse equation of feudal social order with chattel bondage that was put forward by proslavery southerners—Norton emphasizes careful research and interpretation of the period: the *use* of the Middle Ages for the present, not ahistorical reveling in an imagined medieval past.

Owing perhaps to the influence of Norton and the general culture of medievalism that pervaded Boston during this time, Emerson greatly improved his knowledge of medieval English history throughout the 1860s and 1870s. Emerson's 1869 and 1871 notebooks of readings for the unpublished lecture "Chivalry" demonstrate a deep knowledge of both primary and secondary sources pertaining to the English Middle Ages, including Robert of Gloucester's *Chronicle* (ca. 1260), Chaucer's poetry, and a number of postmedieval scholarly and poetic works.[22] Emerson was particularly interested in how chivalry acted as a civilizing agent after the collapse of the Roman Empire and during the emergence of the Christian Middle Ages. For Emerson, "chivalry effected the Union of Europe & Christendom, & the opportunity of close acquaintance with the elaborate courtesy of Asia & Arabia," while at the same time offering the necessary precondition for his century's conception of culture. Against a still-pervasive narrative that sees the Middle Ages as a time of superstition and intellectual conformity that was swept away by the rediscovery of classical learning in the Renaissance, Emerson posits the military and religious leaders of medieval Europe as the originators of his century's cultural impulse. He observes that his audience will likely associate culture—"the favorite word of our times"—with classical and Renaissance thinkers: "Plato & Pericles, Cicero & Caesar, the geniuses of medieval Italy; & the English of the Elizabethan age . . . Sir Philip Sidney, Shakespeare, &

Bacon, Milton." Emerson, however, attributes the emergence of culture more to "the martial & religious geniuses who in the Cid & the English mind gave us the flower of Chivalry *Morte d Arthur*."²³ Given the North's recent military victory in the Civil War, it would be difficult for Emerson's audience not to connect the "martial & religious geniuses" of medieval Europe to the "martial & religious geniuses" of their own time.

"Chivalry" was not the first time Emerson equated the liberal project of emancipation with the chivalric impulse. In "Seventh of March Speech on the Fugitive Slave Law" (1854), Emerson frames the struggle to abolish slavery in similar terms: "Liberty is the crusade of all brave and conscientious men. It is the epic poetry, the new religion, the chivalry of all gentlemen. This is the oppressed Lady whom true knights on their oath and honor must rescue and save."²⁴ By equating the Northern abolitionist with the chevalier, Emerson reworks a familiar trope of the southern slavocracy to his own political ends. A brief write-up of "Chivalry" from the *Daily Alta California* of May 18, 1871, relates that Emerson ended the lecture by asserting that the spirit of medieval chivalry he believed animated the very notions of cultural and civilization in the West had not vanished: "Mr. Emerson read extracts from Tennyson's *Morte d'Arthur* and other works of knightly poetry and fiction, and concluded with expressing his views on the chivalry of the present day—the power it is and may become."²⁵ As in "Progress of Culture," Emerson asserts in "Chivalry" that the spirit of the Middle Ages was flourishing in his own time, and in the United States.

WEALTH AND FEUDAL AUTHORITY:
ENGLISH TRAITS, *THE CONDUCT OF LIFE*, AND *THE NATURAL HISTORY OF INTELLECT*

The full implications of Emerson's recuperation of feudal England as a model for liberal America can only be seen when placed against the doctrine of natural aristocracy espoused first in *English Traits* and then more forcefully in *The Conduct of Life* and *The Natural History of Intellect*. In these works, Emerson theorizes an immense underclass that incorporates most of humanity, one whose primary function is to support a new aristocracy of preternaturally gifted nobles who will emerge from the "creative economy" of laissez-faire. As Emerson bluntly puts it in *The Conduct of Life*: "Some men are born to own. Others are not" (*EL*, 995).

Emerson's appropriation of the feudal past does not square readily with

U.S. liberalism as it was understood in his own century. Indeed, U.S. liberalism had since the Revolutionary Generation defined itself in stark opposition to England's feudal past. Most educated Americans of the eighteenth and nineteenth centuries accepted that, first, "the feudal system was introduced into England only at the time of the Norman Conquest"; second, "Anglo-Saxon England . . . was a land of yeoman farmers"; and, third, the American Revolution had "eliminated the last remnants of the feudal system and restored the freedoms of the period before 1066."[26] If we accept the common narrative that defines the English Middle Ages as the period after Hastings, when the feudal system was transplanted to English soil and the culture of chivalry replaced the tribalism of the Anglo-Saxons, and before the establishment of the Tudor dynasty and the birth of the "early modern" period during the Wars of the Roses (1455–1485), we can begin to imagine the enormity of the historical task U.S. liberalism set for itself. A full four centuries of English history and culture were taken as a period of tyranny, superstition, and oppression.

The American Revolution was meant to restart the story of human progress from 1776. Only a liberal polity and its handmaiden, an entrepreneurial capitalist society, could prevent a reversion to medieval darkness and despair. As we saw in the introduction, this idea is central to U.S. exceptionalist thought, and it continues to exercise an influence on the self-image of the United States as the telos of a certain bourgeois narrative of human history. Emerson, like many of his contemporaries, followed the Revolutionary Generation in believing that the United States had done away with the vestiges of feudal power. The young Emerson "was prepared to consider 'trade' to be 'the principle of liberty . . . [which] . . . settled America, & destroyed feudalism, and made peace and keeps peace.'"[27] This idea persisted throughout Emerson's career. In the 1863 lecture "Fortune of the Republic," Emerson notes that "America was opened after the feudal mischief was spent," and that the antifeudal demands of English Chartism "have all been granted here to begin with" (*EAW*, 143, 144).

It is all the more surprising, then, that Emerson so drastically revises the narrative of America's victory over feudalism in *English Traits*, a difficult text that has since its publication been understood both as a paradoxical critique of British global influence and as a celebration of its "civilizing" accomplishments in the nineteenth century.[28] In *English Traits*, Emerson posits liberalism as being in a close dialectical relationship to feudalism: liberalism in a sense perfects feudalism, and feudalism contains the seed out of which liberalism would spring. In "Race," Emerson asserts that the Celts and Saxons "had no violent feudal tenure," restating the myth of native English liberty we see throughout U.S. liberal thought (*EL*, 791). The Battle of Hastings is expectedly characterized as a clash between noble Saxons and piratical Normans: "Twenty thousand thieves landed at Hastings. These founders of the House of Lords were greedy and ferocious dragoons, sons of greedy and ferocious pirates" (799). Ultimately, though, Emerson comes to claim all of these elements as necessary components in England's supremacy. He reminds us that "the English uncultured are a brutal nation," and that "the mildness of the following ages has not quite effaced" the elements of racial character introduced by Norman and Danish miscegenation (800). Only through the fusing of these national elements could the English achieve the character they assumed in the centuries after Hastings.

Emerson next moves from the historical basis for his reading of English history to its role in forming the English physique. When first seeing an Englishman in the flesh, "The American has arrived at the old mansion-house, and finds himself among uncles, aunts, and grandsires. The pictures on the chimney-tiles of his nursery were picture of these people. Here they are in the identical costumes and air, which so took him" (801). Emerson posits "The American" as a lineal descendant of the Englishman, a mixed feudal/liberal warrior who can find his double anywhere in the world. Emerson's aside on the English face uses racial taxonomy as a metaphor for the intermixing of liberal and feudal elements: "On the English face are combined decision and nerve, with the fair complexion, blue eyes, and open and florid aspect. Hence the love of truth, hence the sensibility, the fine perception, and poetic construction. The fair Saxon man, with open front, and honest meaning, domestic, affectionate, is not the wood out of which cannibal, or inquisitor, or assassin is made, but he is moulded for law, lawful trade, civility, marriage, the nurture of children, for colleges, churches, charities, and colonies" (802). Emerson's reading of the English face mixes elements of the liberty-loving Saxon ("open front") with martial elements drawn from Norman and Danish precedent ("decision and nerve"). The intermixing of these contradictory qualities is the hallmark of a robust Englishness: "The English delight in the antagonism which combines in one person the extremes of courage and tenderness" (802). But the English face's "fair complexion, blue eyes, and open and florid aspect" marks the limit of this intermixing: a blow (to be sure) against the construction of a pure Anglo-Saxon (and therefore "Anglo-American") identity, but one that inscribes a new, hereditary narrative within the broader story of historical progress and development. Nobility here is an inherited trait; the American exists in a familial relation to the Englishman; and the American errand is taken not as a decisive breaking away from the English past, but instead as a completion and perfection of Englishness. Later, in "Ability," Emerson summarizes his new racial historiography in one sweeping sentence: "A century later, it came out, that the Saxon had the most bottom and longevity, had managed to make the victor speak the language and accept the law and usage of the victim; forced the baron to dictate Saxon terms to Norman kings; and, step by step, got all the essential securities of civil liberty invented and confirmed" (*EL*, 806). There is an antagonism at work, but finally Saxon liberty is defined *within the political and economic bounds* of Norman feudalism, not as its negation.

The problem with feudalism, then, is not the power structures that subtend it, but the luxuriousness to which the old feudal elite fell victim: "Great estates are not sinecures, if they are to be kept great. A creative economy is the fuel of magnificence." Stultification, not feudalism, is the enemy here. The increase in national wealth that results from the expanding regime of capital has led to a contrary end: "Large domains are growing larger. The great estates are absorbing the small freeholds. In 1786, the soil of England was owned by 250,000 corporations and proprietors; and, in 1822, by 32,000" (865). Somehow English economic policy had led to the strengthening of the key tenant of feudal economics, real estate law, and the key institution of feudal culture, the grand estate. Emerson's celebration of the monopolizing tendency of the English estate stands in stark contrast to the "semi-socialist" (in Robin Blackburn's words) free land policies of Emerson's Republican North, which encouraged a multiplication of small farms owned and operated by individual proprietors.[29] Trade, which in the 1840s Emerson viewed as a force to destroy feudal power and the concentration of wealth it entails, is on the contrary leading to greater and greater concentrations of wealth in fewer hands. And it is precisely the people who will manage this great concentration of wealth that Emerson dubs his "great knighthood of virtue" in "Progress of Culture."

Emerson's reassessment of English history in *English Traits* resonates with Thomas Carlyle's social vision as developed in *Past and Present* (1843). *English Traits* can be read as Emerson's attempt to rewrite Carlyle's withering critique of the excesses and abuses of the British bourgeoisie in U.S. liberal terms. While comparing the works of these lifelong friends is nothing new, the not-so-quiet influence of *Past and Present* on *English Traits* (and vice versa) is worth reconsidering in light of Emerson's late-career neofeudalism. Like Emerson, Carlyle seeks an aristocracy of virtuous, intelligent, and self-determined overmen to save humanity from economic and spiritual chaos: "The Wiser, Braver: these, a Virtual Aristocracy everywhere and everywhen, do in all Societies that reach any articulate shape, develop themselves into a ruling class, an Actual Aristocracy, with settled modes of operating."[30] "The Wiser, Braver" are the eminent capitalists Emerson elliptically refers to in *English Traits* and addresses explicitly in *The Conduct of Life*. Carlyle declares in "Captains of Industry" that "the Leaders of Industry, if Industry is ever to be led, are virtually the Captains of the World! if there be no nobleness in them, there will never be an Aristocracy more" (*PP*, 271). Obedience to these great men and their wills is the only hope for the world's laboring masses, whom Carlyle characterizes as ready to offer "noble loyalty in return for noble guidance" (273). But duty cuts both ways. Just as Emerson condemns lazy owners who treat their property as a "sinecure," Carlyle compares a "High Class without duties" to "a tree planted on precipices; from the roots of which all the earth has been crumbling" (179). In order to survive the onslaught of bourgeois modernity, the aristocracy needs the proletariat, and the proletariat needs the aristocracy—or, the feudal past requires the collusion of the liberal present in order to survive, and the liberal present requires the grandeur and wisdom of the feudal past to keep from lapsing into chaos and "Mammonism."

Past and Present and *English Traits* both theorize the necessity for a new generation of "Captains of Industry" to lead the laboring classes into a neofeudal regime of fixed social relations with mutual obligations flowing between the upper and lower classes. But like so many of the revolutionary texts of the late 1840s, they fail to provide concrete details for the application of their doctrines. *The Conduct of Life* is Emerson's attempt to put the theories he developed in *English Traits* into practice. *The Conduct of Life* thus stands as the crucial intermediate step between the "high theory" of *English Traits* and the aestheticized medievalism of "Progress of Culture."

In keeping with the medievalism of the other texts of this time, Emerson peppers *The Conduct of Life* with lengthy explications of quotations from Chaucer's *Canterbury Tales* and *House of Fame*. "Fate" finds Emerson citing

The Knight's Tale as his source for the observation that fate is a "strap or belt which girds the world" (*EL*, 944). In order to illustrate the effects literature may enact on political life, Emerson opens "Culture" by claiming that renowned early modern jurist Lord Edward Coke (1552–1634) used Chaucer's *Canon Yeoman's Tale* as a precedent for the development of English laws regarding alchemy (*EL*, 1015). Alluding to the past—its literature, laws, customs, and institutions—is not a mere rhetorical device for Emerson. Instead, the laws and codes of the Old World shape the future of the new. As Laura Dassow Walls notes, Emerson's stance here shares much in common with the notion of "clerisy" that Emerson would have encountered in Samuel Taylor Coleridge's works: "At the top of the hierarchy would be the 'savants,' 'scholars,' and 'priests,' who could constitute a Coleridgean clerisy, there to protect, guide, and enlighten the otherwise calamitous masses."[31] Clerisy likewise aligns Emerson with Charles Eliot Norton, who, as we saw above, viewed Harvard College and its "great knighthood of virtue," the children of the new U.S. corporate nobles, as the best defense against mass social upheaval. Only an elite caste educated in the liberal arts may properly shape and lead the nation as its new nobility.

Ultimately, Emerson calls for the emergence of a neofeudal corporate aristocracy in America. Emerson's corporate "semigod" holds within him all of human history, as he intones with mystic fervor in the epigraph to "Culture":

> Can rules or tutors educate
> The semigod whom we await?
> He must be musical,
> Tremulous, impressional,
> Alive to gentle influence
> Of landscape and of sky,
> And tender to the spirit-touch
> Of man's or maiden's eye:
> But, to his native centre fast,
> Shall into Future fuse the Past,
> And the world's flowing fates in
>   His own mould recast. (*EL*, 1014)

The "semigod" fusing past and present is analogous to Emerson's characterization of England as "an old pile built in different ages" in *English Traits* (*EL*, 929). This "semigod" learns proper conduct through the gradual influence of culture. However, the ability to learn culture is now defined as a heritable trait: "There must be capacity for culture in the blood.... The obstinate prejudice in favor of blood, which lies at the base of the feudal and monarchical fabrics of the old world, has some reason in common experience" (1040). Culture by primogeniture leads Emerson to a profound conclusion in the jumble of maxims and proclamations collected as "Considerations by the Way": "Masses are rude, lame, unmade, pernicious in their demands and influence, and need not to be flattered but to be schooled. I wish not to concede anything to them, but to tame, drill, divide, and break them up, and draw individuals out of them.... If government knew how, I should like to see it check, not multiply the population" (*EL*, 1081). We again see an emphasis on Coleridgean clerisy: the masses will be schooled and drilled, shaped by a higher order of men. Emerson restates this passage's claim in words that echo the familiar style of Nature: "Nature makes fifty poor melons for one that is good, and shakes down a tree full of gnarled, wormy, unripe crabs, before you can find a dozen dessert apples" (1080). Whereas Emerson in 1844 proclaimed that "the uprise and culmination of the new and antifeudal power of commerce, is the political fact of most significance to the American at this hour," Emerson at the dawn of the Gilded Age looks for a "strong man ... [to make] estates, as fast as the sun breeds clouds" (*EL*, 974), a man who, like the feudal baron before the system's decadence in modernity, would author the world.

Emerson's authoritarian turn in *The Conduct of Life* relies on a racialism that prefigures notions of white supremacy as we understand them in our own historical moment.[32] Nell Irvin Painter convincingly argues that Emerson's racialism was formed in large part by his ongoing admiration of Carlyle's Germanic thought and style.[33] Contrary to, say, Cornel West, who claims that Emerson was merely a "typical nineteenth-century North Atlantic 'mild racist,'"[34] Painter portrays Emerson as a thinker who as early as the 1850s had relegated nonwhites and workers to "dismal roles in a mechanistic world."[35] The "dismal roles" reserved for working people—who are represented in *English Traits* and *The Conduct of Life* as an immense genetic underclass that incorporates most of humanity, "white" or no—exist to support a new aristocracy of biologically preordained nobles who will emerge from the "creative economy" of laissez-faire.

For Emerson, the North's coming victory over the slave power in the South represented the destruction of an *artificial* system of class distinction (the slavocracy and the economy it subtended). The destruction of this artificial system of privilege paved the way for the emergence of a "natural" aristocracy whose talent, distinction, and leadership he believed would shape U.S. social life in profound ways. As Rowe notes, Emerson's antislavery writings indict the "unnaturalness of... a love of power" that breeds "the luxury of [the slave owner's] vassalage."[36] Like Norton and the other antimodernists described by Lears, Emerson critiques a backward, decadent economy that breeds moral decline, whether in England or America. However, against the antimodernist impulse of his times, Emerson attempts to find a "place of grace" within the economic and moral schema of liberal capitalism. That "place of grace" would be based, for Emerson, in the leadership of a clerisy whose wealth and goodness would "trickle down" to the unlearned masses. As he puts it in "Fortune of the Republic," "It is a rule that holds in economy, as well as in hydraulics, that you must have a source higher than your tap" (*EAW*, 137). The Old World and its feudal lords have become weak, are "absorbed in maintaining... their luxury," and so are incapable of leading global progress; but the American aristocracy, which draws its strength from commerce and finance, is young, robust, and ready to serve as "the great charity of God to the human race" (141, 152).

Emerson's final series of lectures at Harvard, delivered in 1871 and posthumously collected as *The Natural History of the Intellect*, show how deeply this new racial historiography influenced his later thought. Emerson opens the lectures with an appeal to the Aristotelian and Thomist idea of the prime mover.[37] Already, we find ourselves in a medieval cosmology: the prime mover radiates its creative power down successive chains of being, and human intellects "mimic in their sphericity, the first mind, and share its power" (*NH*, 4). Emerson further anchors his argument in nineteenth-century medievalist terms by deploying metaphors that are feudal in nature. The first hint is Emerson's use of the word "realm," which hadn't entered English until after the Norman Conquest (OED), to describe talent's eminence within the creative man: "intellections are external to intellect, a heaven within man, a realm of undiscovered sciences, of slumbering potencies, a heaven of which the feats of talent are no measure" (*NH*, 5). This immediately brings to mind Emerson's claim in *The Conduct of Life* that the creative man "[makes] estates, as fast as the sun breeds clouds." Recalling the estates moment from *The Conduct of Life* is important in understanding the pattern of images that follow in lectures 1 and 2. Emerson connects the power of all-seeing, all-creating intellect with that of the agrarian lord, the man who, like a Dutch patroon, shapes the land to fit his will: the ideal scholar "admires the Dutch who burnt half the harvest, and enhanced the remainder beyond the value of the whole" (*NH*, 7). In lecture 2, Emerson applies this early genetic experimentation to the cultivation of the self: "Man, a higher plant, repeats in his mental functions germination, growth, state of melioration, crossings, blight, parasites, and all the accidents of the plant" (10).

The moment could be excused as rhetorical excess from a writer who frequently stumbled toward metaphors for thought and soul throughout his career. But the mention of Louis Agassiz in the first paragraph of lecture 2 leads me to believe that Emerson was fully aware of his metaphor's power and meaning. Agassiz, a Swiss biologist and founder of Harvard's Lawrence Scientific School, put forward a polygenetic theory of human evolution.[38] Polygenism in biology implies that humanity is made up of inherently antagonistic strains, making Emerson's evocation of "crossings, blight, [and] parasites" take on protoeugenicist undertones. The racist implications of this notion are clear. In *The Conduct of Life*, Emerson asserts that "some men are born to own," while "others are not." But he doesn't yet say who those men are. Here, Emerson shows his hand. Those who are "born to own" were produced through generations of cultivation and refinement, like a rare orchid. The rest of us, subject as our family lines were to "crossings, blight, [and] parasites," must in turn be cultivated by the great men.

Emerson performs a careful operation in these opening two lectures. First, he defines a pyramidal structure of intellect, a scheme that, like the medieval view of sovereignty, sees authority emanating down from the prime mover to its temporal representatives in industry, the academy, and the state. This in itself isn't innovative. What is unique is how Emerson fixes the feudal idea of order within a pseudo-Darwinian framework through Agassiz. Like a master geneticist creating new strains of a crop, the "creative or ... male mind" takes various "instrumentalities," including "the codes of heraldry and states" (*NH*, 19). Through a dialectical process in which "thought buries itself only in the new thought of larger scope which sprang from it," "the old instrumentalities and incarnations are decomposed and recomposed into new" (20). Emerson's mention of Hegel earlier in the lecture leaves no room for doubt as to the dialectical process Emerson believes the "heroes" of the United States are undertaking. Enlightenment, in its political and scientific sense, "decomposed" the old feudalism and scholasticism of the Middle Ages—not to destroy the former, but to create a higher synthesis of the two eras.

After this high-flown combination of Aristotelian sociology, Hegelian logic, and Darwinian biology, Emerson opens lecture 3 with a comment on Gilded Age businessmen. "Instinct and Perception," delivered on February 21, 1871, sees Emerson pander to the future "captains of industry" in his audience: "It is a few heads which carve out this vast business the world so bustles in . . . Every peasant turns butter, every acre of ground measures out corn, when the hero arrives" (21–22). Unless they were hobbyists sneaking out in the dark of night to some isolated dairy farm in rural Massachusetts, there's little chance the members of the Class of 1871 spent much time churning butter. Emerson is speaking to the world-authoring heroes, not the peasantry. A 1921 report produced by the class of 1871 gives us a very clear picture of Emerson's audience. The report is predictably full of lawyers, scientists, teachers, and businessmen. The report is also deeply interested in lineage: one lawyer is said to have "descended from an old English family," and there is a page celebrating the birth of U.S. senator Henry Cabot Lodge's great-grandson, making the class of 1871 "the only Class where the first great-grandchild is a direct descendant in [a family] line."[39] It's hard to read these passages without suspecting that the class of 1871 were attempting to establish a latter-day Society of the Cincinnati among the men educated to be members of the "knighthood of virtue."

The high hopes ran both ways. Men such as those in the class of 1871 would return Emerson's adulation by cementing his central place in U.S. letters. As historian Richard Teichgraeber argues, we owe Emerson's status "as America's first secular saint" to the "great men" of the Gilded Age, who praised Emerson for his "loftiness of character" and that character's influence on the "culture-bearing entrepreneurs and institutions" of the late nineteenth century.[40]

EFFECTS: CORPORATE KINGS, EDUCATION, AND A NEW FEUDALISM

In a journal entry from 1871, Emerson considers neofeudalism through its practical effects: "The multiplication of monarchs known by telegraph & daily news from all countries to the daily papers, & the effect of freer institutions in England & America, has robbed the title of King of all its romance. . . . It is rich men, in America, who are now considered as the more stable &

the more enviable of the two notabilities. We shall come to add "Kings" in the "Contents" of the Directory" (*JMN*, 16:252). The passage would later be incorporated into his lecture on "Aristocracy," minus the crass and uncharacteristically blunt evocation of "rich men, in America."[41] Corporate chiefs, whose ranks are "more stable & more enviable" than the old feudal lords, have come to supplant aristocracy in form and function.

In *The Conduct of Life*, Emerson puts the matter this way: "What is the benefit done by a good King Alfred . . . compared with the involuntary blessing wrought on nations by the selfish capitalists who built the Illinois, Michigan, and the network of the Mississippi valley roads" (*EL*, 1085). In lecture 10 of his 1871 Harvard lecture series, Emerson harangues his audience for not understanding the secret of history he spent his last decade decoding: "When you say, The times, the persons are prosaic; where is the feudal . . . architecture? Where the Romantic manners? Where the Papal or Calvinistic religion, which made a poetry in the air for Milton or Byron or Belzoni? Our surroundings are as barren as a dry goods shop;—you expose your atheism. Is a railroad or a shoe factory or an insurance office, a bank or a bakery outside of the system and connection of things, or further from God, than is a sheep-pasture or a clam-bank?" (*NH*, 69). Like his contemporaries, Emerson understood the all-eroding, all-revolutionizing power of capitalist modernity, but, unlike his antimodernist and socialist peers, Emerson embraced this power as a means by which to reinstate what he believed was the natural balance and harmony of social life under high feudalism. Only an atheist could deny that a shoe factory or a Memorial Hall was not the spiritual equal to a Tintagel Castle or a Westminster Abbey.

These statements have, as Emerson might say, "some reason in common experience": a new capitalist aristocracy did emerge during Emerson's lifetime, but the results were not perhaps as beneficent as Emerson had hoped. Another example from literature may be closer to the truth: Mark Twain's pragmatic arch-liberal Hank Morgan becomes, by the end of *A Connecticut Yankee in King Arthur's Court* (1889), a ruthless plutocrat whose kingdom is maintained through elaborate spy networks and forced industrial labor, and whose reign ends in a disastrous massacre. Hank displaces feudalism only to introduce a new authoritarian regime in the heart of "second-stage industrialization"; the ideological premises may be different, but the political structures and social effects remain, in essence, the same.[42]

The irony in Northern liberalism's embrace of feudal precedent is underscored in the centerpiece illustration accompanying Henry Van Brunt's *Harvard Register* article on the construction of Memorial Hall. Servants in matching tuxedoes set tables under the vaulted ceiling while busts of luminaries and paintings of fallen soldiers watch from the walls. The servants occupy the same visual plane as the tablecloths, chairs, cups, tables, candelabras, and other incidental details of the scene; striped pants align the servants with the outsized verticality of the gothic architecture, rendering them, in essence, functional decorations. Northern cultural authority constructed in Memorial Hall a cathedral to itself, and these peonized subjects—along with the long-vanished builders of the cathedral, the weavers of tablecloths, the throwers of dinnerware, the lumberjacks sawing logs, and all the rest—toiled to construct and support fantastic structures dreamt up by self-styled lords of finance and management.

There is an even more bitter coda: Harvard's ideological apparatus came dangerously close to collapsing into an openly repressive apparatus when in 1877 Charles W. Eliot martialed the Harvard riflemen to defend property around Cambridge from a feared worker's insurrection.[43] The image of trained riflemen rallying on a campus that had only just recently put the finishing touches on an immense neogothic cathedral invites us to interrogate the North's liberal claims, to see another narrative at play beneath the surface of this era's progressivism.

All of this—the history of medievalism in the North, the riflemen and servants at Memorial Hall, and Emerson's late-career feudal turn—invite us to reconsider the academic institutions in which future "thought leaders" train and many scholars work. Ideologues like Emerson and Norton became "founding fathers" of liberal-arts study in the United States, and prestigious northern educational institutions continue to shape national policy and culture in dramatic ways.[44] The ethos of our universities can therefore be said to replicate the logic laid out in "Progress of Culture" and *The Conduct of Life*: establishing the "great knighthood of virtue" through the training of "semigods" for the private sector. This idea of training the "great knighthood of virtue" is a powerful calling for the nation's elite and has influenced private support for universities since at least Andrew Carnegie. Carnegie was, in many ways, the living exemplar of Emerson's semigod: a ruthless self-made man who, in his later years, gave himself up to the education of the public. My own life has been fundamentally shaped by Carnegie's philanthropic endeavors; a lifelong love of the humanities was born out of summers spent at the Carnegie Center for Literacy and Learning in Lexington, Kentucky. Yet, despite fond childhood memories of time spent in the Gilded Age mansion that housed the Carnegie Center for Literacy and Learning, I have to recognize that Carnegie's dedication to the humanities is part of his broader belief in a triumphal destiny for a very limited number of Americans. Kathleen Davis offers a telling material example of this doctrine: "If you were to approach the south wall of Bucknell University's Carnegie Building, you would see four names inscribed above its lintels: Charlemagne, Alfred, Washington, Lincoln." As Davis puts it, "The culmination of the Charlemagne-to-Lincoln genealogy . . . etched on the Bucknell library wall, monumentalizes . . . racial and economic history together with the politics of its philanthropy."[45] Even if, as Emerson says of England in *English Traits*, America is "aristocracy with the doors open," it remains ever and intractably an aristocracy, with a vast underclass as its boon and support (*EL*, 861). Underscoring the ancient character of this modern dynamic, in 1898 Andrew Carnegie did what any proper king would: retired to Skibo Castle (constructed ca. 1186) to dole out his charitable contributions at a lordly remove from the masses.

That Emerson's redemptive vision during this period tends toward an authoritarian capitulation to the superior prowess of great, educated men casts a shadow over the often-rosy assessment classical liberalism and its tradition of dissent receive in polite U.S. political thought. The Emerson of *English Traits, The Conduct of Life, The Natural History of the Intellect*, and "Progress of Culture" embodies the "ripe" democrat Emerson described in his chapter on Napoleon in *Representative Men* (1850): "The democrat is a young conservative; the conservative is an old democrat. The aristocrat is the democrat ripe, and gone to seed,—because both parties stand on the one ground of the supreme value of property, which one endeavors to get, and the other to keep" (*EL*, 744). It is unsettling that Emerson forgot the lesson he draws from his earlier analysis of the aristocratic element latent within America's democratic social structures: "As long as our civilization is essentially one of property, of fences, of exclusiveness, it will be mocked by delusions" (745). That the "delusions" bred by the property system are so central to pseudo-meritocratic and exclusionary systems of social promotion seems more and more evident.

ෆ CONCLUSION ෂ

The Kentucky Castle

> America, filling the present with greatest deeds and problems, cheerfully accepting the past, including feudalism, (as, indeed, the present is but the legitimate birth of the past, including feudalism,) counts, as I reckon, for her justification and success.
> —Walt Whitman, *Democratic Vistas* (1871)

When Rex Martin died in August 2003, newspapers celebrated his long career as a land developer—and puzzled over the castle he left sitting, unfinished, on a hillside near Versailles, Kentucky. Martin began construction on his castle in 1969. Trouble soon followed. Writing six years after Martin broke ground, journalist J. R. Kimmins made a petite epic of the builder's folly: "Louis XVI would have had someone's head. The kindly King Arthur wouldn't have stood for it. But plain old Rex Martin, a native of the Eastern Kentucky coalfields, has had to put up with fire, floods, and a lack of stone masons in his efforts to build a real castle." Martin promised Kimmins that his project would be completed "by spring." His timeline was off by a few decades. The castle would not be completed until the mid-2000s, well after Martin's death.

Martin's project faltered in the late 1970s. One of the towers collapsed in 1984. By 1988, Martin was in the market for a buyer. Martin had, in the two decades separating the groundbreaking from the attempted sale, suffered a divorce and become a recluse, dealing with clients through "'a Mr. Marshall' of Georgia, who will not leave a number." The *Herald-Leader* wondered whether the sale would push Martin to "finally . . . have an 'open castle' and allow the common folk to see what's inside?" That seemed unlikely. When contacted by the region's paper of record, Caroline Bogaert Martin, the builder's ex-wife, gave a succinct statement: "Umm, I really don't want to talk about it."[1]

Coverage of Martin's death in 2003 was largely concerned with the homestead's fate. A headline in the *Paducah Sun* reads: "Central Kentucky landmark surrounded by romance, myths, 8- to 10-foot wall." With the builder's passing, the castle's future was in doubt; the builder's son, Rex Martin Jr., told the paper he had no interest in living in his father's fantasyland. "My father was a businessman," he insisted. "The castle was just something fun for him. It wasn't anything that made him any money."[2] The son would not complete the work of the father. James Fenimore Cooper would not approve.

The younger Martin soon found a buyer in Tom Post, a lawyer from Miami, Florida, who hoped to use the space as a bed-and-breakfast. Post's ambitions were frustrated by a fire in 2004 that left much of the structure in ruins.[3] The Kentucky State Fire Marshal's office believed there was "a high probability that the fire was intentionally set." Bereaved locals "left flowers and posters" at the castle's gate.[4]

It is quite a career for a building that began its life as a "basically utilitarian" home. Yet it is precisely *in* the homeliness and averageness of Martin's ambition that secret to the semifeudal organization of the United States becomes apparent. It is in the most intimate, private spaces—including our imaginations—that the feudal idea of order flowers. The castle makes evident the latent feudal underpinnings of the U.S. culture of personal land ownership and social mobility. If one works hard enough, one can have a fairytale land of their very own.

Why Rex Martin chose to build a castle is no mystery. As we have seen throughout this study, the American bourgeoisie, both big and little, have since the country's founding longed for the status and power of the old feudal elites. What troubles me about the Martin castle story is, first, that, in a state as poor as my home state, untold millions have been dumped into one builder's dream project; and, second, that people who would never own castles of their own (but perhaps believed one day they would) could be moved to form such strong affective and imaginative bonds with one rich man's folly. Why would Woodford and Fayette County locals lay flowers at the gate of a torched Camelot when the castle and its owner did everything it could to distance itself from the very community that mourned its passing? Put another way, how can we account for the sense of resignation and deference that comes with the feudal idea of order—that is in fact its very essence?

For thinkers at the radical limits of nineteenth-century liberalism, this would be an intolerable situation. In his 1852 address "The Meaning of July Fourth for the Negro," Frederick Douglass describes the nation that first enslaved him and then made him a celebrated public intellectual as a young stream that has not yet become an immovable river. "There is consolation in the thought that America is young," Douglass writes, adding that "great streams are not easily turned from channels, worn deep in the course of ages. . . . They . . . gradually flow back to the same old channel, and flow on as serenely as ever." He concludes the metaphor with a warning: "While the river may not be turned aside, it may dry up, and leave nothing behind but the withered branch, and the unsightly rock, to howl in the abyss-sweeping wind, the sad tale of departed glory. As with rivers so with nations."[5] Douglass's apocalyptic image speaks across centuries to our own moment, when the immovability and traditionalism of U.S. politics threatens us to face down, with sober senses, abysses of our own making: abysses of economic inequality, racial injustice, rampant consumption of natural resources, and looming authoritarianisms.

As with all ideological forms, the feudal idea of order and its concomitant sense of resignation and inevitability have been baked into U.S. culture, past and present. I opened this conclusion with Martin's castle because, as a child, the unfinished home made a strong impact on my imagination. At the time, Martin's home struck me as an "authentic" medieval castle. It now strikes me as a poor imitation of the facade of a Medieval Times restaurant. Then and now, it offers an important lesson about the temporal powers of wealth. If one has enough money, one can seemingly suspend time and space.

Martin's castle sparked a childhood fascination with the medieval that was reinforced in nearly every facet of 1980s popular culture. The decade of my childhood and the decade of Emerson's dotage thus spoke another secret language to one another. Developments in financial markets, technologies, business structures, class roles, and social philosophies during the Gilded Age and the Progressive Era foreshadowed the emerging neoliberal consensus of the 1980s.[6] At the same time, both eras lionized the grim work of amassing of great fortunes by crafting fables in which the entrepreneur was really a temporarily embarrassed hero of old.

Fantasy novels such as J. R. R. Tolkien's perennially popular *The Lord of the Rings* (1954–1955) and popular films such as the *Star Wars* series (1977–1983) and *The Dark Crystal* (1982) made knights of all stripes fashionable again. Toy sets encouraged children to dabble in lordliness by building manors and defending one's plastic avatar's honor in combat. With the advent of home video games, such as the *King's Quest* series (1980–2016), *Dragon's Lair*

(1983), *Gauntlet* (1985), and *The Legend of Zelda* (1986), children could play out simplified versions of medievalist fantasies in a much more immediate and immersive way. These "commodified representation[s] of medieval life" reinforced the corporate structures from which they emerged.[7] The logic of medievalist movies and video games is sympathetic with neoliberalism and its cult of the self-determining businessman-hero: the films, games, and ideas of the time tell a "capitalist fairytale in which anyone who works hard and strives enough can rise through society's ranks and acquire great wealth."[8] These games directly impacted the sensorium, immersing players in medievalist worlds in a way not possible before. At the same time, we marveled at the technological ingenuity and business savvy of the Silicon Valley businesses that brought these fantasies to our screens. Like Hank Morgan, when we slept, we dreamed of industrialists and castles.

Just as many surviving medieval romances concern the lives of the ruling classes and their defenders, the medievalist play of my childhood favored aristocratic characters and courtly scenarios. No eight-year-old in 1989 pretended to be John Ball, leader of the Peasants' Revolt that roiled London in 1381.

It is too simplistic to argue that a feudal idea of order is only an imposition from above. No hoary conspiracy of Hollywood studios, academics, and video-game publishers tricked me into pinning my hopes on a neofeudal future. I was an active participant in the construction of this identity, taking the products of U.S. medievalism (in the form of toys, games, architecture, literature, and cinema) and adapting them to my own circumstances. Play and imagination are powerful tools in the inculcation of social values precisely because they demand that the player or dreamer internalizes the logics of the imaginary world. Like the construction of "white working class" identity that David Roediger's influential *The Wages of Whiteness* (1991) explores, the construction of "feudal identity" requires "historical actors who make (constrained) choices and create their own cultural forms."[9] Corporations, publishers, schools, and governments may provide the raw material for our fantasies, but individual agents construct and perpetuate the forms suggested by these institutions. As Adorno and Horkheimer put it, "The mythic scientific respect of the peoples of earth for the *status quo* that they themselves unceasingly produce, itself finally becomes positive fact."[10] Appropriately, when I have discussed *Medieval America* with my peers, I have more often than not been met with a disheartened *"Well, yes, and?"* It is hard for those of us who spent their twenties and thirties living in cities with seemingly ossified class relations, locked out of housing markets and subject to the whims of ever-emboldened landlords, not to feel the suzerainty of our superiors.

Still, it is strange that so many subjects of a nation forged in revolutionary struggle—a nation whose history "opened with one of those great, really liberating, really revolutionary wars of which there have been so few," as Vladimir Lenin put it in 1918—could be so adept at "unceasingly" producing the status quo of relations between master and slave, lord and serf, husband and wife, and tenant and owner.[11] As I've argued, feudalism, with its sense of mutual obligations in hierarchies and rich cultural history, has been a primary mechanism by which bare economic relations were prettified for Americans both of the ruling and ruled classes. Even as early luminaries of U.S. intellectual life—from Jefferson, Franklin, Crèvecoeur, and Tocqueville through to Frederick Jackson Turner and the "liberal consensus" scholars of the mid-twentieth century—insisted that the United States had enacted a sharp break from the feudal past, the legal and cultural apparatuses of the young republic were mobilized to establish feudal zones within the U.S. constitutional framework.

Even the most mundane aspects of lived experience are structured along feudal lines. Consider, for example, the distinct sovereignties one enters in the average U.S. shopping center. Each store is owned by a corporation whose armed guards hold sovereign power over the shopper. More important, certain civil rights are tacitly given up at the threshold of the Apple Store, Walmart, or Sephora; in entering each of these postmodern fiefdoms, the shopper becomes subject to laws and codes of behavior that can be radically different from those of the legacy state structures in which they reside.[12]

As corporations continue to grow in influence by managing the services once run by one's state and federal governments, the sense of the United States as a patchwork of competing sovereignties, each with its own small army, will become more evident. Likewise, federal and state governments' outright war on unions—a war that has been ongoing throughout Democratic and Republican regimes but that seems to capture the public's imagination only when the right wing is in power—threatens to return the U.S. labor force to the abject conditions described in Karen Orren's *Belated Feudalism*. Without vigorous defense of workers' rights, each atomized worker may enter into master/servant style contracts like those prevalent in the United States prior to the Progressive Era and the ascendancy of trade unions. Mandatory arbitration in employment contracts, which forces workers to enter into company-mandated "alternative dispute resolution," could have the pernicious effect of creating neofeudal subjects to people our patchwork neofeudal cities. Whereas in the past mandatory arbitration contacts were "limited to business-to-business or management/union contexts," such contracts are now offered on "on a take-it-or-leave-it basis" to individual employees and consumers.[13] One may, realistically, move from the landlord's demesne in the morning to the employer's demesne for the majority of the day, taking brief respites in one's preferred corporate demesne. In such a scenario, the developed world resembles an interlocking series of Martin Castles, each siloed off from a universal standard of law and subject to the imperatives of their respective owners.

The Martin Castle's ultimate fate is a sign of how tightly the feudal idea of order is bundled with the U.S. national imaginary. The compound has finally found its footing as a boutique hotel, the Kentucky Castle, where for a few nights guests can imagine what it would be like to live in feudal splendor. The hotel's main selling point, a "farm to table" restaurant that the website promises is "the most romantic restaurant in Kentucky," indicates how the longing for a feudal past can integrate itself within a liberal-capitalist framework.[14] From the outside, "farm to table" is a bid for sustainability, one material expression of the innocuous "slow food" movement that emerged in the early 2000s. Viewed another way, the Kentucky Castle's "farm to table" restaurant is the dream of feudalism distilled to its very essence: the guest, who is lord for the day, can eat foods grown and prepared by serfs laboring within the autarkic bounds of the manor, untouched by the circulation of exchange values in the capitalist food regime of factory farms, big-box grocery megastores, and chain restaurants. That the Kentucky Castle is no less capitalistic than these institutions, despite its "romantic" atmosphere, is the fact that the illusion of feudal splendor seeks to disguise.

Imagining the interpersonal and libidinal potentials within the walls of the isolated dream-autarky provides the Kentucky Castle with its most potent sales pitch: "In our hectic world it's hard to connect with those most important to you. Slow down and let the most romantic restaurant in Kentucky set the stage for a night they'll never forget. Reserve the most beautiful hotel in Kentucky for the ultimate wedding experience that your fiancé deserves. Bring your team or family closer together inside our walls where we treat your family like our family. Be their hero and plan a night or weekend where they have your complete attention in a setting they'll never forget."[15] Like all advertising copy, this pitch relies on repetition and ambiguity to encourage readers to see themselves reflected in the products and services offered. Whether corporate leaders or heads of a family, the Kentucky Castle promises to make them "hero[es]" who command the absolute attention of their audience. Authoritarian longing bubbles just under the surface of the advertisement's final line. If in "our hectic modern world" one's spouse, employee, child, or friend is distracted by the machinations of the attention economy, then the Kentucky Castle offers a dreamworld where all eyes will be on the person with enough capital to book a room and a table for the night. The hotel even weaponizes childhood fantasy through its "Kentucky Fairytale" program, a local Make-a-Wish-style program that promises to give children afflicted with terrible diseases one night of magic in a medievalesque setting. For children who are not ill, the Kentucky Castle offers itself for private functions at a reasonable price. If I were a child today, I would certainly beg my parents for a castle birthday party.

In the epigraph that opens this conclusion, Walt Whitman celebrates the ability of the United States to assimilate the dross of dead generations as his nation's greatest strength. Whitman evinces a hereditary historical imagination not unlike that of Cooper's landlords in *Satanstoe* or the Emerson of "Progress of Culture" and *English Traits*. Encouraged in childhood to imagine itself as the "legitimate" child of feudalism, the mature United States is a jumble of disordered legal, creative, and interpersonal regimes. Whether we view ourselves as lords or as laborers on lord's lands, we daily perpetuate a constellation of images and ideas that prevent truly democratic social forms from emerging, retreating instead to the crumbling towers of the American past.

NOTES

INTRODUCTION

Epigraphs are from Alexis de Tocqueville, *Democracy in America and Two Essays on America*, ed. Isaac Kramnick, trans. Gerald Bevan (New York: Penguin Classics, 2003), 23; Karl Marx and Frederick Engels, *The German Ideology: Part 1*, ed. C. J. Arthur (New York: International, 1970), 67.

1. J. Hector St. John Crèvecoueur, *Letters from an American Farmer: Reprinted from the Original Edition* (New York: Albert & Charles Boni, 1925), 191.

2. Thomas Jefferson, *Jefferson: Writings*, ed. Merrill D. Peterson (New York: Literary Classics of the United States, 1984), 32. For a detailed, numerical analysis of the effectiveness of Jefferson's scheme, see Holly Brewer, "Entailing Aristocracy in Colonial Virginia: 'Ancient Feudal Restraints' and Revolutionary Reform," *William and Mary Quarterly* 54, no. 2 (April 1997): 307–346.

3. Nathaniel Hawthorne, "Earth's Holocaust," in *Hawthorne: Tales and Sketches*, ed. Roy Harvey Pearce (New York: Library of America, 1982), 888.

4. For a brief survey of the waning symbolic power of the crown over the course of the eighteenth century, see Jeremy Black, *George III: America's Last King* (New Haven, Conn.: Yale University Press, 2006), 180–181.

5. Henry Steele Commager, *The Empire of Reason: How Europe Imagined and America Realized the Enlightenment* (London: Weidenfeld & Nicolson, 1978), 129–174; J. G. A. Pocock, *The Ancient Constitution and the Feudal Law* (Cambridge: Cambridge University Press, 1987); Gordon S. Wood, *Empire of Liberty: A History of the Early Republic, 1789–1815* (Oxford: Oxford University Press, 2009), 46.

6. "The Constitution," in *The Debate on the Constitution: Part Two, January to August 1788*, ed. Bernard Bailyn (New York: Library of America, 1993), 944.

7. William Doyle, *Aristocracy and Its Enemies in the Age of Revolutions* (New York: Oxford University Press, 2009), 101–103.

8. George Bancroft, *History of the Colonization of the United States* (Boston: Charles C. Little & James Brown, 1843), 310.

9. Francis Parkman, *France and England in North America*, vol 1., ed. David Levin (New York: Literary Classics of the United States, 1983), 1287.

10. Frederick Jackson Turner, "The Significance of the Frontier in American History," in *Rereading Frederick Jackson Turner: "The Significance of the Frontier in American History" and Other Essays*, ed. John Mack Faragher (New Haven: Yale University Press, 1998), 33.

11. Richard Hofstadter, *The Age of Reform: From Bryan to FDR* (New York: Alfred A. Knopf, 1955), 10.

12. Harriet Beecher Stowe, *Dred: A Tale of the Great Dismal Swamp*, ed. Robert S. Levine (New York: Penguin Classics, 2000), 36–37.

13. Thomas Jefferson, "Jefferson to Madison, Sep. 6 1789," in *Republic of Letters: The Correspondence Between Thomas Jefferson and James Madison 1776–1826*, vol. 1, ed. James Morton Smith (New York and London: W. W. Norton, 1995), 634.

14. Jefferson, "Jefferson to Madison," 635.

15. Louis Hartz, *The Liberal Tradition in America*, 2nd ed. (New York: Mariner, 1991), 3, 24.

16. C. Wright Mills, *White Collar: The American Middle Classes* (New York: Oxford University Press, 2002), 4.

17. Donald Pease, *The New American Exceptionalism* (Minneapolis: University of Minnesota Press, 2009), 164.

18. Henry Nash Smith, *Virgin Land: The American West as Symbol and Myth*, revised edition (Cambridge, Mass.: Harvard University Press, 2007), 48.

19. Leo Marx, *The Machine in the Garden: Technology and the Pastoral Ideal in America*, 35th anniversary ed. (New York: Oxford University Press, 2000), 138.

20. Leslie A. Fiedler, *Love and Death in the American Novel* (Chicago: Dalkey Archive, 1997), 76.

21. Sacvan Bercovitch, *The Rites of Assent: Transformations in the Symbolic Construction of America* (London: Routledge, 1992), 31.

22. John Carlos Rowe, *The New American Studies* (St. Paul: University of Minnesota Press, 2002), 3–16.

23. For two recent examples of the liberal consensus model's influence on contemporary literary criticism, see Nancy Glazener, *Literature in the Making: A History of U.S. Literary Culture in the Long Nineteenth Century* (Oxford: Oxford University Press, 2016), 13–14; and Christopher Hanlon, *America's England: Antebellum Literature and Atlantic Sectionalism* (Oxford: Oxford University Press, 2013), 28.

24. Kim Moreland, *The Medievalist Impulse in American Literature: Twain, Adams, Fitzgerald, Hemingway* (Charlottesville: University Press of Virginia, 1996), 12.

25. Tocqueville, *Democracy in America*, 209.

26. Tocqueville, 68.

27. François Guizot, *The History of Civilization in Europe*, ed. Larry Siedentop, trans. William Hazlitt (Indianapolis: Liberty Fund), 86.

28. Alexander Hamilton, "Speech in the New York Ratifying Convention on the Distribution of Powers, June 27, 1788," in *Alexander Hamilton: Writings*, ed. Joanne B. Freeman (New York: Library of America, 2001), 508.

29. Wood, *Empire of Liberty*, 76–91.

30. David Wooton, introduction to *Locke: Political Writings*, ed. David Wooton (Cambridge, Mass.: Hackett, 2003), 44, 48.

31. David Armitage, *Foundations of Modern International Thought* (New York: Cambridge University Press, 2013), 96.

32. John Locke, *The Fundamental Constitutions of Carolina,* in *Locke: Political Writings*, ed. David Wooton (Cambridge, Mass.: Hackett, 2003), 210–231. See especially §22: "Any lord of a manor may alienate, sell, or dispose to any other person and his heirs for ever, his manor, all entirely together, with all the privileges and leet-men thereunto belonging" (215); §22: "In every signory, barony, and manor, all the leet-men shall be under the jurisdiction of the respective lords of the said signory, barony, or many, without appeal from him" (215); and §110: "Every freeman of Carolina shall have absolute power and authority over his Negro slaves, of what opinion or religion soever" (310).

33. Edmund Fawcett, *Liberalism: The Life of an Idea*, 2nd ed. (Princeton, N.J.: Princeton University Press, 2014), 14.

34. Fawcett, *Liberalism*, 25.

35. Browning, " Tyranny of a Construct," 1065.

36. Susan Reynolds, *Fiefs and Vassals: The Medieval Evidence Reinterpreted* (Oxford: Clarendon, 1994), 1.

37. Reynolds, *Fiefs and Vassals*, 8; Elizabeth A. R. Browning, "The Tyranny of a Construct: Feudalism and Historians of Medieval Europe," *American Historical Review* 79, no. 4 (October 1974): 1064.

38. Pocock, *Ancient Law and the Feudal Constitution*, 56, 107.

39. Adam Smith, *An Inquiry into the Nature and Causes of the Wealth of Nations*, ed. Kathryn Sutherland (Oxford: Oxford University Press, 1993), 235.

40. Smith, *An Inquiry*, 234, 264.

41. Smith, 267.

42. Ellen Meiksins Wood, *Liberty and Property: A Social History of Western Political Thought from the Renaissance to the Enlightenment* (London: Verso, 2012), 14.

43. Wood, *Liberty and Property*, 39.

44. Karl Marx, *Early Writings*, trans. Rodney Livingstone and Gregor Benton (London: Penguin, 1992), 90.

45. Karl Marx, *Capital: A Critique of Political Economy, Vol. 3*, trans. David Fernbach (London: Penguin, 1993), 934.

46. F. L. Ganshof, *Feudalism*, 3rd ed., trans. Philip Grierson (Toronto: University of Toronto Press, 1964), 90–91.

47. Doyle, *Aristocracy and Its Enemies*, 17.

48. See, for example, Leonard Reed's influential essay "I, Pencil: My Family Tree as Told

to Leonard R. Read" (1958). Read, founder of the libertarian Foundation for Economic Education, tells the story of capitalist production as a child's fantasy of kindhearted small-scale owners collaborating with their equally kindhearted (and contented) employees to produce a familiar object.

49. Wood, *Liberty and Property*, 220.

50. Wood, 220.

51. Leon Trotsky, *History of the Russian Revolution*, trans. Max Eastman (Chicago: Haymarket, 2008), 4.

52. Tenets one through five have been freely interpreted from Ganshof's *Feudalism* (1961–1964), especially his work concerning the ceremonial and hierarchical aspects of vassalage and English feudal law and its relation to the state. See Ganshof, *Feudalism*, 69–106 (on ceremonies and obligations of vassalage) and 164–166 (on feudalism and the English state). Tenet one, that the feudal elite see themselves as a distinct race of humans, is borrowed from Doyle, *Aristocracy and Its Enemies*, 6–7.

53. Carl L. Becker, *The Heavenly City of the Eighteenth-Century Philosophers*, 2nd ed. (New Haven: Yale University Press, 2003). Becker's genealogy of natural law philosophy, which he traces from Aristotle through Aquinas and to the eighteenth-century Enlightenment philosophers, is particularly useful (see pp. 53–58).

54. "Desultory Thoughts of a Recluse," *United States' Telegraph*, August 10, 1833, n.p.

55. "To the Working Men," *Providence Patriot, Columbian Phenix* (Providence, R.I.), Saturday, January 25, 1834; Issue 56.

56. Georg Lukács, *History and Class Consciousness: Studies in Marxist Dialectics*, trans. Rodney Livingstone (Cambridge, Mass.: MIT Press, 1968), 47.

57. Fredric Jameson, *Allegory and Ideology* (London: Verso, 2019), xvi.

58. Fredric Jameson, *The Political Unconscious: Narrative as a Socially Symbolic Act* (Ithaca, N.Y.: Cornell University Press, 1981), 21.

59. Karl Marx, *The 18th Brumaire of Louis Bonaparte* (New York: International, 2004), 18.

60. George Lukács, *The Historical Novel*, trans. Hannah and Stanley Mitchell (New York: Penguin, 1981), 23–24.

61. Moreland, *Medievalist Impulse*, 5–6.

62. T. J. Jackson Lears, *No Place of Grace: Antimodernism and the Transformation of American Culture 1880–1920* (Chicago: University of Chicago Press, 1981); Tison Pugh, *Queer Chivalry: Medievalism and the Myth of White Masculinity in Southern Literature* (Baton Rouge: Louisiana State University Press, 2013).

63. Lukács, *Historical Novel*, 205.

64. Frederick B. Pike, *The United States and Latin America: Myths and Stereotypes of Civilization and Nature* (Austin: University of Texas Press, 1992), 178–179.

65. Corey Robin, *The Reactionary Mind: Conservatism from Burke to Sarah Palin* (Oxford: Oxford University Press, 2011), 52.

CHAPTER ONE. PLANTATION ROMANCE AND SOUTHERN MEDIEVALISM IN POE'S MAGAZINE FICTION

The epigraph is from Hamilton Wright Mabie, *Essays in Literary Interpretation* (Cambridge, Mass.: John Wilson and Son, 1893), 7–8.

1. Quoted in Scott Peeples, *The Afterlife of Edgar Allan Poe* (Rochester, N.Y.: Camden House, 2004), 18.

2. Mabie, *Essays*, 19.

3. See John Carlos Rowe, *At Emerson's Tomb: The Politics of Classic American Literature* (New York: Columbia University Press, 1997), 61; F. O. Matthiessen, *American Renaissance: Art and Expression in the Age of Emerson and Whitman* (New York: Oxford University Press, 1941), 10.

4. Joan Dayan, "Amorous Bondage: Poe, Ladies, and Slaves," *American Literature* 66, no. 2 (June 1994): 239–273; Betsy Erkkila, *Mixed Bloods and Other Crosses: Rethinking American Literature from the Revolution to the Culture Wars* (Philadelphia: University of Pennsylvania Press, 2005); Bernard Rosenthal, "Poe, Slavery, and the *Southern Literary Messenger*: A Reexamination," *Poe Studies* 7, no. 2 (December 1974): 29–38.

5. M. Anna Fariello, "Personalizing the Political: The Davis Family Circle in Richmond's Hollywood Cemetery," in *Monuments to the Lost Cause: Women, Art, and the Landscapes of Southern Memory* (Knoxville: University of Tennessee Press, 2003), 116–132.

6. F. L. Ganshof, *Feudalism*, trans. Philip Grierson (Buffalo, N.Y.: University of Toronto Press, 1996), 7–12.

7. Thomas Piketty, *Capital in the Twenty-First Century* (Cambridge: Belknap Press of Harvard University, 2014), 159–161.

8. Walter Benjamin, "On The Concept of History," in *Selected Writings, Volume 4: 1938–1940*, ed. Howard Eiland and Michael W. Jennings, trans. Edmund Jephcott (Cambridge, Mass.: Harvard University Press, 2003), 392.

9. John Pendleton Kennedy, *Swallow Barn: or, A Sojourn in the Old Dominion*, rev. ed. (New York: George P. Putnam, 1852), 70. Hereafter cited parenthetically as *SB*.

10. George Fitzhugh, *Sociology for the South, or the Failure of Free Society* (Richmond, Va.: A. Morris, 1854), 289.

11. Coleman Hutchison, *Apples and Ashes: Literature, Nationalism, and the Confederate States of America* (Atlanta: University of Georgia Press, 2012), 8.

12. Tison Pugh, *Queer Chivalry*, 7.

13. Susan J. Tracy, *In the Master's Eye: Representations of Women, Blacks, and Poor Whites in Antebellum Southern Literature* (Amherst: University of Massachusetts Press, 2009), 36.

14. Tracy, *In the Master's Eye*, 29.

15. Jeremy Wells, *Romances of the Whiteman's Burden Race, Empire, and the Plantation in American Literature, 1880–1936* (Nashville: Vanderbilt University Press, 2011), 39–40.

16. Tracy, *Master's Eye*, 16.

17. Perry Anderson, *Passages From Antiquity to Feudalism* (London: Verso, 2013), 147.

18. Frederick Douglass, "The Meaning of July Fourth for the Negro, Speech at Rochester, New York, July 5, 1852," in *Frederick Douglass: Selected Speeches and Writings*, ed. Philip S. Foner and Yuval Taylor (Chicago: Lawrence Hill Books, 1999): 195.

19. Fitzhugh, *Sociology for the South*, 47–48.

20. James C. Cobb, *Away Down South: A History of Southern Identity* (Oxford: Oxford University Press, 2005); William R. Taylor, *Cavalier and Yankee: The Old South and American National Character* (Oxford: Oxford University Press, 1961). See especially Cobb, p. 44ff.

21. Mark Twain, *Life on the Mississippi*, in *Mississippi Writings*, ed. Guy Cardwell (New York: Library of America, 1982), 500. Tracy makes a similar claim when she asserts that southern writers were attracted to Scott because "his novels, in their recognition of the value of organic society, seemed to share their ... affirmation of conservative values." See Tracy, *In the Master's Eye*, 37.

22. Fitzhugh, *Sociology for the South*, 240.

23. Fitzhugh, 287.

24. Pugh, *Queer Chivalry*, 6.

25. Taylor, *Cavalier and Yankee*, 162–69.

26. Caroline Lee Hentz, *The Planter's Northern Bride* (Philadelphia: T. B. Peterson & Son, 1854), 332.

27. Thavolia Glymph, *Out of the House of Bondage: The Transformation of the Plantation House* (New York: Cambridge University Press, 2008), 63.

28. Lacy K. Ford, *Deliver Us From Evil: The Slavery Question in the Old South* (Oxford: Oxford University Press, 2009), 5–10.

29. Herbert Aptheker, *Essays in the History of the American Negro* (New York: International, 1983), 10–11.

30. William Gilmore Simms, *The Sword and the Distaff: Or, "Fair, Fat and Forty." A Story of the South, At the Close of the Revolution* (Philadelphia: Lippincott, Grambo, 1853), 418.

31. "Thomas Jefferson to John Holmes, April 22, 1820," in *Writings*, ed. Merrill D. Peterson (New York: Library of America, 1984), 1434.

32. Daniel Walker Howe, *What God Hath Wrought: The Transformation of America, 1815–1848* (New York: Oxford University Press, 2007), 158.

33. Howe, *What God Hath Wrought*, 127–128.

34. Edward E. Baptist, *The Half Has Never Been Told: Slavery and the Making of U.S. Capitalism* (New York: Basic Books, 2016), 40.

35. Edgar Allan Poe, "Nathaniel Hawthorne," in *Essays and Reviews*, ed. G.R. Thompson (New York: Library of America, 1984): 572.

36. Poe, "Nathaniel Hawthorne," 579.

37. Joel R. Kehler, "New Light on the Genesis and Progress of Poe's Landscape Fiction," *American Literature* 47, no. 2 (May 1975): 173, 176.

38. Quoted in John Robert Moore, "Poe's Reading of *Anne of Geierstein*," *American Literature* 22, no. 4 (January 1951): 493.

39. Edgar Allan Poe, "The Domain of Arnheim," in *Poetry and Tales*, ed. Patrick F. Quinn (New York: Library of America, 1984), 855. Hereafter cited parenthetically as "DA."

40. T. O. Mabbott, introduction to "The Landscape-Garden," in *The Collected Works of Edgar Allan Poe—Volume II: Tales and Sketches*, ed. T. O. Mabbott (Cambridge: Belknap Press of Harvard University, 1978), 700.

41. Lucian Minor, "Minor's Address," *Southern Literary Messenger* 2, no. 1 (December 1835): 66–67.

42. For an account of Poe's knowledge of Minor's "Address," see Dwight Thomas and David K. Jackson, *The Poe Log: A Documentary Life of Edgar Allan Poe, 1809–1849* (Boston: G.K. Hall, 1987), 176–179.

43. Thomas and Jackson, *Poe Log*, 236–241.

44. James Ewell Heath, "Southern Literature," *Southern Literary Messenger* 1, no. 1 (August 1834): 1–3.

45. Quoted in David Kelly Jackson, *Poe and the Southern Literary Messenger* (New York: Haskell, 1970), 29.

46. Edgar Allan Poe, "Berenice," in *Poetry and Tales*, ed. Patrick F. Quinn (New York: Library of America, 1984), 226. Hereafter cited parenthetically as "Berenice."

47. Jackson, *Poe and the Southern Literary Messenger*, 60–61.

48. J. Gerald Kennedy, "Inventing the Literati: Poe's Remapping of Antebellum Print Culture," in *Poe and the Remapping of Antebellum Print Culture*, ed. J. Gerald Kennedy and Jerome McGann (Baton Rouge: Louisiana State University Press, 2012), 21.

49. Kennedy, "Inventing the Literati," 24.

50. Quoted in Andrew Levy, *The Culture and Commerce of the American Short Story* (New York: Cambridge University Press, 1996), 16.

51. Edgar Allan Poe, "Calavar; or The Knight of the Conquest: A Romance of Mexico," *Southern Literary Messenger* 1, no. 6 (February 1835): 315.

52. Edgar Allan Poe, "Rienzi, the Last of the Tributes. By the Author of 'Eugene Aram,' 'Last Days of Pompeii,' &c. &c. Two Volumes in one. Philadelphia: Republished by E.L. Carey and A. Hart," in *Essays and Reviews*, ed. G. R. Thompson (New York: Library of America, 1984), 145.

53. Quoted in Terrence Whalen, *Edgar Allan Poe and the Masses: The Political Economy of Literature in Antebellum America* (Princeton, N.J.: Princeton University Press, 1999), 53.

54. Michael Beard, "The Epigraph to Poe's 'Berenice,'" *American Literature* 49, no. 4 (January 1978): 611–613.

55. During Reconstruction, *Anne of Geierstein* became instrumental in the formation of

the Ku Klux Klan, who took its wild descriptions of eldritch ritual tribunals and put them into practice. See Moore, "Poe's Reading of *Anne of Geierstein*," 493–496. Moore cites James Taft Hatfield, "Goethe and the Ku-Klux Klan," *PMLA* 37, no. 4 (December 1922): 735–739 as evidence for Scott's influence on the southern terrorist organization.

56. Joan Dayan, "The Identity of Berenice, Poe's Idol of the Mind," *Studies in Romanticism* 23, no. 4 (Winter 1984): 502.

57. William Freedman, "'Berenice' and the Art of Incorporative Exclusion," *Poe Studies/Dark Romanticism* 36, nos. 1–2 (January–December 2003), 68.

58. Edgar Allan Poe, "King Pest," in *Poetry and Tales*, ed. Patrick F. Quinn (New York: Library of America, 1984), 241. Hereafter cited parenthetically as "KP."

59. William Whipple, "Poe's Political Satire," *University of Texas Studies in English* 35 (1956): 84, 86–87.

60. Whalen, *Edgar Allan Poe and the Masses*, 86–108.

61. Louis Renza, "Poe's King: Playing it Close to the Pest," *Edgar Allan Poe Review* 2, no. 2 (Fall 2001): 3–18.

62. Edgar Allan Poe, "The Devil in the Belfry," in *Tales and Sketches*, ed. Patrick F. Quinn (New York: Library of America, 1984), 303, 306. Hereafter cited parenthetically as "DB."

63. Edgar Allan Poe, "The Masque of the Red Death," in *Poetry and Tales*, ed. Patrick F. Quinn (New York: Library of America, 1984), 485. Hereafter cited parenthetically as "MRD."

64. Paul Haspell, "Bells of Freedom and Foreboding: Liberty Bell Ideology and the Clock Motif in Edgar Allan Poe's 'The Masque of the Red Death,'" *The Edgar Allan Poe Review* 13, no. 1 (Spring 2012): 54.

65. Zachary Z. E. Bennett, "Killing the Aristocrats: The Mask, the Cask, and Poe's Ethics of S&M," *Edgar Allan Poe Review* 12, no. 1 (Spring 2011): 42–58; Rick Rodriguez, "Sovereign Authority and the Democratic Subject in Poe," *Poe Studies* 44, no. 1 (October 2011): 39–56.

66. Ronald Gottesman, "Hop-Frog and the American Nightmare," in *Masques, Mysteries, and Mastodons: A Poe Miscellany*, ed. Benjamin F. Fisher (Baltimore: Edgar Allan Poe Society, 2006), 136.

67. Joan Dayan, "Amorous Bondage: Poe, Ladies, and Slaves," *American Literature* 66, no. 2 (June 1994): 239–273; Gottesman, "Hop-Frog and the American Nightmare"; Paul Christian Jones, "The Danger of Sympathy: Edgar Allan Poe's 'Hop-Frog' and the Abolitionist Rhetoric of Pathos," *Journal of American Studies* 35 (2001): 239–254.

68. Edgar Allan Poe, "Hop-Frog," in *Tales and Sketches*, ed. Patrick F. Quinn (New York: Library of America, 1984), 900. Hereafter parenthetically cited as "HF."

69. John Carlos Rowe, *Literary Culture and U.S. Imperialism* (New York: Oxford University Press, 2000), 73.

70. Baptist, *Half Has Never Been Told*, 26.

71. Betsy Erkkila, "The Poetics of Whiteness: Poe and the Racial Imaginary," in *Romancing the Shadow: Poe and Race*, ed. J. Gerald Kennedy and Lilian Weissberg (Oxford: Oxford University Press, 2001), 58.

72. Robin, *Reactionary Mind*, 29.

73. Robin, *Reactionary Mind*, 44.

74. For a survey of this "psychobiographical" interpretation of Poe's work, including its centrality to poststructuralist literary theory, see Rowe, *At Emerson's Tomb*, 49–50.

75. Robin, *Reactionary Mind*, 29.

76. Edgar Allan Poe, "The Fall of the House of Usher," in *Poetry and Tales*, ed. Patrick F. Quinn (New York: Library of America, 1984), 317. Hereafter cited parenthetically as "Usher."

77. For an overview of southern novelists' views of Anglo-Saxonism (later Anglo-Normanism), including the influence of Anglo-Saxon heritage on William Gilmore Simms, see Reginald Horsman, *Race and Manifest Destiny: The Origins of American Racial Anglo-Saxonism* (Cambridge, Mass.: Harvard University Press, 1981): 164–176.

CHAPTER TWO. MELODRAMA OF PRIMITIVE ACCUMULATION

The epigraph is from Stephen Jay Gould, *The Mismeasure of Man* (New York: W. W. Norton, 1996), 28.

1. James Fenimore Cooper, *Satanstoe; or, The Littlepage Manuscripts. A Tale of the Colony*, 2 vols. (New York: Burgess, Stringer, 1845), 9. Hereafter cited parenthetically as *S*.

2. Reeve Huston, "The Parties and 'The People': The New York Anti-Rent Wars and the Contours of Jacksonian Politics," *Journal of the Early Republic* 20, no. 2 (Summer 2000): 241–271.

3. Huston "Parties and 'The People,'" 242.

4. This process is similar to the "settler common sense," a term coined by literary scholar Mark Rifkin to describe how settler logic perpetuates itself through law, politics, domestic life, and personal relations. See *Settler Common Sense: Queerness and Everyday Colonialism in the American Renaissance* (Minneapolis: University of Minnesota Press, 2014), xvi, 14–16.

5. For a detailed discussion of how English settlers attempted to articulate their land rights in terms of both the common law tradition and natural rights philosophy, see Craig Yirush, *Settlers, Liberty, and Empire: The Roots of American Political Theory, 1675–1775* (New York: Cambridge University Press, 2011).

6. John Adams, "Dissertation on the Canon and Feudal Law," in *The Portable John Adams*, ed. John Patrick Diggins (New York: Penguin, 2004), 213.

7. Jefferson, *Writings*, 44.

8. Jefferson.

9. See Holly Brewer, "Entailing Aristocracy in Colonial Virginia: 'Ancient Feudal Restraints' and Revolutionary Reform," *William and Mary Quarterly* 54, no. 2 (April 1997): 307–346// especially pp. 309–310 and 315; Roger G. Kennedy, *Mr. Jefferson's Lost Cause: Land, Farmers, Slavery, and the Louisiana Purchase* (Oxford: Oxford University Press, 2004), 31–32. As Kennedy observes, "Most of the Tidewater aristocracy and nearly all the newer Piedmont oligarchy stayed in the saddle and cantered easily into the post-

Revolutionary world," making Jefferson's dream of an agrarian nation peopled with small freeholds a victory mostly in Jefferson's "symbolic imagination."

10. Kennedy, *Mr. Jefferson's Lost Cause*, 30.

11. David Thomas, "Anglo-American Land Law: Diverging Developments From a Shared History: Part II: How Anglo-American Land Law Diverged After American Colonization and Independence," *Real Property, Probate, and Trust Journal* 34, no. 2 (Summer 1999): 325.

12. The two most recent book-length studies of the Anti-Rent War are Reeve Huston, *Land and Freedom: Rural Society, Popular Protest, and Party Politics in Antebellum New York* (Oxford: Oxford University Press, 2002); and Charles W. McCurdy, *The Anti-Rent Era in New York Law and Politics, 1839–1865* (Chapel Hill: University of North Carolina Press, 2001).

13. McCurdy, *Anti-Rent*, 170.

14. Huston, *Land and Freedom*, 71.

15. Martin Bruegel, "Manorial Society and the Market in the Hudson Valley, 1780–1850," *Journal of American History* 82, no. 4 (March 1996): 1399.

16. Huston, *Land and Freedom*, 111.

17. Bruegel, "Manorial Society," 1395.

18. Bruegel, 13.

19. See Harry L. Watson, *Liberty and Power: The Politics of Jacksonian America* (New York: Hill & Wang, 2006), 50, 176–195.

20. Reeve, "New York Anti-Rent Wars," 249.

21. Huston, *Land and Freedom*, 21, 204.

22. Philip J. Deloria, *Playing Indian* (New Haven: Yale University Press, 1999), 41–43.

23. Deloria, *Playing Indian*, 44.

24. Vine Deloria, Jr., *Custer Died for Your Sins: An Indian Manifesto* (Norman: University of Oklahoma Press, 1988), 4, 174–177, 194–195.

25. Granville Hicks, "Landlord Cooper and the Anti-Renters," *Antioch Review* 5, no. 1 (Spring 1945): 95–109.

26. See Eric J. Sundquist, *Home as Found: Authority and Genealogy in Nineteenth-Century American Literature* (Baltimore: Johns Hopkins University Press, 1979), xx.

27. Alan Taylor, *William Cooper's Town: Power and Persuasion on the Frontier of the Early American Republic* (New York: Vintage, 1996), 59, 99–100.

28. James Fenimore Cooper, *The American Democrat, Political Writings of James Fenimore Cooper*, ed. Bradley J. Birzer and John Wilson (Washington, D.C.: Regnery, 2000), 364.

29. See John P. McWilliams Jr., *Political Justice in a Republic: James Fenimore Coopers America* (Berkeley: University of California Press, 1972), 199, 340, for the ways in which *The American Democrat* defends a "strict constructionist" view of the U.S. Constitution.

30. "Federalist #18," "'Publius,' The Federalist XLV," in *The Debate on the Constitution: Part Two: January to August 1788*, ed. Bernard Bailyn (New York: Library of America, 1993), 103.

31. James Fenimore Cooper, *The Letters and Journals of James Fenimore Cooper: 1845–1849*, ed. James Franklin Beard (Cambridge, Mass.: Belknap Press of Harvard University Press, 1968), 388.

32. Daniel Marder, "Cooper's Second Cycle," *South Central Review* 2, no. 2 (Summer 1985): 31, 24; Marius Bewley, "Fenimore Cooper and the Economic Age," *American Literature* 26, no. 2 (May 1954): 169.

33. Cooper, *Letters and Journals*, 7.

34. James Fenimore Cooper, *The Chainbearer; or, The Little Page Manuscripts*, 2 vols. (New York: Burgess, Stringer, 1845), iii–iv. Hereafter cited parenthetically as *C*.

35. William N. Fenton, *The Great Law and the Longhouse: A Political History of the Iroquois Confederacy* (Norman: University of Oklahoma Press, 1998), 7–8.

36. Fenton, *Great Law and the Longhouse*, 358.

37. Karl Marx, *The Ethnological Notebooks of Karl Marx*, 2nd ed., ed. Lawrence Krader (Assen, the Netherlands: Van Gorcum, 1974): 138.

38. Manuel Yang, "Specter of the Commons: Karl Marx, Lewis Henry Morgan, and Nineteenth-Century European Stadialism," *borderlands* 11, no. 2 (2012): 7.

39. See especially Vine Deloria Jr.'s take on Martin Luther King Jr.'s Poor People's March in Deloria, *Custer Died for Your Sins*, 185–187; Russell Means, "The Same Old Song," in *Marxism and Native Americans*, ed. Ward Churchill (Boston: South End, 1992), 19–34; and Leslie Marmon Silko, *The Almanac of the Dead* (New York: Simon & Schuster, 1991).

40. See Byrd's discussion of Lenin, Gramsci, and "internal colonization" in Jodi Byrd, *The Transit of Empire: Indigenous Critiques of Colonialism* (Minneapolis: University of Minnesota Press, 2011), 130–131; Coulthard's rereading of the "primitive accumulation" and colonialism in Marx's *Capital* in Glenn Coulthard, *Red Skins, White Masks: Rejecting the Colonial Politics of Recognition* (Minneapolis: University of Minnesota Press, 2014), 7–13; and Estes's discussion of Wounded Knee and landed wealth in Nick Estes, "Wounded Knee: Settler Colonial Property and Indigenous Liberation," *Capitalism Nature Socialism* 24, no. 3 (2013): 190–202.

41. James Fenimore Cooper, *The Redskins; or, Indian and Injun*, 2 vols. (New York: Burgess, Stringer, 1846), 121. Hereafter cited parenthetically as *R*.

42. See Charles O'Donnell, "Progress and Property: The Later Cooper," *American Quarterly* 13, no. 3 (Autumn 1961): 402–409 for the unconvincing claim that the Littlepage novels are finally a condemnation of the "original sin" of native displacement.

43. Deloria, *Playing Indian*, 40.

44. Susan Schenckel, *The Insistence of the Indian: Race and Nationalism in Nineteenth-Century American Culture* (Princeton, N.J.: Princeton University Press, 1998): 16

45. Richard Slotkin, *Regeneration Through Violence: The Mythology of the American Frontier, 1600–1860* (Norman: University of Oklahoma Press, 1973), 484–485.

46. Slotkin, *Regeneration Through Violence*, 486.

47. Scheckel, *Insistence of the Indian*, 19, 26–29.

48. Monika M. Elbert and Lesley Ginsberg, introduction to *Romantic Education in Nineteenth-Century American Literature*, ed. Monika M. Elbert and Lesley Ginsberg (New York: Routledge, 2014), 1–2.

49. Elbert and Ginsberg, introduction, 3–4.

CHAPTER THREE. MARRIAGE, CHIVALRY, AND FEUDAL LAW

Epigraphs are from J. Elizabeth Jones, "Of Husband and Wife," in *History of Woman Suffrage*, 3 vols., ed. Elizabeth Cady Stanton, Susan B. Anthony, and Matilda Joslyn Gage (Rochester, N.Y.: Charles Mann, 1889), 110; Harriet A. Jacobs, *Incidents in the Life of a Slave Girl*, ed. Jean Fagan Yellin (Cambridge, Mass.: Harvard University Press, 1987), 29. Hereafter cited parenthetically as *I*.

1. Saidiya V. Hartman, *Scenes of Subjection: Terror, Slavery, and Self-Making in Nineteenth-Century America* (New York: Oxford University Press, 1997), 102.

2. Jean Fagan Yellin, *Harriet Jacobs: A Life* (New York: Basic Books, 2004), 101–102.

3. Jacobs's nuanced critique of Seneca Falls rhetoric foreshadows Angela Davis's thoroughgoing Marxist analysis of the early women's rights movement and abolitionism. See Angela Y. Davis, *Women, Race, and Class* (New York: Vintage, 1981), 46–86.

4. Giorgio Agamben, *The Kingdom and the Glory: For a Theological Genealogy of Economy and Government*, trans. Lorenzo Chiesa and Matteo Mandarini (Stanford,: Stanford University Press, 2011), 51.

5. Nancy F. Cott, *Public Vows: A History of Marriage and the Nation* (Cambridge, Mass.: Harvard University Press, 2000), 62.

6. Tapping Reeve, *The Law of Baron and Femme*, 3rd ed., ed. Amasa J. Parker and Charles Baldwin (Albany, N.Y.: William Gould, 1862), iii–iv.

7. A. J. Minnis, *Medieval Theory of Authorship: Scholastic Literary Attitudes in the Later Middle Ages* (Philadelphia: University of Pennsylvania Press, 1984).

8. Cott, *Public Vows*, 14.

9. Cott, 17.

10. Ruth Bloch, *Gender and Morality in Anglo-American Culture, 1650–1800* (Los Angeles: University of California Press, 2003), 79.

11. Carol Shammas, *A History of Household Government in America* (Charlottesville: University of Virginia Press, 2002), 65.

12. Shammas, *History of Household Government*, 3. Also see Mark E. Brandon, *States of Union: Family and Change in the American Constitutional Order* (Lawrence: University of Kansas Press, 2003), 35–37. Brandon convincingly connects laws pertaining to master and servant to those concerning husband and wife through readings from Blackstone's *Commentaries* (see also in Brandon page 49 on the relationship between guardian and ward).

13. Quoted in Stanton et al. *History of Woman Suffrage*, 774.

14. Sidney Lanier, *The Boy's Froissart: Being Sir John Froissart's Chronicles of Adventure Battle and Custom in England France Spain Etc.* (New York: Charles Scribner's Sons, 1879), v.

15. Barry Gaines, "The Editions of Malory in the Early Nineteenth Century," *Papers of the Bibliographical Society of America* 68 (1974): 1–17.

16. John Olin Eidson, *Tennyson in America: His Reputation and Influence from 1827 to 1858* (Athens: University of Georgia Press, 1943); Christina Henderson, "A Nation of the Continual Present: Timrod, Tennyson, and the Memorialization of the Confederacy," *Southern Literary Journal* 45, no. 2 (Spring 2013): 20; James H. Hood, "Overreading Tennyson: Antebellum American Appropriations of the Lady Poems," *Victorian Poetry* 32, no. 1 (Spring 1994): 82.

17. Elisha P. Hurlbut, *Essays on Human Rights and Their Political Guaranties* (New York: Greeley & McElrath, 1845), 144.

18. Mark Brandon, *States of Union*, 32.

19. Quoted in Stanton et. al, *History of Woman Suffrage*, 580.

20. Stanton et al., 110.

21. Elizabeth Stockton, "E. D. E. N. Southworth's Reimagining of the Married Women's Property Reforms," in *E. D. E. N. Southworth: Recovering a Nineteenth-Century Popular Novelist*, ed. Melissa J. Homestead and Pamela Washington (Knoxville: University of Tennessee Press, 2012), 244.

22. Stockton, "E. D. E. N. Southworth's Reimagining," 243.

23. Michelle Ann Abate, "Launching a Gender B(l)acklash: E. D. E. N. Southworth's *The Hidden Hand* and the Emergence of (Racialized) White Tomboyism," *Children's Literature Association Quarterly* 31, no. 1 (Spring 2006): 48.

24. Veronica Stewart, "Narrative Freedom in E. D. E. N. Southworth's *The Hidden Hand, or, Capitola the Madcap*," *LIT* 8, no. 2 (1997): 153–172.

25. Sari Edelstein, "Metamorphosis of the Newsboy": E. D. E. N. Southworth's *The Hidden Hand* and the Antebellum Story-Paper," *American Fiction* 37, no. 1 (Spring 2010): 45.

26. Abate, "Gender b(l)acklash," 50.

27. Edmund Burke, *Reflections on the Revolution in France*, ed. J. G. A. Pocock (Indianapolis: Hackett, 1987), 66.

28. Paul Christian Jones, "'This dainty woman's hand . . . red with blood': E. D. E. N. Southworth's *The Hidden Hand* as Abolitionist Narrative," *Transcendental Quarterly* 15, no. 1 (March 2001): 77.

29. Elizabeth Cady Stanton, "Divorce versus Domestic Warfare," in *Elizabeth Cady Stanton: Feminist as Thinker*, ed. Ellen Carol Dubois and Richard Cándida Smith (New York: New York University Press, 2007), 255.

30. Anna Julia Cooper, *A Voice From the South*, in *The Voice of Anna Julia Cooper*, ed. Charles Lemert and Esme Bhan (Oxford: Rowman & Littlefield, 1998), 53.

31. The only scholarly edition of Cooper's works, Lemert and Bhan's *Voice of Anna Julia*

Cooper, incorrectly claims the proslavery Methodist bishop Henry Bidleman Bascom as Cooper's source for this passage. However, a Google Books search reveals that Cooper is directly quoting from the rhetorician John Bascom's works, not the bishop's.

32. John Bascom, *Philosophy of English Literature: A Course of Lectures Delivered in the Lowell Institute* (New York: G. P. Putnam's Sons, 1876), 37.

33. Chris Nyland, "Adam Smith: Stage Theory and the Status of Women," working paper, Department of Economics, University of Wollongong, 1991.

34. Cooper, *Voice*, 60–61.

35. Cooper, 63.

36. Albert H. Tricomi, "Harriet Jacobs's Autobiography and the Voice of Lydia Maria Child," *ESQ* 53, no. 3 (2007): 217–252.

37. Thomas Doherty, "Harriet Jacobs's Narrative Strategies: *Incidents in the Life of a Slave Girl*," *Southern Literary Journal* 19, no. 1 (Fall 1986): 83.

38. Jennifer Rae Greeson, "The 'Mysteries and Miseries' of North Carolina: New York City, Urban Gothic Fiction, and *Incidents in the Life of a Slave Girl*," *American Literature* 73, no. 2 (June 2001): 277–309.

39. Doherty, "Narrative Strategies," 86.

40. Greeson, "Mysteries and Miseries," 292.

41. Fiedler, *Love and Death*, 71.

42. Fiedler, 76, 145.

43. Sharon Block, "Lines of Color, Sex, and Service: Comparative Sexual Coercion in the Early Republic," in *Sex, Love, Race: Crossing Boundaries in North American History*, ed. Martha Hodes (New York: New York University Press, 1999), 156.

44. Christina Accomando, "'The laws were laid down to me anew': Harriet Jacobs and the Reframing of Legal Fictions," *African American Review* 32, no. 2 (Summer 1998): 239.

45. Hurlbut, *Essays on Human Rights*, 146.

46. Bruce Mills, "Lydia Maria Child and the End to Harriet Jacobs's *Incidents in the Life of a Slave Girl*," *American Literature* 64, no. 2 (June 1992): 255.

CHAPTER FOUR. RESISTANCE TO THE FEUDAL-LIBERAL ALLIANCE

1. Robert J. Walker, "Letter of Mr. Walker, of Mississippi, Relative to the Annexation of Texas in Reply to the Call of the People of Carroll County, Ky., to Communicate His Views on That Subject," in *The U.S. Mexican War: A Binational Reader*, ed. Christopher Conway, trans. Gustavo Pellón (Indianapolis: Hackett, 2010), 39–40.

2. Quoted in Michael Levin, *Marx, Engels, and Liberal Democracy* (New York: Palgrave Macmillan, 1989): 28.

3. Horsman, *Race and Manifest Destiny*. See especially chapter 11, "Anglo-Saxons and Mexicans" (208–228) and chapter 12, "Race, Expansion, and the Mexican War" (229–240).

4. Richard Griswold del Castillo, *The Treaty of Guadalupe Hidalgo: A Legacy of Conflict* (Norman: University of Oklahoma Press, 1990), 82–83.

5. *The Constitutions of California and the United States, with Related Documents, 2017–2018* (Sacramento: California State Legislature, 2017), 115.

6. Howe, *What Hath God Wrought*, 809–810.

7. Shelley Streeby, *American Sensations: Class, Empire, and the Production of Popular Culture* (Berkeley: University of California Press, 2002), 195.

8. Robert A. Wilson, *Savage Anxieties: The Invention of Western Civilization* (New York: Palgrave Macmillan, 2012).

9. James Knox Polk, "James K. Polk: Third Annual Message—December 7, 1847," American Presidency Project, http://www.presidency.ucsb.edu/ws/print.php?pid=29488 (accessed March 21, 2016).

10. James Knox Polk, "James K. Polk: Third Annual Message—December 7, 1847," American Presidency Project, http://www.presidency.ucsb.edu/ws/print.php?pid=29488 (accessed March 21, 2016).

11. John O'Sullivan, "The Great Nation of Futurity," *Democratic Review* 6 (Washington, D.C.: Langree & O'Sullivan, 1839), 426.

12. John O'Sullivan, "Annexation," *United States Magazine and Democratic Review* 17, no. 1 (July–August 1845): 5–10. In *The U.S. Mexican War: A Binational Reader*, ed. Christopher Conway, trans. Gustavo Pellón (Indianapolis: Hackett, 2010), 53.

13. Jáksic, *Hispanic World*, 4.

14. Waddy Thompson, *Recollections of Mexico* (New York: Wiley & Putnam, 1846), 18. For Thompson's influence on anti-Catholic sentiment in the run-up to the U.S.-Mexico War, see John C. Pinheiro, *Missionaries of Republicanism: A Religious History of the Mexican-American War* (New York: Oxford University Press, 2014), 135.

15. "Spain in the Fifteenth Century," *Southern Literary Messenger* 7, no. 3 (March 1841): 242.

16. Severn Teackle Wallis, "Spain: Her History, Character and Literature. Vulgar Errors—Their Extent and Sources," *Southern Literary Messenger* 7, no. 7 (July 1841): 441–442.

17. Washington Irving, *The Alhambra*, in *Irving: Bracebridge Hall, Tales of a Traveler, The Alhambra*, ed. Andrew Myers (New York: Library of America, 1991), 753, 770.

18. *Xicoténcatl*, trans. Guillermo I. Castillo-Feliú (Austin: University of Texas Press, 1999), 131.

19. Lorenzo de Zavala, *Journey to the United States of North America*, ed. John-Michael Rivera, trans. Wallace Woolsey (Houston: Arte Público, 2005): 3. Views like Zavala's animated much American and Mexican historiography in the later nineteenth century. For two early examples, see Gorham D. Abbott, *Mexico, and the United States: Their Mutual Relations and Common Interests* (New York: G.P. Putnam & Son, 1869): 31; and Matías Romero, *Mexico and the United States* (New York: G.P. Putnam & Son, 1898), quoted in Clayton Charles Kohl, "Claims as a Cause of the Mexican War" (PhD diss., New York University, 1914), vii.

20. Zavala, *Journey*, 368.

21. See Horsman, *Race and Manifest Destiny*, 25–42 for a description of this historical

project as it concerned Anglo-Saxon superiority and the imperial destiny of the United States.

22. Brian DeLay, *War of a Thousand Deserts: Indian Raids and the U.S.-Mexican War* (New Haven: Yale University Press, 2008), 4–5.

23. Jenny Franchot, *Roads to Rome: The Antebellum Protestant Encounter With Catholicism* (Berkeley: University of California Press, 1994), 13.

24. Susan Griffin, *Anti-Catholicism and Nineteenth-Century Fiction* (Cambridge: Cambridge University Press, 2000), 11, 94.

25. Griffin, *Anti-Catholicism and Nineteenth-Century Fiction*, 92.

26. Robert Walter Johannsen, *To the Halls of the Montezumas: The Mexican War in the American Imagination* (Oxford: Oxford University Press, 1985), 252.

27. Philip Young, *History of Mexico; Her Civil Wars, and Colonial and Revolutionary Annals; From the Period of the Spanish Conquest, 1520, to the Present Time, 1847: Including an Account of the War With the United States, Its Causes and Military Achievements* (Cincinnati: J. A. & U. P. James, 1847), 56.

28. Young, *History of Mexico*, 57.

29. Maria DeGuzmán, *Spain's Long Shadow: The Black Legend, Off-Whiteness, and Anglo-American Empire* (Minneapolis: University of Minnesota Press, 2005), 64.

30. Quoted in Iván Jáksic, *The Hispanic World and American Intellectual Life, 1820–1880* (New York: Palgrave MacMillan, 2007), 153.

31. Schmidt, "Mexico."

32. Schmidt, 131.

33. Schmidt, 132.

34. Schmidt, 121

35. Horsman, *Race and Manifest Destiny*, 37–38, 124–138.

36. Greer et al., *Rereading the Black Legend*, 3.

37. These two sentences summarize much of Pierre Villar's argument regarding Spain's economic stagnation in the sixteenth and seventeenth centuries. See Pierre Villar, *A History of Gold And Money: 1450–1925*, trans. Judith White (London: Verso, 2011), 37–38.

38. Vilar, *A History of Gold and Money*, 48. The arbitrariness of gold as a commodity has often been explained away by its rarity or usefulness, but these explanations are largely attempts to naturalize quirks of capitalist economic practice through the language of science. As Marx pithily puts it in *Capital: Volume 1*: "So far no chemist has ever discovered exchange-value either in a pearl or a diamond" (177).

39. We should also remember that the Dutch were Spanish subjects until they won independence from Hapsburg Spain after the Eighty Years' War in 1648, meaning that the Dutch benefited from the "price revolution" initiated by Spanish gold even as they fought against Spanish rule.

40. Marx's discussion of indigenous displacement can be found in *Capital: Volume 1*, trans. Ben Fowkes (London: Penguin, 1990), 873–876. Against the familiar narrative—pop-

ularized by Smith and still prevalent in American primary and secondary education—that capital stems from the resources of a "diligent, intelligent and above all frugal élite," Marx tells us that "in actual history, it is a notorious fact that conquest, enslavement, robbery murder, in short, force, play the greatest part" in capitalism's origins (873–874). Many readers of this book will likely see no controversy here, and rightly so. The historical record is clear: capitalism's origins were a bloodbath, capitalist hierarchies are still enforced in the developed world with what is euphemistically called "soft power," and enforced in the developing world with what is glossed over as "hard power." But, before taking this narrative as common knowledge, we should remember that respected liberal historians and political thinkers still find it difficult to admit. Joyce Appleby, for instance, in her best-selling popular history *The Relentless Revolution: A History of Capitalism* (New York: W. W. Norton, 2011), emphasizes England's privileged role in capitalist development: "How counterintuitive that this poor, cold, small, outlandish country would be the site of technological innovations that would relentlessly revolutionize the material world!" (11).Appleby's argument goes on to celebrate how England's "technological wizards transformed the world of work" by "[establishing] new administrative structures to deal with industry and labor" (137, 114). Appleby glances at the facts on the ground of force in her narrative, but only grudgingly, and always with a booster's "glass half full" appreciation for what England's technological wizards purportedly gave the world.

41. William Prescott, *History of the Conquest of Mexico* (New York: Random House, 2010), 368.

42. Thompson, *Recollections*, 8–9.

43. Quoted in Jáksic, *Hispanic World,* 141.

44. Schmidt, "Mexico," 119.

45. See James Muldoon, *The Americas in the Spanish World Order* (Philadelphia: University of Pennsylvania Press, 1994), 65–70.

46. See Magali Marie Carerra, *Imagining Identity in New Spain* (Austin: University of Texas Press, 2003) for eighteenth-century attempts to regular Spanish class and racial intermixture in Mexico.

47. Joselyn M. Almeida, *Reimagining the Transatlantic (1780–1890)* (Burlington, Vt.: Ashgate, 2011), 28–32.

48. For Las Casas's role in the expansion of the African slave trade, see D. A. Brading, *The First America: The Spanish Monarchy, Creole Patriots, and the Liberal State, 1492–1867* (Cambridge: Cambridge Universtiy Press, 1998), 61; and David Brion Davis, *Inhuman Bondage: The Rise and Fall of Slavery in the New World* (Oxford: Oxford University Press, 2006), 55–56. For Las Casas's eventual rejection of the African slave trade, see Federick P. Bowser, *The African Slave in Colonial Peru* (Stanford, Calif.: Stanford University Press, 1974), 325.

49. Jodi Byrd, *Transit of Empire: Indigenous Critiques of Colonialism* (Minneapolis: 2011), xii.

50. J. G. A. Pocock, *Barbarism and Religion: Volume 4, Barbarians, Savages, and Empire*

(Cambridge: Cambridge University Press, 2004), 176. Pocock's formula is taken up and expanded upon in Tony C. Brown, *The Primitive, the Aesthetic, and the Savage: An Enlightenment Problematic* (Minneapolis: University of Minnesota Press, 2012), 69.

51. Jodi Byrd, *Transit of Empire*, 17

52. Ridge, *Trumpet*, 72. The Cherokee Nation's difficult relationship to slavery was produced by centuries of interaction with English and Spanish colonial forces. Theda Perdue, *Slavery and the Evolution of Cherokee Society, 1540–1866* (Knoxville: University of Tennessee Press, 1979) remains an invaluable record of these complex interactions. For the role of Cherokee divisions in Confederate warfare, see Clarissa Conner, *The Cherokee Nation in the Civil War* (Norman: University of Oklahoma Press, 2007), especially 94–115.

53. John Rollin Ridge, "California," in *Poems* (San Francisco: Henry Payot, 1869), 87–92.

54. John Rollin Ridge, "Poem, Delivered before the Agricultural, Horticultural, and Mechanics' Society of the Northern District of California, on Wednesday Evening, August 5th, 1869," in *Poems*, 114–127.

55. John Rollin Ridge, "Poem, Delivered at Commencement of Oakland College, Cal., June 6th, 1861," in *Poems*, 78–83.

56. John Rollin Ridge, *A Trumpet of Our Own: Yellow Bird's Essays on the North American*, ed. David Farmer and Rennard Strickland (San Fransciso: Book Club of California, 1981), 69.

57. Ridge, *A Trumpet of Our Own*, 76.

58. Mark Rifkin, "'For the wrongs of our poor bleeding country': Sensation, Class, and Empire in Ridge's *Joaquín Murieta*," *Arizona Quarterly* 65, no. 2 (Summer 2009): 37.

59. Larissa Tracy and Jeff Massey, introduction to *Heads Will Roll: Decapitation in the Medieval and Early Modern Imagination*, ed. Larissa Tracy and Jeff Massey (Leiden: Brill, 2012), 4–11.

60. Erica Stevens, "Three-Fingered Jack and the Severed Literary History of John Rollin Ridge's *The Life and Adventures of Joaquín Murieta*," *ESQ* 61, no. 1 (Winter 2015): 73–112.

61. Philip Fisher, "Democratic Social Space: Whitman, Melville, and the Promise of American Transparency," in *The New American Studies: Essays from Representation*, ed. Philip Fisher (Berkeley: University of California Press, 1991), 101.

62. Dana D. Nelson, *The World in Black and White: Reading "Race" in American Literature* (Oxford: Oxford University Press, 1994), 109.

63. Eric J. Sundquist, *Empire and Slavery in American Literature, 1820–1865* (Jackson: University Press of Mississippi, 1995), 188.

64. Herman Melville, *Typee: A Peep at Polynesian Life, During a Four Months' Residence in A Valley of the Marquesas*, in *Herman Melville: Typee, Omoo, and Mardi*, ed. G. Thomas Tanselle (New York: Library of America, 1982), 231.

65. Herman Melville, *The Confidence-Man: His Masquerade*, ed. Harrison Hayford, Hershel Parker, and G. Thomas Tanselle (Evanston, Ill.: Northwestern University Press, 2002): 95.

66. Delano, *Narrative*, 327.

67. Eric Wertheimer, *Imagined Empires: Incas, Aztecs, and the New World of American Literature* (Cambridge: Cambridge University Press, 1999), 158.

68. Alberto Flores Galindo, *In Search of An Inca: Identity and Utopia in the Andes* (New York: Cambridge University Press, 2000), 7–9.

CHAPTER FIVE. FEUDALISM, INDIVIDUALISM, AND AUTHORITY IN EMERSON'S LATER WORKS

Epigraphs are from *Ralph Waldo Emerson: Essays and Lectures*, ed. Joel Porte (New York: Library of America, 1983), 278; hereafter cited parenthetically as *EL*; *The Collected Works of Ralph Waldo Emerson*, ed. Alfred R. Ferguson, Joseph Slater, Wallace E. Williams, Douglas Emory, Philip Nicoloff, Robert E. Burkholder, Barbara L. Slater, Ronald A. Wilson, Joel Myerson, Albert J. von Frank, and Thomas Wortham, 10 vols. (Cambridge, Mass.: Harvard University Press, 1971–2013), 8, 214; hereafter cited parenthetically as *CW*.

1. John Peacock, "Self-Reliance and Corporate Destiny: Emerson's Dialectic of Culture," *ESQ* 29, no. 2 (1983): 59.

2. Peacock, "Self-Reliance and Corporate Destiny," 63.

3. "The Graduates of Harvard College, at Their Meeting of Friday," *Boston Daily Advertiser*, July 18, 1865, 2.

4. *The Letters of Ralph Waldo Emerson*, vol. 5, ed. Ralph L. Rusk and Eleanor Tilton (New York: Columbia University Press: 1939–96), 469; hereafter cited parenthetically as *Letters*.

5. Bainbridge Bunting, *Harvard: An Architectural History* (Cambridge, Mass.: Belknap Press of Harvard University, 1998), 92.

6. Quoted in Robert B. Shaffer, "Ruskin, Norton, and Memorial Hall," *Harvard Library Bulletin* 3, no. 2 (Spring 1949): 231.

7. Joyce Appleby, *Liberalism and Republicanism in the Historical Imagination* (Cambridge, Mass.: Harvard University Press, 1992), 6.

8. Christopher Hanlon, *America's England*, 54.

9. See Lears, *No Place of Grace*, 20–22, 38.

10. Russ Castronovo, *Fathering the Nation: American Genealogies of Slavery and Freedom* (Berkeley: University of California Press, 1995), 106–157; Christopher Newfield, *The Emerson Effect: Individualism and Submission in America* (Chicago: University of Chicago Press, 1996), especially 5–14 on "corporate individualism"; John Carlos Rowe, *At Emerson's Tomb*, 17–41.

11. *The Journals and Miscellaneous Notebooks of Ralph Waldo Emerson*, ed. Linda Allardt, William H. Gilman, Alfred R. Ferguson, Harrison Hayford, Ralph H. Orth, J. E. Parsons, A. W. Plumstead, et al., 16 vols. (Cambridge, Mass.: Harvard University Press, 1960–82), 7:342; hereafter cited parenthetically as *JMN*.

12. "Newness" as a description of the nationalist temperament of the 1840s is borrowed

from Irving Howe, *The American Newness: Culture and Politics in the Age of Emerson* (Cambridge, Mass.: Harvard University Press, 1986).

13. For an in-depth analysis of Emerson's debt to the political tradition of "classical liberalism," see Neal Dolan, *Emerson's Liberalism* (Madison: University of Wisconsin Press, 2009), especially 28–32 on Emerson, Hume, and Adam Smith.

14. Robert D. Richardson, *Emerson: The Mind on Fire* (Los Angeles: University of California Press, 1995), 544, 553.

15. Karl Marx, *Capital Volume I*, trans. Ben Fowkes (New York: Penguin, 1990), 940.

16. Friedrich Nietzsche, "On the Uses and Disadvantages of History for Life," in *Untimely Meditations*, ed. Daniel Breazeale, trans. R.J. Hollingdale (Cambridge: Cambridge University Press, 1997), 62–63.

17. My account of "The American Scholar" follows what has been the majority opinion of the essay's intent since Oliver Wendell Holmes famously declared it our "Intellectual Declaration of Independence." But Robert Burkholder has also convincingly argued that Emerson's vision may not be as radical as we may think. See Robert E. Burkholder, "The Radical Emerson: Politics in 'The American Scholar,'" *ESQ* 34, no. 1 (1st and 2nd Quarters 1998): 45.

18. Nancy Bentley, *Frantic Panoramas: American Literature and Mass Culture, 1870–1920* (Philadelphia: University of Pennsylvania Press, 2009), 70. See also Alan Trachtenburg, *The Incorporation of America* (New York: Hill & Wang, 1982), 144, for Trachtenburg's similar discussion of the function of enculturation for the education of the working and middle classes.

19. James Turner, *The Liberal Education of Charles Eliot Norton* (Baltimore: Johns Hopkins University Press, 1999), 243.

20. Turner, *Liberal Education*, 180.

21. Charles Eliot Norton, "Emancipation in the Middle Ages," Harvard University, Houghton Library, MS Am 2117.

22. As Paul Giles notes, Emerson used Chaucer and other medieval writers throughout his career: "He engages systematically with early English culture, exhuming it for his own purposes and reorganizing it in terms of a dialectic between past and present." Paul Giles, *The Global Remapping of American Literature* (Princeton, N.J.: Princeton University Press, 2010), 76.

23. Ralph Waldo Emerson, "Chivalry," Harvard University, Houghton Library, bMS Am 1280.211 [Lectures, 1869–1870] (Folders 1 and 2).

24. *Emerson's Antislavery Writings*, ed. Len Gougeon and Joel Myerson (New Haven: Yale University Press, 1995), 88; hereafter cited parenthetically as *EAW*.

25. "Ralph Waldo Emerson's Last Lecture," *Daily Alta California*, May 18, 1871, 1. The reviewer may be mistaken about Emerson quoting Tennyson; the "Chivalry" notebooks contain a number of longhand quotations from various historical sources and romances, but no excerpts from Tennyson's 1833 poem.

26. Horsman, *Race and Manifest Destiny*, 9.

27. Len Gougeon, *Virtue's Hero: Emerson, Antislavery, and Reform* (Athens: University of Georgia Press, 2010), 113.

28. Robert E. Burkholder, "The Contemporary Reception of *English Traits*," *Emerson: Centenary Essays*, ed. Joel Myerson (Carbondale: Southern Illinois University Press, 1982), 156–172; Susan L. Roberson, "Emerson's *English Traits* and the Paradox of Empire," *New England Quarterly* 84. no. 2 (June 2011): 265–285.

29. Robin Blackburn, *An Unfinished Revolution: Karl Marx and Abraham Lincoln* (New York: Verso, 2011), 18–19.

30. Thomas Carlyle, *Past and Present*, ed. Chris R. Vanden Bossche, Joel J. Brattin, and D. J. Trela (Berkeley: University of California Press, 2005), 242; hereafter cited parenthetically as *PP*.

31. Walls, *Emerson's Life in Science*, 221.

32. For an overview of thought on Emerson's relationship to race, see Len Gougeon, "Race," in *Ralph Waldo Emerson in Context*, ed. Wesley T. Mott (New York: Cambridge University Press, 2014), 196–203. Gougeon argues that Emerson evidences a racial "egalitarianism" that was not entirely continuous with his major sources for racial "science," Chambers's *Vestiges of Creation* and Robert Knox's *Races of Men* (198). It is not within the scope of this chapter to assess Gougeon's claim for Emerson's "racial egalitarianism" against his stated views on race in *English Traits*. However, Gougeon's reluctance to accept the evidence at hand concerning Emerson's stiffening racial vision may owe more to one scholar's adoration of "virtue's hero" than it does an accurate account of Emerson's social doctrines. For a different perspective on Emerson's view of race in *English Traits*, see Susan Castillo, "'The Best of Nations'? Race and Imperial Destinies in *English Traits*," *Yearbook of English Studies* 34 (2004): 100–111; and Philip Nicoloff, *Emerson on Race and History* (New York: Columbia University Press, 1961).

33. Nell Irvin Painter, *The History of White People* (New York: W. W. Norton, 2011), 174–175.

34. Cornel West, *The American Evasion of Philosophy: A Genealogy of Pragmatism* (Madison: University of Wisconsin Press, 1989), 28. West borrows his formulation (Emerson as a "mild racist") from Nicoloff's *Emerson on Race and History*. But West somewhat misrepresents Nicoloff's argument. While indeed concluding that Emerson was a "mild racist," Nicoloff nonetheless emphasizes that his writings "[espoused] a particular racial doctrine" with frightening consistency. See Nicoloff, *Emerson on Race*, 120.

35. Painter, *History of White People*, 203.

36. Rowe, *At Emerson's Tomb*, 26.

37. Ralph Waldo Emerson, *Natural History of the Intellect*, ed. Maurice York and Rick Spaulding (Chicago: Wrightwood, 2008), 4; hereafter cited parenthetically as *NH*.

38. For a discussion of the polygenism and racial thought in the nineteenth century, and Agassiz's contributions to the polygenism hypothesis, see David Livingstone, *Adam's Ances-*

tors: Race, Religion, and the Politics of Human Origins (Baltimore: Johns Hopkins University Press, 2011), 169–180.

39. *Report of the Class of 1871 of Harvard College* (Cambridge, Mass.: Riverside Press, 1921): 15, 208.

40. Richard F. Teichgraeber, *Building Culture: Studies in the Intellectual History of Industrializing America, 1867–1910* (Columbia: University of South Carolina Press, 2010), 50, 52.

41. Ralph Waldo Emerson, *Lectures and Biographical Sketches* (Boston: Houghton, Mifflin, 1893), 88.

42. For a discussion of Twain's satire and its relation to historical sense in the late nineteenth century, see Stephen Pasqualina, "Delirium So Real: Mark Twain's Spectacular History," *J19: The Journal of Nineteenth-Century Americanists* 7, no. 1 (Spring 2019): 103–130.

43. Rowe, *At Emerson's Tomb*, 31.

44. Consider how, in the wake of the 2008 economic catastrophe, Harvard faculty in the business and economics departments began to question the role their institutions had in shaping the men and women who nearly led the world toward a second Great Depression. See, for instance, Philip Delves Broughton's "Harvard's masters of the apocalypse," *Sunday Times* (London), March 1, 2009, http://www.thesundaytimes.co.uk/sto/news/uk_news/article153373.ece.

45. Kathleen Davis, "Tycoon Medievalism, Corporate Philanthropy, and American Pedagogy," *American Literary History* 22, no. 4 (Winter 2010): 789.

CONCLUSION

The epigraph is from Walt Whitman, *Poetry and Prose*, ed. Justin Kaplan (New York: Library of America, 1982), 929.

1. Michelle Berman, "Mystery House," *Lexington Herald-Leader*, November 6, 1988, A1–A12.

2. Beverly Fortune, "Lexington Builder Remembered for His Castle," *Paducah Sun*, August 7, 2003, 11A.

3. Erica Flack, "Flames Destroy Woodford County Castle," WAVE3 News, May 11, 2004, https://www.wave3.com/story/1856042/flames-destroy-woodford-county-castle/.

4. "Kentucky Castle Fire Likely Arson," Firehouse, May 28, 2004, https://www.firehouse.com/home/news/10530945/kentucky-castle-fire-likely-arson.

5. Frederick Douglass, "The Meaning of July Fourth for the Negro, Speech at Rochester, New York, July 5, 1852," in *Frederick Douglass: Selected Speeches and Writings*, ed. Philip S. Foner and Yuval Taylor (Chicago: Lawrence Hill, 1999), 188–205; 189.

6. Eli Cook, "The Neoclassical Club: Irving Fisher and the Progressive Origins of Neoliberalism," *Journal of the Gilded Age and Progressive Era* 15, no. 3 (July 2016): 246–262.

7. KellyAnn Fitzpatrick and Jil Hanifan, "Medievalism and Representations of Corporate Identity," *Studies in Medievalism XXI: Corporate Medievalism* (2012): 27–36.

8. Fitzpatrick and Hanifan, "Medievalism and Representations," 33.

9. David R. Roediger, *The Wages of Whiteness: Race and the Making of the American Working Class* (New York: Verso, 2007), 9.

10. Theodor Adorno and Max Horkheimer, *Dialectic of Enlightenment*, trans. John Cumming (New York: Verso, 1997), 41.

11. Vladimir Lenin, "Letter to American Workers," in *Lenin's Collected Works* (Moscow: Progress, 1965), 62–75; 28.

12. For a detailed study of the ways contemporary U.S. governance reflects a feudal structure of sovereignty, see Vladimir Shlapentokh and Joshua Woods, *Feudal America: Elements of the Middle Ages in Contemporary Society* (University Park: Penn State University Press, 2011).

13. Jean R. Sternlight, "Creeping Mandatory Arbitration: Is It just?", *Stanford Law Review* 57, no. 5 (April 2005): 1631–1675; 1636.

14. "About," Kentucky Castle, https://www.thekentuckycastle.com/about (accessed August 25, 2019).

15. "Kentucky Hotel | Versailles | The Kentucky Castle," Kentucky Castle, https://www.thekentuckycastle.com (accessed August 25, 2019).

INDEX

abolition: conservative visions of, 110, 116; Emerson's writings on, 175; in relation to medieval history, 160, 168; westward expansion and, 129; women's suffrage and, 34, 96. *See also* slavery
absolutist state, 14
Adams, Henry, 20
Adams, John, 63–64
Adorno, Theodor, 98
Agassiz, Louis, 176
"Agriculture" (Ridge), 145–146
American Democrat, The (J. F. Cooper), 68–70, 79, 82–83
American Revolution: effects on women, 96, 100–101, 105; erasure of feudal past, 2, 8, 13, 62–67, 169, 189n2; in *The Littlepage Manuscripts*, 72, 77–79; proslavery thinkers' use of, 31, 33, 36–37; Society of the Cincinnati, 3, 177; Virginia's role in, 31, 197n9
"American Scholar, The" (Emerson), 162–163
Anglo-Americans: liberalism versus feudalism debate, 7, 62, 93, 162; views on Cherokee Nation, 148; views on history, 1–4, 8, 20, 92, 132, 147, 171; views on Mexico, 131–141; westward expansion and, 89, 144
Anne of Geierstein (Scott), 29, 44, 195n55
anti-Catholicism, 135
Anti-Rent War, 61–62, 65–68, 71–91
Aristotle: biology and, 143; in Emerson, 175, 177; *oikonomia*, 100, 103
Arthuriana, 101. *See also* chivalry
autarky, 27, 38, 53, 186
Aztecs, 135, 139–147

Bancroft, George, 3
Bascom, John, 112–113
Beecher, Lyman, 128–129
beheading, 148–149, 156–157
Benito Cereno (Melville), 130, 149–157
Benjamin, Walter, 29
"Berenice" (Poe), 40–45, 55
Bird, Robert Montgomery, 42–43
Blackstone, William, 99, 102. *See also* common law
Boston, Mass., 55, 67, 159, 167
Burke, Edmund: gender and, 56–57, 109; hereditary political power and, 64; ritual and, 14, 148; in *Swallow Barn*, 30, 32

Calavar (Bird): 42–43
"California" (Ridge), 144–145
Capital (Marx): volume 1, 137, 162, 204n38; volume 3, 14
capitalism: feudalism and, 14–15, 17; liberalism and, 4, 6, 166, 175, 186; medievalism and, 20; relationship to Spanish history, 137–138; slavery and, 33; trade and, 22;
Carlyle, Thomas, 34, 171–174
Carnegie, Andrew, 179–180
Chainbearer, The (J. F. Cooper), 77–83
Chaucer, Geoffrey, 112–113, 167, 172–173
Child, Lydia Marie, 119, 127
chivalry: in antebellum south, 27, 33–34, 51; Emerson's views of, 167–168; in *The Hidden Hand*, 98–111; indigenous sovereignty and, 142–144; marriage law and, 97–103; relationship to chattel slavery, 35, 95, 97–99, 117
"Chivalry" (Emerson), 167–168

Commentaries on the Laws of England (Blackstone), 99, 102. *See also* common law
common law, 5–6; feudal idea of order and, 15–16; land law and, 61, 63–65, 197n5; marriage codes and, 96–106, 114, 122, 124
Conduct of Life, The (Emerson), 172–175
Confidence-Man, The (Melville), 156–157
Cooper, Anna Julia, 112–114, 201n31
Cooper, James Fenimore, 60–94; *The American Democrat*, 68–70, 79, 82–83; *The Chainbearer*, 77–83; *Leatherstocking Tales* (sequence of novels), 92–93; *The Redskins*, 83–92, 94; *Satanstoe*, 61, 72–77
coverture, 98, 102–106, 115, 118, 123. *See also* feudalism
Critique of Hegel's Doctrine of the State (Marx), 13

Debow's Review, 136
decadence, 6, 10, 54–56, 86, 107, 164–166, 174
Declaration of Independence, 37, 61, 102–103, 110, 208n17
de Crèvecoeur, Hector St. John, 1–2, 185
"Devil in the Belfry, The" (Poe), 47–50
"Dissertation on Canon and Feudal Law" (J. Adams), 63–64
"Domain of Arnheim, The" (Poe), 39–40
Douglass, Frederick, 32–33, 182

"Earth's Holocaust" (Hawthorne), 2
Eighteenth Brumaire of Louis Bonaparte, The (Marx), 19–20
Emerson, Ralph Waldo, 158–180; "The American Scholar," 162–163; "Chivalry," 167–168; *The Conduct of Life*, 172–175; *English Traits*, 169–172; involvement in Memorial Hall project, 159–161; *The Natural History of the Intellect*, 175–177; "Progress of Culture," 163–166; "Self-Reliance," 158, 161–162

Engels, Friedrich, 1, 8, 128, 134
English Traits (Emerson), 169–172
Enlightenment: gender and, 96, 100; indigenous sovereignty and, 91, 132, 140; Marxist interpretations of, 13–15; relationship to feudalism, 5, 16–17, 62–71, 176–177, 192n53

"Fall of the House of Usher, The" (Poe), 53–59
Federalist no. 17 (Madison), 70
feudalism: allodial title, 63, 65, 67, 76; entail, 5, 63, 197n9; feudal idea of order, 15–18, 186; marriage law and, 96, 112–113 primogeniture, 1, 63, 174; relationship to liberalism, 2, 10, 70, 121, 169–170, 178, 185 (*see also* liberal consensus); relationship to medievalism and middle ages, 7–8, 18–22, 162, 177, 192n52; scutage, 14; southern views of, 27, 73–75; U.S. historiography and, 4, 8–15, 154, 164–165, 169; U.S. land law and, 62–71
Filmer, Robert, 10, 100
Fitzhugh, George, 20–21, 27, 30–34
freehold (land law), 63–64, 171, 197n9
Froissart, Jean, 51

German Ideology, The (Marx), 1, 8
gothic: architectural style, 39, 158, 159–160, 164–165, 179; in *Benito Cereno*, 154; in early feminist writing, 102; in *Incidents in the Life of a Slave Girl*, 111, 116, 120–122; literary genre, 3, 20, 44, 82, 105–106; in relation to Spain, 134
Gould, Stephen Jay, 60, 62
Great Dismal Swamp, The (Stowe), 4–5
"Great Nation of Futurity, The" (O'Sullivan), 132
Guizot, Francois, 9–10, 15, 112

Hartz, Louis, 5–6
Hawthorne, Nathaniel: "Earth's Holocaust," 2; Poe's reviews of, 37–38

Heath, James Ewell, 41–43
Hegel, Georg, 13, 25, 176–177
Hentz, Caroline Lee, 28, 30, 35, 54
Hidden Hand, The (Southworth), 93–98, 103–111, 125
Hofstadter, Richard, 4
"Hop-Frog" (Poe), 23, 29, 51–55, 105
Hurlbut, Elisha P., 101–102, 124

Incidents in the Life of a Slave Girl (Jacobs), 22, 95–98, 111–123, 125–127
indigeneity, 22–23, 62, 67, 80, 89–90, 130–157; Iroquois nation, 79–80, 87; white appropriations of, 67, 83–84, 87–91
Iroquois nation. *See* indigeneity
Irving, Washington, 133–134, 161
Ivanhoe (Scott), 34

Jackson, Andrew, 46, 48
Jacobs, Harriet, 22, 95–98, 111–123, 125–127
Jefferson, Thomas: Declaration of Independence, 37, 61, 102–103, 110, 208n17; on slavery, 36, 43; understanding of feudalism in United States, 1–2, 12, 63–64, 189n2, 197n9; views on history, 4–6, 160, 185
Jones, J. Elizabeth, 95–96, 102

Kennedy, John Pendleton, 21, 27; *Swallow Barn*, 28, 30, 35, 40, 84
Kentucky Castle, 181–187
"King Pest" (Poe), 29, 45–46

"Landor's Cottage" (Poe), 39, 56
"Landscape Garden, The" (Poe), 38–39
Lanier, Sydney, 101
landlords, in New York, 61,
Leatherstocking Tales (J. F. Cooper), 92–93
Lenin, Vladimir, 185
liberal consensus: definition, 5–6; literary criticism's relationship to, 6–8; rejection of feudalism, 158–163, 182–184; synthesis with feudalism, 9–11, 19, 70–71, 93, 121, 166–170. *See also* feudalism
Life and Adventures of Joaquín Murieta, The (Ridge), 141–149
Lincoln, Abraham, 166, 180
Locke, John, 10–11, 100

Mabie, Hamilton Wright, 25–26, 59
Madison, James: letter to, 5; *Federalist* no. 17, 70
Magna Carta, 164
Malory, Thomas, 101
Marx, Karl: *Capital* (volume 1), 137, 162, 204n38; *Capital* (volume 3), 14; *Critique of Hegel's Doctrine of the State*, 13; *The Eighteenth Brumaire of Louis Bonaparte*, 19–20; *The German Ideology*, 1, 8; indigenous sovereignty and, 80, 199n40, 204–205n40; letter to Vera Zasulich, 80
"Masque of the Red Death, The" (Poe), 29, 48–55
"Meaning of July Fourth for the Negro, The" (Douglass), 32–33, 182
medievalism: antimodernism and, 7, 20–21, 160–161; plantation romance and, 30–40; in twentieth century, 183–184. *See also* feudalism
Melville, Herman: *Benito Cereno*, 130, 149–157; *The Confidence-Man*, 156–157
Memorial Hall, 23, 160–161, 178–179
Mexico: arguments for conquest by United States, 128–129, 138; association with Spain, 131–141; indigenous groups in, 139–141; race and, 129–130, 136–137, 151; as threat to U.S. sovereignty, 91
"Mexico" (Schmidt), 136–139,
Mohawk Valley (N.Y.), 61–62, 65–66, 70–76, 90–94

Natural History of the Intellect, The (Emerson), 175–177
noblesse oblige, 53, 110, 115, 165. *See also* chivalry; feudalism

Norman Invasion, 12, 34, 147, 160, 169, 170–171
"North American Indians, The" (Ridge), 146–147
Norton, Charles Eliot, 160, 166–167, 173–175, 179

Onondaga people, 73, 78, 84, 90
O'Sullivan, John, 132

paternalism. *See* slavery
Poe, Edgar Allan: "Berenice," 40–45, 55; "The Devil in the Belfry," 47–50; "The Domain of Arnheim," 39–40; "The Fall of the House of Usher," 53–59; "Hop-Frog," 23, 29, 51–55, 105; "King Pest," 29, 45–46; "Landor's Cottage," 39, 56; "The Landscape Garden," 38–39; "The Masque of the Red Death," 29, 48–55; work at *Southern Literary Messenger*, 26, 29, 40–47, 133
Polk, James Knox, 131–132, 136
Prescott, William H., 136–139
"Progress of Culture" (Emerson), 163–166

Redskins, The (J. F. Cooper), 83–92, 94
Reeve, Tapping, 99
Ridge, John Rollin: "Agriculture," 145–146; "California," 144–145; *The Life and Adventures of Joaquín Murieta*, 141–149; "The North American Indians," 146–147

Satanstoe (J. F. Cooper), 61, 72–77
Schmidt, Gustavus, 136–139
Scott, Walter: 33–34, 43, 101, 108, 147; *Anne of Geierstein*, 29, 44, 195n55; *Ivanhoe*, 34; *Waverly*, 155
"Self-Reliance" (Emerson), 158, 161–162
Simms, William Gilmore, 28, 30, 35, 54
slavery: economics of, 28, 37, 114–115; indigenous displacement and, 152–153, 206n52; paternalism and, 34–36; Poe's relationship to, 42; southern culture and, 27–40, 167; uprisings against, 35; women's rights movement and, 96–97. *See also* abolition
Smith, Adam, 12–13, 78, 113
Southern Literary Messenger, 133. *See also* Poe, Edgar Allan
Southworth, E. D. E. N., 93–98, 103–111, 125
Splash Mountain (theme park attraction), 27
Stanton, Elizabeth Cady, 98, 102, 104, 111–114,
Stowe, Harriet Beecher, 4–5
Swallow Barn (Kennedy), 28, 30, 35, 40, 84

Tocqueville, Alexis de, 1, 8–9
Trotsky, Leon, 15

Van Buren, Martin, 48

Waverly (Scott), 155
White, Thomas Willis, 41
Whitman, Walt, 10, 181, 187

www.ingramcontent.com/pod-product-compliance
Lightning Source LLC
Chambersburg PA
CBHW032213230426
43672CB00011B/2546